P9-DFM-188

Also by Marshall I. Goldman

What Went Wrong with Perestroika

Gorbachev's Challenge:
Economic Reform in the Age of High Technology

The U.S.S.R. in Crisis:
The Failure of an Economic System

Environmental Pollution in the Soviet Union:
The Spoils of Progress

LOST OPPORTUNITY

Why Economic Reforms in Russia Have Not Worked

MARSHALL I. GOLDMAN

W. W. Norton & Company
New York • London

Printed in the United States of America
First Edition

The text of this book is composed in Aldus with the display set in Clarendon Condensed.
Composition and manufacturing by The Maple-Vail Book Manufacturing Group.
Book design by Charlotte Staub

Library of Congress Cataloging-in-Publication Data

Goldman, Marshall I.
Lost opportunity : why economic reforms in Russia have not worked / Marshall I. Goldman.
p. cm.
1. Russia (Federation)—Economic policy—1991– 2. Russia (Federation)—Economic conditions—1991– 3. Russia (Federation)—Politics and government—1991– I. Title.
HC340.12.G65 1994
338.947—dc20 94-16500

ISBN 0-393-03700-2

W. W. Norton & Company, Inc., 500 Fifth Avenue, New York, N.Y. 10110
W. W. Norton & Company Ltd., 10 Coptic Street, London WC1A 1PU

1 2 3 4 5 6 7 8 9 0

To

Jessica
Samuel Todd
Jacob
Sam
Jonah
David
Elie

Keep up the tradition.

Contents

Preface ix

1 The Reform That Never Was 1

2 The Rise of Boris Yeltsin 31

3 The Breakup of the Soviet Union 50

4 Economic Advice 64

5 Shock Therapy 94

6 Privatization 122

7 Lessons of History: Postwar West Germany and Japan 145

8 Gradualism or Shock Therapy: Hungary versus Poland 160

9 China as a Model 190

10 Economic Aid: Great Expectations—Massive Disappointments 213

11 The Clash between Economics and History 229

Notes 259

Bibliography 277

Index 281

Preface

After the collapse of the Soviet Union and the end of Mikhail Gorbachev's presidency, newspapers and journals were filled with articles detailing the demise of Sovietology. Those of us in Soviet studies never completely understood the reason for all the fuss. As far as we were concerned, the field was more exciting than ever. The challenges for the former republics of the Soviet Union were as difficult as ever, except that now instead of one country having to deal with the problems there were fifteen. More than that, in the new openness of 1992, unprecedented opportunities for research and study emerged. What before had been provincial centers became world capitals overnight. Even within Russia there was change. Remote regions of Russia remained remote, but now they were eager to engage in contact with business executives and scholars from the outside world. Some even raised the prospect of independence from Russia—or at least more autonomy in dealing with Moscow. The strong showing of Vladimir Zhirinovsky, a representative of the extreme right, in the December 1993 election added to the complexity of the transformation challenge and confirmed the inherent difficulty of trying to transform a country with Russia's reactionary background. Intellectually, the region of the former Soviet Union has never been more exciting. In fact it has become an open laboratory for the study of how to transform centrally planned totalitarian systems into market-oriented democracies, a task not likely to be accomplished within a day or two.

While this has been an exciting process for Western Sovietologists to observe, chronicle, and analyze, it has also been personally disorienting. Now that there is no Soviet Union, I am a scholar without a country. I am not even sure what to call myself. Without a Soviet Union, how can I continue to call myself a Sovietologist? One option is to refer to the region as the Commonwealth of Independent States (CIS); that, after all, is what was formed by most of the republics in an attempt to provide some continuing coordination. Therefore, if I was a Sovietologist when there was a Soviet Union, this would make me and my colleagues Cistologists. Actually, that term more accurately conveys the sense of what it is like to deal with that part of the world in the post-Gorbachev era.

In the chapters that follow, we will examine how it came about that Boris Yeltsin rose to power and took on the task of reforming the Russian economy. Since Yeltsin has written two autobiographies and several biographers have described his political battle with Gorbachev, we will focus primarily on Yeltsin's economic policies.[1] In contrast to Gorbachev, who was unable to decide what reforms and which reformers to support, Yeltsin accepted the idea of shock therapy administered by Yegor Gaidar, a young economist he eventually appointed acting prime minister. We will consider the role of economic advisers, both Russian and foreign, and why Yeltsin selected Gaidar, a man he met only after the coup began in August 1991. We will then examine the suitability of shock therapy as a reform strategy for Russia. To gain perspective, we will also look at economic reform in Germany, Japan, Eastern Europe, and China. Finally, we will consider what Russia should do next and what the outside world can and should do to assist Russia in its reform efforts. This analysis also involves a consideration of exhortations of those like Richard Nixon who have warned that failure to provide all-out help may lead to a collapse of the reforms and to the subsequent quest for scapegoats. Will there be a search for those "who lost Russia"? This means asking not only was it ours but was it Yeltsin's or even Gorbachev's to lose?

Explaining all these issues is not easy, especially when events in the former Soviet Union move so quickly. Yet for those of us who study the region, it is almost like academic tenure—you know there will still be a job tomorrow because there will always be something new to explain.

This marks my fourth book with W. W. Norton and my editor and friend Donald Lamm. Each time I say to myself, This book will be the end of the series, but each time something new and even more exciting takes place, and we begin the whole process over again and I continue to rely on his judgment.

As this manuscript goes off to the publisher, it would be inexcusable for me not to thank the relays of typists and students who helped me prepare it. First there is Kim Thomas, who may have crippled herself in the process. In addition, Josh Barrow, Toyia Battle, and Cyrus Mody went over repeated drafts to make corrections. The use of a word processor may offer many advantages but it is also likely to require many more adjustments than were needed in the old days of simple typewriters. Kristin Kaulbach, too, offered some very helpful suggestions.

When expressing my thanks, I want to repeat my by now ritualized appreciation to Wellesley College, the Russian Research Center at Harvard, and Shelby Cullom Davis and especially Kathryn, whose chair I hold at Wellesley. While my expressions of gratitude may seem perfunctory, my appreciation is deeply felt. It is hard for me to think of a place that could have been more supportive of my work these last thirty-five years than Wellesley College. That is a long time to spend at any one place, and there are not many of us these days who do. Perhaps if other academic institutions were as congenial and compatible with such a fine quality of life, others would have an equally long tenure. The same could be said about the Russian Research Center. Nobody ever wants to leave the place. For many it is an extension of their families—especially families in which there is a vibrant intellectual interaction. Finally, the support of the Davis family has made it possible for me to undertake research I might otherwise have had to forgo. It is also wonderfully rewarding to have someone outside your immediate family take such pride in your endeavors.

While such thanks by now have a regular place in book acknowledgments, there is something different about this particular project. My wife, Merle, usually edits everything I write, but this time she outdid herself. Since we have been collaborating more and more on the process of reform in China and Russia, that may seem to be only natural. However, asking a spouse to collaborate or edit a manuscript is an unnatural process. Only those who have tried will understand why. There are not many families I know of in which nasty arguments these days center on whether Confucianism helps or hurts economic development and why Russia is unlikely to become democratic before China does. In any case, after forty years of marriage, we have finally found a way to edit each other's work. In this instance she deserves a tribute for an extraordinary effort.

Lost Opportunity

1.

The Reform That Never Was

Rarely have events moved with such speed. On Thursday, October 8, 1992, Mikhail Gorbachev found himself facing a phalanx of Moscow policemen, sent by Boris Yeltsin to block Gorbachev's way into what the day before had been the headquarters complex of his International Foundation for Social Economic and Political Studies, or Gorbachev Foundation. To add to the humiliation, the Yeltsin government had just ordered that Gorbachev could not leave Russia. Ultimately, he did get permission to fly to Berlin to attend the funeral of Willy Brandt, the former West German chancellor, but then he was not allowed to fly on to Italy. In the end the ban was lifted entirely, but Gorbachev had been made, as he put it, "the first refusenik of the Yeltsin government."

Ten months earlier Gorbachev had headed what a few years before had been regarded as one of the most intimidating governments in the world. Under his leadership the Soviet Union had agreed to a series of far-reaching arms agreements, and in October 1991 Gorbachev was being applauded in the West as the Nobel laureate who ended the Cold War. Yet, whatever his standing in the outside world, he was no hero at home. Reflecting the depth of the contempt for Gorbachev in Russia, a Moscow actor, who played the role of Gorbachev in a local theatrical production, had just recently been attacked and beaten by Muscovites. They had mistakenly assumed that the actor was really Gorbachev.[1] He had gone from being a world hero to being a local scapegoat in less than twelve months.

Ironically, Gorbachev's chief tormentor was Boris Yeltsin. Yeltsin had been nothing more than a provincial party functionary when Gorbachev personally brought him to Moscow in 1985. And a scant two years later, in 1987, Gorbachev had drummed Yeltsin out of the leadership ranks "forever" because of what the Communist Party leadership regarded as his inept, insubordinate, and embarrassing behavior when he broke party ranks and attacked fellow members of the Politbureau.

Gorbachev could be forgiven for his failure to understand how his world had been turned upside down so quickly. Normally, it takes a revolution or an earthquake to set off such Richter scale readings in a country's political and economic life. "An earthquake" is how historians will probably characterize the Gorbachev era, from his rise to power in March 1985 to his forced abdication on December 25, 1991, and his replacement by that same Boris Yeltsin.

From the mid-1930s until Gorbachev came to power, the Soviet Union had been the world's most stolid, stultified, and even reactionary country. It may have advertised itself as a revolutionary society, but at least as far as domestic life was concerned, it prized nothing so much as the status quo. Change occurred in the outside world, not within the Soviet Union.

Yet in the late 1980s change suddenly came to Russia. For years Russians used to joke that just as Americans could stand in front of the White House and criticize the president, so they could stand in front of the Kremlin and also criticize the U.S. president. But under Gorbachev the Soviet people gradually lost their fear of the state, and by 1988 many Soviet citizens did indeed stand in front of the Kremlin and ridicule Gorbachev. At the same time, the country itself began to fall apart. By January 1992, instead of one Union of Soviet Socialist Republics, there were fifteen independent countries, including some that almost immediately went to war with their neighbors and former fellow Soviets.

The disappearance of the Soviet Union had equally far-reaching effects on the outside world. Almost overnight what was generally agreed to be the world's most powerful and threatening military force found its influence reduced to what at times seemed that of a banana republic. When a Soviet leader, especially Gorbachev, met with an American president, it was truly a summit meeting with implications for the whole world. When Yeltsin as the president of Russia suggested in November 1992 to President-Elect Bill Clinton that Russia and the United States resume the holding of summits, many questioned the need for them. Other than offering economic help to Russia, such meetings seemed to have little value. Even though it still had a nuclear arsenal, there was little likelihood by late 1992 that Russia might in the near future again threaten the United States' military dominance. Russia as the successor to the Soviet Union was no longer a superpower. Moreover, virtually all the newly independent republics of the former Soviet Union found themselves having to deal with separatist movements within or outside their own boundaries. The monolithic Soviet Union transformed itself into a multitude of squirming ethnic tadpoles, each seeking to head off in its own direction.

Whereas once everything in the Soviet Union was centrally controlled and stable, if not stagnant and reactionary, now almost everything seems to have become autonomous and decentralized. Before, almost all prices were centrally set; in 1992 the majority of prices in Russia were decontrolled and left to find their own level. Before, all foreign trade was monopolized through the Soviet Ministry of Foreign Trade; now each republic is an independent country and sets its own rules, and in Russia and in most of the other new countries, individuals, as well as companies and corporations, can import and export.

Visually, the changes are jolting. A General Motors dealership operates on Gorkii Street, now Tverskaia Street, around the corner from a McDonald's restaurant located in Pushkin Square. Given the awe in which almost all Russians hold Pushkin, this intrusion of Western materialism seems to many to verge on the sacrilegious. As if this were not enough, the annual doubling of the crime rate, even the advent of kidnapping, reflects the seedy side of life that has accompanied the reform process.

The period from mid-1991 to mid-1992 was especially turbulent. By the summer of 1991 the Soviet public seemed to have lost its remaining enthusiasm for Gorbachev and his apparently diminishing commitment to the reform process. Nonetheless, the defeat of the August 1991 putsch of communist hard-liners reawakened a sense of optimism. For a brief time there was even a sense of euphoria. Having lost their fear of authorities, Russians had acted courageously and stood by Boris Yeltsin, their democratically elected president, in his moment of danger when he triumphed against the hard-liners. There was relatively little support for Gorbachev, who was blamed for the collapse of the economy and Russia's international standing. Equally important, they were angry that the hard-liners had tried to take the law into their own hands. But soon their anger, and the feeling of triumph from having stood up to the tanks, began to fade. By the end of 1992 the day-to-day drudgery of dealing with an increasingly unsuccessful economic reform had transformed the euphoria into hostility and despair.

In October 1993 accumulated frustrations provoked by an obstructionist parliament led Yeltsin to order its disbandment. This sparked another confrontation between traditionalists and reformers. After open reluctance on the part of the military to support him, made worse by the recurrence of an attack of mental depression, Yeltsin and the reformers ultimately prevailed, but the struggle was a bloody one; whereas in August 1991 only three lives were lost, in October 1993 scores of people were killed in the struggle for the Russian White House.[2] Of equal concern, in the aftermath of the October battle, Yeltsin ordered the closing of fifteen newspapers and at least eight hard-line political parties. Admittedly, some of those affected had been openly advocating the violent overthrow of the Yeltsin regime, but these shutdowns plus Yeltsin's decision to dismiss the chief judge of the constitutional court and to cancel the scheduled presidential election cast a shadow over the country's freedom of expression. Given Russia's political tradition of overassertive governments, this not only stirred unpleasant memories but also raised questions about the depth of Yeltsin's commitment to openness and tolerance for dissent.

I

Gorbachev's end came with astonishing swiftness. It had seemed for a time that Gorbachev would be considered second only to Lenin as the Soviet Union's greatest leader. Within months of his assuming power in 1985, the public committed itself to Gorbachev and his call for perestroika and glasnost. His frequent appearances evoked applause and increasingly enthusiastic crowds. His arms control agreements with the United States and the accompanying Gorbymania on the world scene brought not only a safer world but also a reflected glory on the Soviet people. During his December 1990 visit to the United States, for example, the American public seemed to show more appreciation for Gorbachev than for its new president, George Bush. The Soviet people, who had in the past chafed at the outside world's disapproval of the Soviet Union's bullying and unbecoming behavior, found it much more appealing to be cheered rather than jeered.

Admittedly, Gorbachev's hold on power when he was general secretary of the Communist Party was not dependent on public opinion or competitive elections. Yet under his leadership the Soviet Union introduced fixed terms for its leaders. This implied that the Soviet public was to be given a chance to renew or reject its leaders at a specified time and that until then its leaders would have a specified term to prove themselves. In that spirit Gorbachev designated himself president for a five-year term ending in 1993. But in 1990 and 1991, as the economy collapsed and the domestic political scene became more and more unsettled, the Soviet people began to lose faith in Gorbachev and he became threatened by his own reforms. Term or no term Gorbachev's hold on power began to weaken.

The outside world found the Soviet people's unhappiness with Gorbachev hard to understand. For almost seven decades it had come to accept the notion that, with the possible exception of Georgi Malenkov (who succeeded Stalin) and Nikita Khrushchev, all Soviet leaders exercised absolute powers surpassing those of most other dictators. Even as late as July 1991, in his last Moscow summit meeting with his friend Mikhail Gorbachev, President Bush gave no outward indication that there was any threat to Gorbachev's serving out the remainder of his term. In fact, however, the August 1991 conspirators had already begun to plan the coup.

Gorbachev even lost the support of some of his oldest and most committed advisers. His minister of foreign affairs, Eduard Shevardnadze, had become so concerned about Gorbachev's unwillingness to support his fellow reformers and stand up to his more outspoken critics that he dramatically resigned his post as foreign minister in December 1990 and prophetically warned about the danger of a coup.

Although Shevardnadze's warning was premature, another one of Gorbachev's closest advisers, Aleksandr Yakovlev, issued a similar warning on August 16, 1991, just three days before the actual attempt. By early July 1991 opposition to Gorbachev had become increasingly blatant. Details of the forthcoming coup were known even to the United States ambassador to the Soviet Union, Jack Matlock. In June 1991, just before George Bush arrived in Moscow for the U.S.-Soviet summit, Ambassador Matlock sought a private audience with Gorbachev to warn him about what he had been told a few days before by one of those close to the conspirators.[3] Secretary of State James Baker offered a similar warning to his Russian counterpart, Aleksandr Bessmertnykh, on June 20, 1991.*[4] Whether President Bush discussed the rumors directly with President Gorbachev has not been revealed, but the American president did seek the advice of several Western Sovietologists in a meeting in Kennebunkport also on June 20, 1991, about the likelihood of a coup. This was just before Bush's departure for Moscow. Whatever Gorbachev's reaction when the putsch actually began, it is clear that he had received some advance warning, including the specific names of the actual conspirators.[5]

II

The Soviet people may have been upset by Gorbachev's penchant for hobnobbing with foreign kings, queens, presidents, and popes, and angered over what they regarded as Raisa Gorbachev's regal ways, but what ultimately brought Gorbachev down was his failure to deal effectively with the country's economic problems. Furthermore, the reforms he did implement set off centrifugal forces that resulted in the breakup of the Soviet empire. It would have been bad enough if the split had been limited to Eastern Europe's breaking away from the Soviet Union, but when the USSR itself began to disintegrate, that was too much for many of the more powerful military and political leaders.

The deteriorating economic conditions provided an opening for various ethnic groups that had long harbored political grievances against Moscow and increased their determination to secede. Given the intensity of their bitterness, it is likely that even if perestroika had been a roaring success, they would still have pressed to secede. Nevertheless, it is also likely that if the

*This was unwise, since Bessmertnykh's subsequent stance during the coup attempt indicated that he was less than firmly opposed to such an attempt.

economy had been flourishing, there would have been less interest in an immediate and, in some cases, complete severance of relations.

Without question, Gorbachev deserves enormous credit for even contemplating the far-reaching economic and political reforms associated with perestroika and glasnost. But he had great, though mistaken, expectations about the way his reforms could be implemented. As he saw it, they could be carried out within the existing Communist framework; he merely had to fine-tune the present system. As perestroika evolved, however, it gave rise to a series of proposals that, if implemented, would have resulted in a radical departure from the centrally planned economy. Though ambitious, Gorbachev's subsequent plans had major shortcomings. Gorbachev never understood that the purpose of economic reform should be to make people's lives better. He was too tied to the old system. To him, at first, perestroika meant increasing the production of machine tools. His campaign for intensification and acceleration *(uskoreniie)* of machinery output was reminiscent of past efforts to increase production of heavy industry.[6] While he did try to increase productivity and streamline the production process, none of these efforts improved daily life. Little or nothing was done to increase the availability of consumer goods. If anything, day-to-day life became worse for most of the public. His 1985 crackdown on the sale of vodka, for example, may have been good for public health but was regarded as another example of his disregard for the public's wants.*

Part of the problem was that Gorbachev had no blueprint for reforming a centrally planned economy. By contrast the Chinese began by concentrating on such economic reforms as turning the land over to the peasants, providing consumer goods, and creating new private businesses and services. But Gorbachev was con-

*This was in part a bad rap for Gorbachev, because it was Yegor Ligachev, the number two man in the Politburo at the time, who lobbied the hardest for the vodka campaign.

vinced that such an approach would not work in the Soviet Union, because of a more deeply rooted centralized bureaucracy and the people's ideological resistance to the notion of private farming and business.[7] To overcome this resistance, he began with political reforms, in order to remove the opponents and demonstrate his commitment to reform.

When he realized in 1987 that his emphasis on machine tool production was a mistake, he shifted the emphasis to establish cooperative and private enterprises. Except during the the New Economic Policy (NEP) period, in the early 1920s, and World War II, there had been no toleration of, let alone official support for, private and cooperative activities. The cooperatives authorized by Gorbachev were to be independent, very different from the existing state-run cooperatives in the countryside, which were intended to give the appearance of being independent, but were not.

Although China and almost all the countries in Eastern Europe had long since accepted the idea of cooperatives, private commercial activities, and even private manufacturing enterprises, this was a bold, though belated, step. If successful, it would have allowed private entrepreneurs to respond to the demands of the country's consumers, something that most of the country's planners had heretofore either neglected or deemed a low-priority matter. Despite his approval, however, Gorbachev did not wholeheartedly support the shift in emphasis. He was fearful that too rapid a shift to the private sector would lead workers to defect en masse from the state sector. The state sector would then collapse, confronting the country with very grave economic difficulties. Gorbachev never overcame that fear. During his tenure he commissioned eleven to twelve economic reform plans but ultimately rejected each one, creating reform gridlock.[8] Like the bridegroom who can never quite bring himself to show up at his wedding, Gorbachev could never bring himself to accept the changes such proposals would inevitably set in motion. Potentially, much could have been done, but because of his reluctance to implement the plans, little was accomplished. In fact, each shift in plans seemed only to exacerbate the economic problems.

For example, Gorbachev's neither-here-nor-there attitude in 1987 toward the cooperative and private sector all but assured that his decision to allow the opening to the private sector would be halfhearted, reluctant, and, as a consequence, counterproductive. By limiting the public's opportunity to open its own businesses to pensioners and students, Gorbachev, in effect, restricted entry. Within two years these limitations were removed, but the restraint on entry, even if temporary, created enormous structural problems that have thwarted more far-reaching attempts at reform ever since.

Gorbachev's resistance to opening new businesses brought to mind the apocryphal story about the Moscow traffic authorities who realized that they had to make drastic changes in the country's traffic patterns. The accident rate had become too high and the traffic jams too recurrent. Having heard that the British traffic system was relatively safe and efficient, they decided to send an engineer to London. Sure enough, he reported back that London seemed to have solved many of its traffic problems. "What are the British doing differently?" demanded those who had not made the trip. "Simple! They drive their cars on the left side of the road, whereas we run ours on the right side." After some careful discussion they decided that, as of January 1, all traffic in Russia would be transferred to the left side of the road. But as the date approached, and more and more criticisms appeared in the press, several authorities began to see that they were asking too much of a people whose cars still had their steering wheel on the left side and who had no practice driving on the left side of the road. So it was decided to switch by stages; those with more experience, such as truck and cab drivers, would switch as planned on January 1. The less experienced drivers, however, would prepare themselves gradually. They would continue on the right side of the road until July 1 and only then make the switch.

In fairness to Gorbachev, it must be said that he probably did not anticipate the impact his actions ultimately had, but the restraints on entry and the resulting lack of competition all but guaranteed that those few pensioners and students who did form their own businesses would become wealthy overnight. For more than fifty years the planned command economic system had so neglected the wants of consumers that almost any new entrepreneur was able to produce for the domestic market goods that were either produced inadequately or not produced at all.

This new wealthy class, however, became an immediate target for Russian and ethnic toughs who formed themselves into bands of racketeers referred to collectively as the mafia. Their growth coincided with the weakening of central state economic and political control. Previously, private manufacturing, and buying or selling, was an economic crime punishable by death. Once it was legalized, the number of police was sharply cut back. This provided a perfect opening for criminal groups that saw a chance to prey on the new entrepreneurs and demand a payoff. That was the only way for the entrepreneurs to avoid a shooting or a firebombing. In short order, these mafia groups came to control virtually all private business, restaurants, and trucking, casting an antisocial aura over the whole private sector. That control concentrated on preventing new groups from entering the market. The fewer sellers there were, the higher the price was likely to be. A good example was offered by the Moscow, Kiev, and Leningrad airports. By ensuring that only a few cars could serve the airports, the mafia forced arriving passengers to pay ten to twenty times the authorized rate. This higher rate naturally attracted other would-be drivers, who quickly discovered that seeking to enter a mafia-controlled market could be hazardous not only to one's car but to one's health. By preventing new suppliers from responding to the incentive of higher prices, the mafia effectively hamstrung efforts to increase the output of consumer goods.

III

Admittedly, any economic shake-up of the magnitude needed to switch the Soviet Union from central planning to a market-based system was bound to destabilize the country. Previous Soviet leaders had sought to ensure that the planned command system would endure forever so that no one would be able to reinstate the market system. This was to be accomplished by means of several specific actions. First, the Soviet Union destroyed the private entrepreneurs and growth sectors. Burning his institutions behind him, Stalin nationalized virtually all industry, agriculture, and service. By the time he was through, he had succeeded not only in suppressing private enterprise but also in eliminating the commercial banking system, as well as commercial legal and accounting practices.

While Stalin undoubtedly seemed to enjoy destroying capitalist institutions, he was motivated by more than sheer sadism. Those around Stalin no doubt sincerely believed that capitalism was wasteful and that the nationalization of all economic activity, along with the introduction of central planning, would bring with it important economic advantages for the Soviet Union. For example, what was the point of having four gas stations on one corner or several different brands of soap, as so often happens under capitalism? It made much more sense and it would be cheaper to have only one station or one brand of soap, controlled by a central planner. The eliminating of private enterprise and the small-scale marketing infrastructure would thus make it possible not only to do away with needless and wasteful competition but also to consolidate existing factories, which in turn would bring with it economies of scale. In theory, economies of scale would mean low-cost production. These factories were likely to be monopolies, but theoretically, with a central-planning system and the absence of private ownership, factory managers would not be able to take advantage of their monopoly position. In any event, unlike Western economies, the Soviet economy deliberately fostered monopolies. As a measure of how pervasive monopolies were, Gossnab, the state supply agency, reported that in 1991, out of 7,664 products manufactured in the machine-building, metallurgical, chemical, timber, and construction sectors, 77 percent, or 5,884, were monopolies.[9]

Just how outsized Soviet industry had become has been highlighted by a comparison of American and Soviet factory size reported by Stanley Fischer of MIT. Measured by the share of total industrial employment, the United States, which is usually considered partial to large-scale enterprises, reported that about 26 percent of all its industrial enterprises had 1,000 or more employees. Yet in the Soviet Union 73.3 percent had 1,000 or more employees.[10] If a Soviet factory or dam or machine tool was not the biggest, there would be some explaining to do. In the Soviet Union small was definitely not beautiful, and anyone who thought so was regarded as unbalanced. Gigantomania, as the people called it, was everywhere.

Looking back over the decades from the 1930s to the 1960s, one could certainly conclude that centrally planned systems, with their faster rate of economic growth, had many advantages over the market system—at least in the short run. However, by the 1970s the impressive growth of the Communist countries had begun to falter. Moreover, such growth, whatever the short-run advantages, entailed long-run costs. As we will explain in more detail, these costs were for many years masked in the Soviet Union by profligate use of proceeds from both the export and the domestic sale of the Soviet Union's oil, gas, and other valuable raw materials, resources the central-planning system utilized in a wasteful way. Sooner or later, as the deposits in the most accessible fields were mined out, the extraction of these raw materials was bound to become more expensive. To make matters worse, the communist bloc as well as the outside world ultimately became less interested in the products favored by the central planners. How many tanks, missiles, tons of steel, and machine tools did a society need? In addition, their attempts to convert the country's heavy industrial and military production to consumer goods proved to be inept. Some Soviet economists, such as Evsei Liberman in the 1960s and Tatiana Zaslavskaia in the 1970s, began to realize that the planning command system had become costly and counterproductive.[11] Invariably, however, their findings were ignored or condemned by the political leadership. Until Gorbachev came along, it was almost treasonable to call for an end to central planning and the introduction of private ownership.

But however inappropriate the central-planning system may have been, junking it was very difficult. For sixty years Soviet leaders had rooted the system of central planning so deeply that it seemed impervious to efforts to pull it apart.

Even if a Soviet reform leader had come along with the perfect reform package, he would have had difficulties implementing it. The magnitude of the Stalinist revamping of the economy, with its distorted if not grotesque industrial structure, was meant to create a permanent change. As a consequence any conversion of the physical plant and change of mental attitudes would require several decades, if not more. Virtually all past economic decisions would have to be reversed, and many party leaders were sure to resist any such reversal. After all, on the surface the Soviet economy appeared not to be doing all that badly. Moreover, there was a real danger in attempting to shift course in such a fundamental way. Perhaps the economy did need some revamping, but over seventy years, it had developed its own logic and momentum. Disrupting that involved serious risks. In some ways it was like the daredevil motorcyclist able to defy gravity by speeding around the walls of a cylinder that is standing perpendicular to the ground. There is little danger for such a daredevil as long as he maintains sufficient speed, but once he hesitates or, much worse, turns off the motor, he and the motorcycle are likely to tumble to the ground. That, in effect, is what happened when the fully engaged Soviet planning system was shut down for repairs and engine overhaul, and switched from central planning to a more market-oriented system. Once Gorbachev disrupted the economic momentum and disconnected parts of the system, the economy all but disintegrated. In the resulting chaos it was difficult to believe that the Soviet Union had once been a powerful and at times impressive economic power, which just a decade earlier had awed the world. Compounding its decline was the fact that Soviet officials lacked the experience and the institutional structures needed to make the transition to a market economy.

Russian officials also came to realize how shortsighted the emphasis on huge monopolistic factories and the exclusion of competition and competitive products from other countries had been. The unintended result was that both Gorbachev and Yeltsin found themselves with an economy dominated by industrial dinosaurs that, whatever their other characteristics, were marked by inflexibility and the production of obsolete products. They were too big, too wasteful, and too conditioned to ignoring market forces to satisfy customers. They were so wasteful, in fact, that instead of adding value to products, as factories are supposed to do, they subtracted value. The raw materials used in production were worth more as raw materials than as a finished product such as an automobile. But until the 1980s there was no need to worry about such matters, since it was hard to conceive of a time in the Soviet Union when the central plan would be superseded by the market.

Such industrial dinosaurs were also ill suited to compete with their counterparts in the international market economies of the late twentieth century, where the key to survival has been flexibility, mobility, high quality, innovation, and good communications. Moreover, in their determination to stifle market procedures, the Soviets outlawed all but an inconsequential part of the private wholesaling and retailing sector. That also meant an end to private banking and credit. For that matter, accounting and commercial law codes became illegal or obsolete. (There is no doubt that American society could do with considerably fewer lawyers and accountants; but eliminating virtually all of them—at least those involved with the commercial sector—would go to the other extreme.)

Stalinist policies also had lasting effects on agricultural productivity that could not be corrected by a governmental decree or two. It was not only that they had ceased to produce machinery for small farms; in the late 1920s and early 1930s, when the Soviets killed and exiled the kulaks and other successful farmers, they effectively eliminated the most efficient farmers. No wonder agricultural production suffered.

The Soviet effort to turn its back on capitalism affected its international economic activity as well. For example, the authorities prohibited private importing and exporting. Like everything else, those functions were nationalized and then centralized. Additionally, in order to enhance the country's isolation from outside economic influences, the authorities decreed that the ruble could no longer be converted into other currencies. This meant that rubles could no longer be carried out of or brought into the country. Possession of foreign currencies by Soviet citizens was also illegal. All of this would ensure that Russia would be at a disadvantage if it ever attempted to leave the world of the planned economy.

Undoing all these measures and attempting to reestablish a market infrastructure and institutional base could not be done overnight. It had taken sixty years to destroy market institutions and replace them with centrally planned behemoths. With good leadership, reversing the process might require less than sixty years. In any event, as Gorbachev and then Yeltsin were to discover, the transformation, especially the radical restructuring and even abandonment of those gigantic manufacturing monopolies, could not be achieved quickly or painlessly.

Russia's challenge was to build not only new economic institutions but new attitudes as well. The market ethic was never as deeply entrenched in the psyche of the prerevolutionary peasant as in that of his West European or Chinese counterpart. Most Russians have almost always seemed more comfortable in a collective or communal, as opposed to an entrepreneurial, environment. Because its economy was much less developed and therefore more self-contained, markets and business played a much smaller role in Russia than in England, France, and Germany. There are few Western or Chinese counterparts to the nineteenth-century village commune, or *obshchina*. That is not to deny the role of the prerevolutionary weekend market fairs and a seasonal event like the Nizhni Novgorod trade fair. Even during the surge of market activity in early-twentieth-century Russia and again during the NEP in 1921–28, the public attitude toward such behavior was often critical and certainly not supportive. The merchants or kulaks of the NEP were generally regarded as sleazy speculators who profited at the expense of the masses. Moreover, these speculators seemed to be drawn disproportionately from minorities or the underclass of the Slavic population.

These antimercantile feelings were reinforced by the frontal attack of Marxist-Leninist doctrine on the market and private business. Traditional Russian attitudes toward private business often seemed to be in harmony with Marxist ideology. Marx regarded service activities as parasitical. Thus there was little if any public protest against the Communist notion of economic crimes as enforced by Stalin, Khrushchev, and other members of the Politburo. Those accused of diverting state resources for personal gain or of operating private businesses were not only arrested but often sentenced to death. That served to discourage interest in taking private initiatives. That economic crimes kept recurring suggests that not everyone was dissuaded, but the threat of death did have a certain inhibiting effect.

For both cultural and ideological reasons, the attitude toward private business in the Soviet Union could hardly be described as friendly. A country's humor often reflects deeply held beliefs. For example, Russians tell the story of the genie who had three wishes to grant. The Frenchman requested a château, a vineyard, and his mistresses. The American wanted his VCR, laptop computer, and handgun. The Russian hesitated and then replied, "My neighbor has a goat. I don't have a goat. Kill my neighbor's goat!" This would seem to be a more accurate measure of Russia's attitude than a recent telephone survey of Moscow residents that alleged that Muscovites have the same attitude toward private business as New Yorkers do.*

Thus a precondition to successful reform is not only a fundamental revamping of the industrial and commercial institutions but also a change of attitudes. Change of this magnitude is daunting. It is like insisting that a right-handed pitcher pitch left-handed. The pitcher will have the wrong kind of conditioned response (a hostile mental attitude toward private trade), and he will also need a new glove, since his old one was designed for his left hand, which is now his throwing hand (the industrial and marketing infrastructure is designed for the planned economy, not a competitive market). Theoretically, such a shift can be made quickly, but the odds of making such a change both quickly and successfully are not very high.

IV

While the planned command economy was becoming less and less suited to satisfying the needs of the Soviet public, some of the main underpinnings of the country's economic strength also became less secure. For example, no matter how gross their errors, Soviet planners had known they could always compensate for their mistakes by importing goods purchased with the export proceeds from the country's abundant oil wealth. But oil production began to decline in 1989.

Since oil was the country's most important hard-currency

*Robert J. Shiller, Maxim Boycko, and Vladimir Korobov, "Popular Attitudes toward Free Markets: The Soviet Union and the United States Compared," *American Economic Review* 81 (1991): 385. It is hard to take such surveys seriously when the interviewing is done by telephone, especially given the Russian phone system, with its fourteen telephone lines for each hundred inhabitants. *WSJ*, Oct. 2, 1992, p. C4. An official Russian report puts the figure lower, at nine per urban resident. *Ekonomika i zhizn*, no. 40 (Oct. 1990): 15. That compares with forty-three phones for each hundred in Western Europe. Of course, it may be that the Shiller survey is accurate and that New Yorkers just don't think much of business.

earner, the drop in oil output was particularly serious. Typically, oil exports accounted for as much as 60 percent of the country's nonmilitary exports. Natural gas exports generated another 10 percent or so. In fact, oil and gas were the real secrets of the Soviet Union's economic and military prowess. The country could afford to build and subsidize its economy's agricultural, industrial, and military dinosaurs because it could always use its oil and gas to pay for the imported food, consumer goods, and machinery that the planners neglected to include in their domestic production plan.

The supply of oil and gas, not the effectiveness of central planning, created the impression of an ascendant economic and military power. It was not only foreign observers who failed to understand this; Soviet officials themselves seemed to have been unaware of just how important raw materials were to the Soviet Union's economic success and how essential it was to husband their use. Blinded by what seemed to be their bottomless wells, Soviet planners encouraged the squandering of energy. Surrounded by what looked like a limitless sea of energy, Soviet apartment dwellers were provided with radiators but no radiator valves and no gas meters to facilitate conservation. The planners had not thought it necessary to arrange for the manufacture of radiator valves or gas meters.[12] German authorities estimate that a more economical household use of gas would have reduced Soviet annual gas consumption by four billion cubic meters. A similar efficiency among Soviet industrial consumers could have saved another thirty to thirty-two billion cubic meters—altogether 6 percent of Russian consumption. Beguiled by the apparent abundance of Soviet energy, some American Sovietologists added to the confusion by actually advocating that the Soviet Union intentionally reduce its agricultural effort and increase oil exports to pay for agricultural imports.[13]

Not surprisingly, it proved impossible for this wastefulness to continue forever. Oil extraction dropped temporarily in 1984–85 but recovered in 1986–87. After 1989, however, it fell again sharply, by 10 percent in 1991 and even more drastically thereafter. By reducing exports to the former republics of the Soviet Union, the Russians were temporarily able to divert more oil exports to Western countries, but the drop in output led to a drop in exports and eventually in hard-currency earnings. With less hard currency available to spend on imports, the Soviet Union cut imports and borrowed increasingly large amounts to finance what it did import. Like nothing else, this drop in imports highlighted the failings of the planning system. The shortcomings could no longer be masked. As much as anything, the drop in oil production explains how the Soviet economy could have appeared to be so robust in the pre-Gorbachev era and then unravel in a matter of months. The Soviet economy was more than a Potemkin village, but from the 1960s on massive infusions of oil dollars were required to prop it up.*

V

Despite all these fetters on reform, if Gorbachev had committed himself immediately in March 1985 to a gradual introduction of new institutions and economic mechanisms, as happened in Hungary or even China, he might have achieved at least partial success. That is not to say that such reforms would necessarily have been successful (even Hillary Clinton would have had trouble reforming the Soviet economy); the magnitude of change required was simply too great. Moreover, too slow a pace facilitates the growth of the mafia, but too rapid a pace is likely to result in inflation or chaos. It would have helped if, as a minimum, Gorbachev had had a better sense of what was required to take the place of the centrally planned system. His failure to understand the kind of institutions and economic mechanisms needed for a successful reform made it inevitable that the break-

*This refers to the traditional Russian practice of deceiving outsiders. When Czarina Catherine the Great came to visit the domain of Count Potemkin, he erected a façade of villages and stationed peasants in front of those staged props to wave as the czarina drove by.

down of the planning system exacerbated rather than alleviated the economic problems.

Gorbachev and his fellow Politburo members seemed unable to grasp some basic economics. They kept insisting there should be no switch to market mechanisms until sufficient consumer goods were already on the shelves. They had trouble comprehending that the best way to achieve equilibrium between supply and demand was to raise prices. That was the most efficient way of shrinking the size of the queue. They feared correctly that the deregulating of prices would very likely spark enormous price increases, inflation, and social unrest.[14] They preferred to wait until state planners had managed by administrative measures to order factory managers to increase the production of the necessary extra merchandise. That, they argued, was the proper way to shrink the size of the queues. On occasion administrators did manage to do this, but more often direct orders failed to produce the desired equilibrium. Gorbachev was not the first Soviet leader to find that administrative orders were not enough to eliminate market deficits.

This series of mistaken and counterproductive moves created an economic situation that worsened with time. Instead of reducing the economic problems, Gorbachev so intensified them that, before long, gradual reform became increasingly difficult, if not impossible, to bring about.

By the time he was through, Gorbachev had managed to produce something seldom experienced before—a supply-side depression. If for no other reason, this will guarantee him a place in economic theory textbooks. Heretofore, most of the world's recessions or depressions have been similar in that, faced with a drop in demand, retailers cut back on their inventories, and some even declare bankruptcy. As a result, orders to the factory are reduced, precipitating layoffs and in some cases factory closings. As unemployment increases and output declines, GNP drops. Such recessions or depressions are demand driven.

Under Gorbachev the situation was very different. Given the shortcomings of central planning, there was no decline in demand or purchasing power. Rather, factories cut back or closed down because they lacked raw materials and components. When Gorbachev began to shrink the powers of Gosplan, the central planning agency, the monopolies that made sense under central planning proved to be a serious bottleneck. There were problems enough with plan fulfillment when Gosplan was all-powerful; when its authority was undermined and when market forces increased, state enterprise monopolies often found that their suppliers for one reason or another could not deliver the components as planned. Since their suppliers were also monopolies, they had nowhere else to turn to meet their production target. In the absence of other sources of supply, their customers in turn were also likely to suffer, and so on in a massive domino effect. The growth of the mafia, which gained control over supplies, led to a similar hardening of the supply arteries in the private sector. Between the state monopolies and the private mafia, it was very difficult to find substitute suppliers or anyone willing to respond to the new market opportunities.

The problem encountered by the Vladimir tractor factory illustrates the effects of the supply-side depression. Located about a two hours' drive from Moscow, the Vladimir factory, like most Soviet enterprises, was designed to be as self-sufficient as possible. Nonetheless, it had to rely on a few outside suppliers, including a tire factory in Armenia. When Armenia and Azerbaijan went to war in January 1990, Azerbaijan declared an embargo on all goods moving in and out of Armenia. That proved to be awkward for the Vladimir plant, because the embargo meant that when it shipped its tractors, it could do so only if it shipped them without tires, not a good way to increase productivity.

Why didn't the tractor factory go to another tire producer? Because the tire factory in Armenia had a monopoly. Why didn't the tractor factory turn to a wholesaler? Because with the downgrading of Gosplan there was no effective wholesaler that could perform such functions.

The farms dependent on the Vladimir tractors were also

affected. In Ukraine, for example, not only did the tractors have no tires; there was no diesel fuel to power them. Ukraine had agreed to sell grain and meat to Russia, but because of the growing inflation the ruble price agreed upon was no longer realistic, so Ukraine refused to make such deliveries. In protest, Russia began to withhold its diesel fuel. Ukraine then cut its shipments of coal to Russia, which retaliated by withholding timber, used among other things to hold up Ukraine's mine shafts. In the aftermath, not only did Ukrainian coal output decline, but 30 to 40 percent of its crop never made its way to the market, because of the lack of fuel. Crop waste has always been high in the Soviet Union, but this supply-side depression increased the degree of waste. In addition, factories suffered as their monopoly suppliers found themselves unable to obtain inputs. The consumer's lot, ever difficult, became harder still. As the growing inflation increased the pressure to hoard, goods disappeared from the state shops. In response the mafia and the black marketers, like good monopolists, did all they could to sustain or increase the shortage of goods. By doing so, they increased their power and profits.

VI

Such was Gorbachev's economic legacy. It is certainly unfair to blame all of the economic shortages on him. As we saw, the economy had been so booby-trapped that anyone attempting to undo the central planning mechanism would trigger the ensuing chaos. Gorbachev's problem was that he and his associates could not find their way out of the chaos they had triggered.

In addition, as the economy began to self-destruct, the residents of the Soviet Union became less and less committed to holding the Union together. Given the way the czars and the party's general secretaries had coerced the 150 or so ethnic groups into the Greater Russian and the Soviet empires, there was always an underlying determination to throw off Muscovite controls. As long as the power of the Soviet Union and Moscow seemed strong and stable, there was little sense in giving in to such nationalistic urges. But as the economy began to falter and Gorbachev began to espouse glasnost and adherence to Western noncoercive norms, the pressures for autonomy grew. To remain in the Union most likely meant to suffer a continuing decline in economic conditions. Independence might not improve economic conditions, but it was not apt to make them worse than they already were or were apt to become, or so it seemed.

Even some Russians began to advocate autonomy. As they saw it, the formation of the Soviet Union had come at great cost to Russia. Of course, the Soviet Union was a mask for Russian imperialism, but was it worth it? To support that empire, Russia had been forced to squander its precious oil, gas, and other raw materials to finance the often ungrateful and unresourceful minority non-Russian republics. By 1991 there seemed to be a growing consensus that the arrangement was not worthwhile. That was virtually the reverse of what the non-Russian ethnic groups of the Soviet Union had been arguing. As they saw it, it was their resources and hard labor that had propped up the Russians. They, not the Russians, were being exploited. In the end the Soviet Union may have been the only empire in the world where those in the metropolitan center, Moscow, felt as exploited as those in the peripheral colonies. That was one of the miracles of the Soviet system. All correctly perceived that they were being exploited, but except for an oversized military-industrial complex, the country had little of a material nature to show for the seventy years of exploitation.

Under these circumstances Gorbachev correctly perceived that he would have to make some concessions in order to hold the Soviet Union together. After several abortive efforts, he arranged for the signing of a new union agreement on August 20, 1991. If this agreement had come into being, it would have resulted in a considerably watered-down version of what had once been one of the most rigidly controlled empires in the world. As it was, Gorbachev had already conceded increasing control of the country's raw materials to the republics and their subdivisions. In the meantime some were also becoming more politically assertive. Several of the Baltic states had already declared their unwillingness to remain in any union—decentralized or not.

Critics argue that if Gorbachev had acted earlier and offered the Baltics and some of the other national groups more autonomy, they would have been satisfied and stayed in the Union. Gorbachev was a great compromiser, but his compromises were always too little and too late. Once the pressures for freedom and more autonomy began to grow, they were hard to contain and it became all but impossible "to stay ahead of the curve." Sooner or later the pressures would build again, until either autonomy was attained or blood was shed in an attempt to prevent the country from splitting apart.

Of course, not all Russians or all other ethnic groups were unhappy with the status quo. In fact, Russian nationalists and those who benefited from the super power status of the Soviet Union feared that once Gorbachev's semi-union plan was signed, it would mark the end of a strong centralized Soviet Union. Concerned for some time about what was happening to the country, they wanted a reassertion of more centralized controls and a shift of additional powers from the periphery to the center. Led by the head of the KGB, Vladimir Kryuchkov, they were determined to take extreme measures to achieve their goals—including a coup, if necessary, and with or without Gorbachev's participation. The decision to sign the new union treaty on August 20 forced their hand. They advanced their plan for a coup and launched it on August 19, 1991.

VII

Despite their faulty planning and comic implementation of the putsch, the conspirators nonetheless came close to achieving their goal. They had no trouble placing Gorbachev under house arrest while he vacationed in the Crimea, and with what they thought was their control of the army, KGB, and police they had the firepower available to storm the office of the Russian president and its parliament, or, as it came to be called, Yeltsin's White House. Their biggest mistake was to let Boris Yeltsin slip out of their hands as he made his way in from his suburban dacha to the White House, in the center of the city. As the only Russian leader who had run in and won a national election, he and probably no one else had the legitimacy and potential for challenging the conspirators. With a display of uncommon bravery and theatrics, Yeltsin defied the conspirators, who, because of the secrecy and uncoordinated nature of their scheme, allowed themselves to be outmaneuvered.

Yeltsin, not Gorbachev, upset their plans. Given the state of the economy and evident political disintegration sparked by Gorbachev's reforms, there was very little popular concern over his fate inside the Soviet Union itself. Unlike Yeltsin, Gorbachev had never run in any popular election. His political positions were always the result of party selection and promotion processes. Yet, because there was a sense that agreed-upon procedures had been violated and that an elected official's powers had been circumscribed, the public opposed the coup. However, that official was Yeltsin, not Gorbachev. I was in Moscow at the time of the coup. There were no rallies for Gorbachev, and no one mounted a barricade in his name. Nor were there graffiti calling for his return. Instead, the shouts and barricades were for "Boris." The graffiti attacked the Communist Party and its Central Committee and, by extension, even Gorbachev. For that matter, many observers thought, perhaps correctly, that Gorbachev was involved at least indirectly with the conspirators.

The coup failed, but only because some KGB and army units refused to follow orders. Nonetheless, it was touch and go in the early hours. Because the Yeltsin forces lacked access to most of the national media, they had difficulty mobilizing popular support. Not too many were willing to take the risk. Initially, they could muster only a few thousand, mostly young people. That was unusual because up until that point most of the demonstrators in Moscow were the middle-aged or pensioners. There was also a surprising number of new entrepreneurs. For the entrepreneurs a return to more centralized control could have meant prison or, at the least, arbitrary interference in their business and personal lives. (Similar concerns had led some Chinese entrepreneurs to join in the Chinese student demonstration in Tiananmen Square in April and May 1989.) For that matter, the French bourgeoisie had risen up against the king for similar reasons two centuries earlier.

When it became apparent on the second day of the coup that the conspirators were not going to use their firepower, increasing numbers of Muscovites ventured out into the streets and around the White House. By Thursday, the fourth day of the coup, a White House rally drew several hundred thousand defenders, and by Friday I could find no one who had supported the coup or who had anything good to say about the conspirators. The sense of euphoria was everywhere. The "people" had stood up for Yeltsin and "democracy." The putsch had failed and the conspirators been arrested. Nevertheless, when the outcome was still in doubt, only a few thousand had been willing to declare themselves on behalf of Yeltsin. Moreover, only a few cities like Sverdlovsk and St. Petersburg mounted similar protests. For the vast majority, it was indifference, support for the coup, or, at best, "Wait until the dust settles." This initial meager turnout contrasted starkly with the demonstrations of several million in China in 1989.

Exciting as the defeat of the coup was, the realization grew that this by no means ended the country's economic and political problems. For one thing, the failure of the coup meant the end of the Union. Although a few days earlier Gorbachev had protested Lithuania's growing insistence on independence, after the coup it was no longer an issue. In the vacuum that occurred after the coup attempt, Lithuania simply became independent, as did many of the other republics. However exhilarating independence was for the different nationalist movements, it also meant that the integrated Soviet economy painstakingly crafted over seventy years was suddenly divided into fifteen or more parts. While it could be argued that in the long run output in the various republics might well increase, in the short run supply flows were severed, further disrupting production and raising prices.

Even though to all appearances the coup had failed, in fact it set in motion Gorbachev's ouster. One after another of his powers as president of the Soviet Union disappeared. Yeltsin's leadership against the conspirators and his increasing assertiveness on behalf of Russia deprived Gorbachev of his authority as the president of a country, the Soviet Union, that was quickly becoming extinct. As early as October 1991 Yeltsin set out a distinctive economic role for Russia. Gorbachev's other main powers, the control of the army and the KGB, were also taken away as Russia and soon the other republics set up their own armies. Moreover, the Soviet army and KGB had been compromised by the coup.

Gorbachev tried to hang on. Ultimately, he lost power because Yeltsin and the other republic leaders simply dissolved the Soviet Union. As a consequence Gorbachev found himself a president without a country. Unintentionally, by depriving Gorbachev of power, Yeltsin accomplished what the August conspirators had failed to achieve. Although Yeltsin's effort was peaceful, on December 25, 1991, when Gorbachev was nudged out of the president's office, it was nonetheless a coup. Gorbachev's term as president was supposed to last for at least another two years. Yeltsin finally triumphed, even if he had to participate in the abolition of the Soviet Union to do it.

Admittedly, given the way he had been abused by Gorbachev, Yeltsin had just cause to seek revenge. Yet his personal vindictiveness did not add to his stature. He was so eager to humiliate Gorbachev that he moved into Gorbachev's personal offices three days before the agreed date. When Gorbachev tried to gain admittance to pack up his belongings, he found to his dismay that Yeltsin had already taken possession and was inside drinking whiskey with Ruslan Khasbulatov, Yeltsin's then close confederate but soon to become antagonist.[15]

VIII

Soon after the coup Yeltsin became increasingly assertive in introducing radical reforms in the Russian part of the Soviet economy. In contrast to Gorbachev, who was unable to decide on what reforms and which reformers to support, Yeltsin accepted the idea of shock therapy administered by Yegor Gaidar, a young economist he ultimately appointed acting prime minister. As we shall see, however, their efforts proved as futile as Gorbachev's. Admittedly, even if they had come up with the right combination of reforms, the process would have been prolonged and agonizing. Russia, after seventy years under communism, simply does not lend itself readily to market and democratic reforms. To make matters worse, those attempting reform have generally failed to appreciate just how complex their task was and what their strategy should have been. A comparison of reforms in other societies, both capitalist and communist, shows that a prerequisite for such reforms is the existence of large enough nonstate marketing, agricultural, and production sectors to respond to newly liberalized price and profit incentives. The existence of these institutions is no guarantee that the reforms will be successful, but the absence of such institutions all but guarantees that the reform effort will fail. The reason for this is that a private-sector response to market stimuli is essential because there must be an immediate increase in the production and availability of consumer goods after the reforms have been set in motion. Only in this way will the public perceive that there are real and immediate benefits to be gained from such reforms. This perception is needed to offset the inevitable dislocation and pain that accompany the restructuring process. What Yeltsin and Gaidar, as well as Gorbachev, never fully understood is that the purpose of the reforms should be to make people's lives better.

Many reformers argue endlessly over what should come first, political reform or economic reform. Obviously, if the economic reforms can be made to work and quickly show results, political reform will be easier to implement. Rapid political reform, however, without an improvement in economic livelihood jeopardizes the success of the economic reforms, particularly if those political reforms unleash long-suppressed demands for regional, individual, or ethnic rights. As reflected by the Zhirinovsky neofascist protest vote in the December 1993 election, the public may become so angry over what it sees as a misconceived reform effort that it not only forces the reform effort back to square one but even insists, as did Zhirinovsky, that the government return to square minus one.

Assuming that there were some way to modulate the pace of reforms, the optimal scenario would be to be set in motion a gradual increase in simultaneous economic and political reforms. Failed economic reform will jeopardize political reforms, just as failure to provide political reforms will ultimately frustrate economic reforms. As we shall see, Poland is one of the few countries that seem to have achieved something close to a balanced mix. This is the elusive goal for all reforming societies, not merely those seeking to unshackle themselves from the legacy of communism. What follows is an analysis of Yeltsin's rise to power and his so far unsuccessful attempt to find the proper blueprint for economic reform and a balance between economic and political reforms.

2.

The Rise of Boris Yeltsin

What is surprising is not that Mikhail Gorbachev fell from power but that Boris Yeltsin rose to it. Gorbachev had been the protégé of two of the most powerful men in the Politburo, Yuri Andropov and Mikhail Suslov. Once in position as the general secretary of the Communist Party, Gorbachev immediately moved to consolidate his power. More rapidly than any general secretary before him, he purged those he viewed as corrupt, inept, or a threat. The first to go was Grigori Romanov, the one-time leader of Leningrad. He was dismissed in July 1985, a mere four months after Gorbachev's selection. The dismissal of other potential challengers followed in October and December.

That was not the end of the purging process. I have a Russian poster in my office printed in 1986 with the photographs of all the members of the Politburo. By late 1990 I had placed *x*'s over all of their faces as one after another was removed from the Politburo and power. Only Gorbachev's face remained, and I crossed it off for a Russian TV program in December 1991.

Yeltsin took a very different road to the Kremlin. Unlike Gorbachev, he had no patron in Moscow. He rose to power largely on the strength of his abilities and his performance as first secretary of the Sverdlovsk Communist Party, the highest-ranking party or government official in the area. Located in the Urals, Sverdlovsk (now called Ekaterinburg, as it was before the revolution) was one of the Soviet Union's largest and most important industrial centers, and the fifth-largest city in Russia.

Yeltsin came to the attention of the Moscow officials for both his administrative talents and his experience in the construction industry, where he had received his initial training. But unlike the majority of his peers, Yeltsin had little interest in taking a job in Moscow. He was comfortable in Sverdlovsk. It was largely free of the day-to-day bureaucratic battles prevalent in Moscow, and for that reason he turned down several promotions, including a job as minister, all of which would have required a move to Moscow. Finally, in April 1985, pressured by Gorbachev, he agreed to leave Sverdlovsk, but he insists he did so with a good deal of reluctance.[1]

Though he considered it to be beneath what his stature merited, Yeltsin's first job in Moscow was that of the head of the section in the Central Committee of the Soviet Communist Party that supervised the construction industry. Yeltsin believed he should have been entitled, at the very least, to the rank of secretary in the Central Committee in charge of construction. Two months later, in June 1985, he was indeed elected to that position, but Gorbachev's delay in promoting him rankled Yeltsin. Yeltsin's memoirs are sprinkled with his complaints about Gorbachev's put-downs.[2]

Before long, however, Gorbachev promoted Yeltsin once again, moving him this time into the middle of the perestroika battle. Gorbachev realized that his reform efforts would go nowhere without the purging of officials who were obstructing the reforms in the Moscow city party organization, particularly its upper ranks. The Moscow party was for eighteen years headed by Viktor Grishin, who had been the second secretary eleven years before that. Under Grishin's control Moscow had become notorious for its corruption and crime-ridden ways.[3] But Grishin had become a political power in his own right not only in the city but also in the national Politburo. In fact, he was one of the chief contenders, along with Gorbachev, to replace Konstantin Chernenko. Once he was in power, one of Gorbachev's first political decisions was to remove Grishin and replace him with a proven and honest administrator willing to take on an entrenched and corrupt bureaucracy. As the former head of Sverdlovsk, one of the few areas relatively free of corruption and self-dealing, Yeltsin seemed the logical choice, and he became responsible for running Moscow in December 1985.[4]

While almost everyone agrees that Yeltsin did an excellent job in Sverdlovsk, there is also agreement that he did a poor job in running Moscow. After his brief assignment in construction, Yeltsin plunged with a passion into the cleanup of Moscow's messy economic and political affairs. One of his first steps as Moscow party secretary was to fire Vladimir Promyslov, its longtime mayor.[5] Promyslov was forced to turn in his resignation two days after the announcement of Yeltsin's appointment.[6] Yeltsin replaced Promyslov with Valery Saikin, previously the manager of the Moscow ZIL truck factory, but it was Yeltsin who took the most public stance in dealing with municipal affairs.

As in Sverdlovsk, in Moscow, Yeltsin became an activist reformer. To dramatize and publicize his actions, Yeltsin arranged for television crews to accompany him on most of his visits. He made a special effort to call attention to the understocked shelves in the front of the store, in contrast to the overstocked storage facilities in the back, where managers, for a bribe, diverted state resources to the privileged and powerful. At the same time, Yeltsin also purged the bureaucrats and managers in the city administration, most of whom were longtime associates of Grishin and Promyslov. Before long Yeltsin had purged twenty-three out of the thirty-three district first secretaries and had arrested over eight hundred corrupt trade officials.[7] In March 1987 Yeltsin claimed he had replaced over one-half of all the leaders in the Moscow party leadership.[8] He even fired some of his own appointees.

Following his own precepts, Yeltsin not only purged the bureaucracy and assaulted traditional party privileges such as access to specially stocked stores; he also made a point of living like the man in the street—riding buses and subways and using ordinary health clinics, instead of the fancy hospitals set aside for the party elite. His effort to end special privileges for party members applied both to local Moscow officials and to the national Communist Party hierarchy, most of which lived in Moscow. These actions alienated a large percentage of the party establishment, people whose backing he would later need.

The party and state apparatus did not take such attacks passively. They responded by openly sabotaging Yeltsin's efforts. Food supplies intended for Moscow were deliberately diverted, destroyed, or left to rot by bitter city employees.[9] Government apparatchiks (sometimes referred to as the government mafia), along with nongovernment mafia members, even threatened his personal safety. At one of his public meetings, a written "question" passed from the audience read, "You, Yeltsin, have started to tackle the Moscow mafia. We've been through this before—Khrushchev wanted to pack all of us off to labor camps. If you go on the way you have, someone else will have your job in two years' time!"[10] As Yeltsin subsequently noted, "This prediction came true." Other Yeltsin opponents insisted, "We have stolen and will continue to steal."[11] On another occasion someone warned him, "Don't snipe at us. . . . We are the elite, and you cannot halt the stratification of society. You are not strong enough. We will rip the puny sails of your perestroika and you will be unable to reach your destination. So moderate your ardor."[12] Some even warned ominously that he "should go back to Sverdlovsk before it was too late."[13] Despite his frenetic pace and fierce determination, in the face of such opposition there was not much he could do. He himself, acknowledged that, as of April 1987, "people have not felt substantial changes."[14]

But the failure to improve Moscow's living conditions could not be blamed entirely on Yeltsin. It would have been surprising if meaningful change had actually occurred. At the time perestroika and glasnost were not succeeding anywhere in the country. In 1987 it was still too early for Yeltsin to see how difficult it was to undo an extended centrally planned command economy and move to a market economy.

Yeltsin himself was truly puzzled by his meager success and eventually exhausted by the experience. Discounting the sabotage against him and the turnover of personnel, Yeltsin had believed he would be as successful in running Moscow as he had been in running Sverdlovsk. But he forgot that in Sverdlovsk he was not an outsider but an insider in love with his city. There was some truth to the accusation "You Boris Nikolaivich unfortunately love neither Moscow nor Muscovites."[15]

Moreover, Yeltsin's talents were better suited to the command system conditions that prevailed at the time in Sverdlovsk. In the old command system Yeltsin issued orders and took it for granted that most of them would be implemented. Given that Yeltsin was an active leader, concerned more with improving conditions for the city than for himself, the odds were that his commands would be supported.

By the time Yeltsin took over leadership in Moscow, however, the system was in transition. The perestroika-glasnost era was just beginning, but already the old command system had begun to disintegrate. The new environment demanded less dictating and more consensus building and bottom-up effort. Yeltsin only partly understood this. His muckraking efforts and public showmanship reflected his understanding of the need to mobilize public support, but he, like Gorbachev, did not know how to translate that public desire for change into constructive action. Nor did it help that in an era of glasnost and perestroika the party bureaucracy and the Moscow municipal "civil service" no longer felt themselves obligated to Yeltsin or intimidated by his commands. They regarded themselves as basically impervious to grassroots anger or desire for action. Even if fired temporarily, they believed in their own staying power and, equally important, in their enduring decision-making authority and control.

Given the magnitude of the necessary changes, even if Yeltsin had been a hometown hero, he would have faced enormous resistance. One of his fiercest opponents was Yegor Ligachev, at the time the number two man in the Politburo and a staunch defender of party prerogatives. Ligachev resisted Yeltsin's insistence that party members should be forced to endure the same day-to-day difficulties faced by ordinary citizens. Yeltsin notes that as many as forty thousand party members enjoyed special privileges. But Ligachev refused to eliminate their access to special food and appliance stores, not to mention dachas and clinics. Yeltsin was just as determined to cut off their access.[16]

That is not to argue that either man was wholly consistent. In Yeltsin's eyes it was immoral to create special class privileges for the party elite. But his sense of morality did not extend to restricting the sale of vodka and other alcoholic products or to the closing of a Moscow brewery.[17] Undoubtedly, his concern for the public's continuing access to vodka reflected not only his populist impulses but also his own fondness for vodka. By contrast, Ligachev, as a dedicated party official, saw no problem in reserving special privileges for officials who worked harder, and bore more sacrifices, than ordinary people. Given his very strict code of personal behavior, however, Ligachev also regarded the Russian affinity for vodka as a national curse. Access to vodka thus became another element in their rivalry.

This clash of views gradually spread from issues to personalities. According to Yeltsin himself, his escalating battles with Ligachev played an important role in his unprecedented decision to resign voluntarily from the Politburo.[18] He was upset that Gorbachev seemed to be siding more and more with Ligachev and abandoning Yeltsin and what Yeltsin regarded as the Gorbachev model of reform.

Confronted with increasing opposition from below and lack of support from above, and beset with growing concern about his abilities to handle the job, Yeltsin suddenly decided he had had enough. Unfortunately for him as well as for Gorbachev, he chose to announce his surprise decision at a meeting of the Central Committee on October 21, 1987, called to approve Gorbachev's preparations for the celebration of the seventieth anniversary of the 1917 Bolshevik Revolution.

If made public, this evidence of internal disorder, dissent, and difficulty with the reform process would have detracted from the festivities and what Gorbachev intended to be a triumphant occasion for communism, the Soviet Union, and himself. If things are going well, Politburo members simply do not resign, especially before momentous occasions such as the seventieth anniversary.[19]

From Gorbachev's point of view, Yeltsin's resignation not only detracted from the seventieth-anniversary celebration; it also undermined Gorbachev's role as a balancer of reformers like Yeltsin and conservatives like Yegor Ligachev. For all these reasons, Gorbachev arranged for the Central Committee to limit itself initially to a simple condemnation of Yeltsin's speech. In the hope of preventing a scandal, it was agreed that Gorbachev would postpone dismissing Yeltsin from the Politburo until after the November 7 festivities.[20] However, word of Yeltsin's resignation leaked out on October 31; just as Gorbachev feared, it detracted from his efforts to glorify the success of perestroika, glasnost, and the revitalization of the communist movement. As punishment, four days after the November 7 ceremonies Gorbachev convened a special inquisition to humiliate Yeltsin.

Although Gorbachev had initially indicated that Yeltsin might someday be allowed to return to power, the condemnation heaped on Yeltsin during the November 11 Moscow city party plenum was so spiteful and vicious that Yeltsin's political career seemed finished. Gorbachev showed no mercy. Two days before attending the November 7 ceremonies and participating in a false picture of solidarity with the other members of the Politburo, Yeltsin suffered chest pains and severe headaches and was taken to the hospital. Nonetheless, Gorbachev insisted that Yeltsin be present at the November 11 meeting so that he would be forced to hear himself denounced, even though it required that Yeltsin be taken from his sickbed in the hospital.[21]

While Soviet politicians with political headaches traditionally seek shelter in hospitals, Yeltsin's health problems were real. Because of his reported tendency to drink too much, he is thought to have a serious liver problem. In addition Yeltsin suffered from a recurring heart problem he developed at the age of twenty-two, when he was improperly treated for rheumatic fever.[22] (After he was elected to the Russian Supreme Soviet in 1990, Yeltsin was involved in a car accident and a plane crash. To cope with the lingering pain, he frequently has had to take powerful drugs, which would leave him with a puffy face and unhealthy appearance.) There were also rumors that he had suffered a mental breakdown. In his 1994 memoirs, Yeltsin candidly acknowledges that he suffers periodically from depression. But however bad Yeltsin may have felt before the proceedings, he must have felt considerably worse afterward. In a throwback to the Stalin show trials of the 1930s, he was barraged by accusations and ad hominem criticisms designed not only to whip up passions among his accusers but to ensure, as in the 1930s, that the target would be destroyed forever as a political force.

As if the accusations, many of them false, had not been enough to break this proud man's spirit, Yeltsin was also forced to acknowledge his shortcomings publicly and to confess that his resignation had detracted from the anniversary ceremonies. This too resembled the confessions of the "wreckers" of the Stalin era, but Yeltsin, unlike them, was not jailed, exiled, or executed. Nonetheless, the ruthlessness of the assault, especially in view of his weakened state, made him determined to seek revenge.

At the time, however, it appeared that Yeltsin was finished as a political player. In fact, Gorbachev telephoned him, Yeltsin recalled, to tell him that "he wasn't going to let me back into politics."[23] But confronted with a surprising show of public support in the form of demonstrations and letters for Yeltsin in places like Moscow as well as Sverdlovsk, Gorbachev relented somewhat. He grudgingly appointed Yeltsin a vice minister of the construction industry. Still, this paper-pushing administrative post was a form of modern-day exile, particularly for a man known for his restlessness and energy. Khrushchev had used similar tactics to humiliate and disgrace his opponents Vyacheslav Molotov and Georgi Malenkov. But whereas Khrushchev assigned them to positions far out in the provinces, Gorbachev allowed Yeltsin to remain in Moscow. (In retrospect, Gorbachev would probably have been wiser to order Yeltsin to return to Sverdlovsk, and out of the center in Moscow, which Yeltsin might also have preferred.) Whatever the location, Yeltsin had for all intents and purposes become a political nonentity. Indeed, just as in 1964 when Khrushchev himself was forced from office, no paper or journal was allowed even to mention the disgraced man's name. Despite glasnost, Yeltsin disappeared from the public eye for eighteen months.[24]

Yeltsin's subsequent reemergence as a political force and eventually Gorbachev's successor is unprecedented in Soviet and Russian history. It heightens the unexpectedness of Yeltsin's rebirth that, before Gorbachev's attack, Yeltsin hardly seemed a likely candidate for the post of president. Yet, after an initial period of withdrawal, Yeltsin took on almost the whole governmental political establishment and especially the Communist Party.

For all their differences, in some ways Yeltsin and Gorbachev had much in common. Born only a month apart, both were products of the kind of peasant families that made up over 80 percent of the population at the time. Another common characteristic was that members of both families had run-ins with Stalin's police.[25] Yeltsin's father was arrested. Both of Gorbachev's grandfathers were arrested. Yeltsin's and Gorbachev's families were both poor. However, the Stavropol region, in the south, Gorbachev's home, was well suited to agriculture, and thus the family had little to fear from the extremes of the weather. By contrast the Sverdlovsk region, in the Urals, where Yeltsin's family lived, was located farther north and east and thus had a shorter growing season with less varied and more problematical harvests.

Despite the harshness of the times and their own humble origins, both boys were sent by their families to acquire a higher education. Gorbachev was helped by the fact that he won a silver medal in his school's academic competition. The determination of the party and government leadership at the time to increase the percentage of peasant children in the university also helped Gorbachev win admittance to the very prestigious Moscow State

University. It was considered then even more than now the combined Harvard and Yale of the Russian educational system.

Although Yeltsin, too, achieved high marks, he did not place as well academically. Happy to remain closer to home, he enrolled in the Urals Polytechnical Institute for training as an engineer. Unlike Gorbachev, Yeltsin was somewhat irreverent and more of a prankster and sportsman. He spent many hours exploring, hiking, and sometimes fighting with his classmates. He was also a fanatic for volleyball—a game he continued to play even after he blew off two fingers of his left hand while experimenting with a stolen hand grenade as a child during World War II.[26]

Gorbachev was more purposeful and focused on Communist Party matters.[27] He joined the party at the age of twenty, in 1951. By contrast Yeltsin did not join the party until 1961, when he decided for nonideological reasons that he had to join to facilitate his rise in the managerial ranks in the Sverdlovsk construction industry. After graduation from Moscow State University, Gorbachev returned to Stavropol and plunged right into party work. Yeltsin devoted himself to construction. He was viewed as a savvy, but physically rough manager. Only in 1969 did he agree to take on work as a senior Communist Party official, responsible for all construction in the Sverdlovsk Oblast province.

Once involved in the party, Yeltsin like Gorbachev began to move up the administrative ladder. Ultimately, both men became head of their party organization or the local maharaja in their respective oblasts. In the 1960s and 1970s they had, in effect, the powers of little dictators. Nevertheless, both were considered capable, honest leaders. Given their similar posts—Gorbachev in the rich agricultural area and Yeltsin in one of the main military industrial districts of the country—they had periodic dealings with each other.[28] Yeltsin has acknowledged that he frequently sought Gorbachev's help with agricultural matters in Sverdlovsk; at the same time he also helped Gorbachev obtain metal and timber for Stavropol.

Gorbachev was called to Moscow in November 1978; as we saw, Yeltsin followed seven years later, but as Gorbachev's subordinate. A careful reading of Yeltsin's autobiography reveals hints of jealousy and resentment at what Yeltsin perceived as Gorbachev's increasingly imperious and arrogant Moscow ways. Yeltsin dates the first "cooling in our relationship" to 1978, shortly after Gorbachev became secretary of the Central Committee apparatus in charge of agriculture.[29] Yeltsin deeply resented Gorbachev's staff's criticisms of agricultural conditions in the Sverdlovsk region. Gorbachev had long known that Sverdlovsk was located in a region ill suited for farming, and Yeltsin was proud that his region had done as well as it had.

Though Gorbachev thought enough of Yeltsin to put him in charge of cleaning up Moscow, it should not have come as a surprise, given their uneasy relationship over the years, that Gorbachev eventually turned on Yeltsin, especially when Yeltsin began to behave erratically. But by challenging the party and its prerogatives and provoking attacks not only from Ligachev but from an increasingly overbearing Gorbachev, Yeltsin inadvertently all but guaranteed his ultimate resurrection. With his attack on the abuse of party privileges and his criticism of Gorbachev's and Ligachev's crackdown on the sale of vodka, Yeltsin became the spokesman for the little guy. When party leaders pounced on him and sought to humiliate him publicly, Yeltsin emerged as a hero and martyr. Yeltsin became the man of the people, put forward to take on Ligachev, the man of the party. Given the increasing cynicism of the Soviet public, the Soviet leaders should perhaps have realized that the more they attacked and sought to belittle Yeltsin, the more popular he would become. This was a reaction to years of deceit and manipulation.

Yeltsin's "political exile," as he described it, was first breached at the Nineteenth Communist Party Conference, on June 2, 1988, where, despite efforts to prevent his selection as a delegate, Yeltsin was nominated at the last minute by party officials in Karelia, far out of the mainstream, as one of their delegates.[30] Yeltsin suggests this action may have been a face-saving gesture on the part of Gorbachev, who came under pressure from some delegates to allow Yeltsin to attend. But while they agreed to let Yeltsin attend, they did all they could to prevent him from participating in the proceedings, which were also being televised nationally.[31] Determined to be heard, on the last day of the conference, Yeltsin left his assigned seat at the rear of the highest balcony, pushed his way onto the main floor of the vast auditorium, and headed for the podium as if to speak. After a futile effort to entice him out of the hall, Gorbachev relented and allowed Yeltsin to address the nation.[32] Once again Yeltsin attacked the party and its privileges. He also urged that he be rehabilitated in his lifetime, rather than wait fifty years as had happened to Stalin's victims.

Not surprisingly, Yeltsin's plea was rejected. Once more he disappeared from the public scene. But while the Soviet media were warned to avoid him, the Western media regarded him as a colorful figure who had spoken openly and frankly and would probably do so again. He was sought out and interviewed by several Western television networks. During the June 1988 U.S.-Soviet summit meeting, I recall, correspondents for ABC News were eager to talk with him. Yeltsin's comments to reporters soon found their way back to the Soviet Union via foreign broadcasts, such as those of the BBC and the Voice of America.[33] This only intensified the anger of party officials, who at the time still regarded unauthorized interviews with Western journalists as close to treasonous.

The effort to ignore him continued, and it was another six months, until November 12, 1988, before Yeltsin was finally invited to speak at a domestic forum.[34] Even then, the organizers of the lecture at the Higher Komsomol School had great difficulty in obtaining permission. Moreover, when he delivered his speech, it was initially ignored by the national and city press, though some provincial papers did reprint portions of it.

In a full-fledged effort to "escape from Coventry," Yeltsin also decided to run in the March 26, 1989, election for a seat in the newly created Soviet Congress of People's Deputies.[35] A third of the 2,250 seats had been set aside for senior Communist Party officials, including Gorbachev, as well as certain influential groups, but the rest of the seats were, at least in principle, open to anyone who wanted to run. Yeltsin, however, was not "anyone." The party authorities did all they could to keep him off the ballot. The Central Committee even established an investigative subcommittee to determine whether Yeltsin was eligible to run as a Communist Party candidate. His resignation speech at the October 1987 party plenum, where he attacked the party leadership, was judged to be "politically mistaken," and thus he was considered unfit to run.[36] But the more they tried to blackball him, the more popular Yeltsin became.[37] His rallies attracted crowds of 100,000 or more. His candidacy was seen as a challenge to Gorbachev. In the end Yeltsin ran for a seat at large in the city of Moscow. He won a stunning victory, garnering 89.6 percent of the vote. The size of Yeltsin's mandate made it politically impossible for Gorbachev to shunt Yeltsin aside any more, though he tried his best.

One of the major responsibilities of the 2,250-member Soviet Congress of People's Deputies was to select 542 of its delegates as representatives in the Supreme Soviet of the Soviet Union. Whereas the Congress was scheduled to meet in full session twice a year, the Supreme Soviet was to meet on a continuing basis. Therefore, in terms of day-to-day legislation, the Supreme Soviet was the more important decision-making body. Unable to keep Yeltsin out of the Congress, Gorbachev tried to keep him out of the Supreme Soviet. A full slate was nominated and elected with no mention of Yeltsin. Only after an already elected delegate resigned specifically to make room for Yeltsin was he able to become a member.[38]

In the bitter process of coming back from the politically dead, Yeltsin shed much of his party loyalty and political and economic ideology. Thus unshackled, he challenged the monopoly role of the Communist Party and began to agitate for a multiparty system.[39] This was a prelude to his dramatic resignation a year later from the Communist Party itself at the Twenty-eighth Party

Congress, in July 1990.[40] Even before that, in 1989, he began to advocate land reform and a switch to the market.[41] He assumed, however, that the transition would be relatively painless and that the land would continue to be owned by the state.[42]

Having won such a large mandate in the election to the All Union Congress of People's Deputies, Yeltsin decided in 1990 to run again, this time for the smaller Russian Congress of People's Deputies. Recognizing how futile it was, Gorbachev and the other party officials made no effort to keep Yeltsin off the ballot. Moreover, he ran as a delegate from his home base of Sverdlovsk, where he again received an overwhelming mandate, 84 percent of the vote. Unlike the All Union Congress, the Russian Congress featured direct election, region by region. No seats were set aside, as in the All Union Congress, for the party and special organizations.[43] Like the All Union Congress, however, the Russian Congress was then expected to elect about one-third of its 1,040 members to serve in the ongoing Russian Supreme Soviet.

Until the 1990 election the Russian Supreme Soviet was regarded as more a joke than a source of power. All decisions of any significance had always come from the All Union Supreme Soviet or Congress. The best people, including Gorbachev, never even bothered to seek membership in the more restricted Russian body. But Yeltsin had a different agenda in mind. Although he did not talk about it openly, he seemed to understand before almost anyone else that as a result of Gorbachev's reforms, and of glasnost in particular, the Soviet Union would not long endure. Once the election process became a meaningful one with secret ballots and competitive candidates, its demise was inevitable. Having to win a contested election, the candidates to the Supreme Soviet would truly have to represent their constituents and express their wishes. Consequently, delegates began to reflect more nationalist feelings and ultimately demanded more autonomy. This realization may explain Yeltsin's repeated insistence that he had no interest in challenging Gorbachev for the role of president of the Soviet Union. His interest was limited to

Russia. Until Yeltsin began to limit his political interest to Russia, any politician who dared to suggest that Russia, and not the Soviet Union, was the political force that counted would have been laughed at.

Yeltsin, however, determined not only to serve in the Russian Congress of People's Deputies and in the Russian Supreme Soviet; he also set his sights on winning election as the chairman of the Russian Supreme Soviet. Holders of this post were chosen by the members of the Russian Supreme Soviet. Even though until 1991 it was often referred to as the presidency, it was not a sought-after position. Like everything limited to the Russian Republic itself, it had not been taken seriously, because earlier only the Soviet Union mattered politically. For most purposes the Soviet Union was Russia. Similar reasoning explains why until 1990 there was no separate Russian Academy of Sciences or Russian Communist Party.[44] Both institutions, like the Russian Supreme Soviet, would have been redundant since the All Union institutions were almost invariably dominated by Russians and reflected Russian views.

However meaningless the position of president or chairman of the Russian Supreme Soviet may have been in the past, Gorbachev quickly concluded that he did not want Yeltsin to win it. For Gorbachev it was probably a matter more of symbolism than of power. The Russian Supreme Soviet in 1990 was still a relatively feeble institution, but Gorbachev did not want Yeltsin to have the title of president, even if only of the Russian Federation. Gorbachev therefore made a determined effort to defeat Yeltsin.

Indeed, Yeltsin had already encountered fierce opposition from party and government apparatchiks, many of whom were also elected to the Russian Supreme Soviet. They had been alienated by his increasingly radical ideas. His chief opponent was Aleksandr Vlasov, the last prime minister of the Russian Republic before the open elections and a candidate member of the All Union Politburo. Gorbachev at first swung his support to Vlasov. When it appeared that Vlasov could not win, Gorbachev arranged to speak at a session of the Russian Supreme Soviet even though he was not a member. He bitterly attacked Yeltsin and backed Ivan Polozkov, from the city of Krasnodar, although Polozkov was a hard-line conservative and an opponent of many of Gorbachev's reforms. Polozkov had been an outspoken critic of, among other things, perestroika and glasnost, and attacked private trade and cooperatives. He was also a strong supporter of the collective farm system.[45] (He later led the way to the creation of the Russian Communist Party and was one of the instigators of the coup in August 1991.) In his determination to stop Yeltsin, however, Gorbachev was prepared to support whoever might defeat him, regardless of his attitude toward reform.

Anticipating that victory would not come easily, Yeltsin began to call for more political sovereignty for the republics, first of all Russia.[46] By this Yeltsin meant, for example, that Soviet law would be implemented only when it coincided with the Russian Republic's own laws. However, legal autonomy was more than Gorbachev was prepared to yield. At the time he wanted to offer no more than "economic autonomy." Yeltsin's initiative gave a foretaste of what would happen when the public gained genuine voting power.

Gorbachev was so obsessed with the possibility of a Yeltsin victory that, on the very eve of his trip to a May 1990 summit meeting in Washington with George Bush, he interrupted his preparations to call a meeting of about 250 Russian Supreme Soviet delegates to urge them to oppose Yeltsin. He told the delegates that Yeltsin sought to "destroy the Union—its defense, its finances—destroy everything."[47] Implicit, but even more important, was Gorbachev's personal rivalry with Yeltsin, this man who refused to be shunted aside.

Whether it was Gorbachev's pressure or the fact that Yeltsin supporters were still not mobilized, the vote for Yeltsin as chairman fell short of the necessary majority. In a second ballot, Yeltsin picked up some more votes, but still not enough to win. At that point the opposition regrouped, and on the third round of votes Polozkov withdrew in favor of Vlasov, but Vlasov also failed to win the necessary number of votes. Finally, Yeltsin won with 4 votes to spare over the 535 needed. In typical fashion he immediately called a press conference to flaunt his victory. This served Yeltsin's purpose at the time, which was to distract Gorbachev at the summit in Washington. Whereas one of the goals of the trip had been to lift Gorbachev out of petty partisanship into the realm of international diplomacy, he was instead forced to respond to questions about Yeltsin's victory.

Although Yeltsin's new base in the Russian Supreme Soviet provided a public forum for his views, his four-vote plurality meant that his support there was far from secure. If proof were needed, on March 7, 1991, those opposed to Yeltsin called an emergency meeting of the Russian Supreme Soviet to oust Yeltsin as president.[48] The effort failed. But Yeltsin the savvy politician turned the tables. Just ten days later, on March 17, he won support for a referendum to decide whether or not to create the post of Russian president and to elect that president directly by a vote of the people.[49] Yeltsin won the referendum. In the subsequent presidential election held June 12, 1991, out of six candidates, Yeltsin won 57.4 percent of the votes in the first round.

Yeltsin's direct election by the people was a historic event. Over forty-five million people voted for him. Other than Richard Nixon, Ronald Reagan (but only in the run for his second term), and George Bush, no one else in history had ever received more votes in a democratic election. Equally important, this was the first time in Russia, before or after the revolution, that the Russian people had ever had a chance to elect their own president. Yeltsin was no longer merely a creature of the Russian Supreme Soviet. He had not just run for election from a specific region as an ordinary delegate to the Russian parliament; he went before the whole country to seek a franchise from the entire Russian public. Gorbachev had done neither. In fact, he had never risked an election among the people at large, whether for representative of the National Congress of People's Deputies or for president. For that matter, he had never run in a popular and contested election for a party post. He had always been elected either on a one-candidate ballot or in an intraparty election organized and run for and by party officials. Unlike Yeltsin in 1991, Gorbachev had never sought or received a popular mandate from the electorate. In the early days of glasnost or perestroika, when he could have won, Gorbachev did not appreciate the symbolism of such a mandate or think it important. Later on, as he came to realize that such a franchise would have been a powerful weapon in his battle to implement his program, it was too late. By 1991, if Gorbachev had tried to run for president, whether against Yeltsin or against some other popular figure, he might well have lost. His failure to risk an earlier public vote in a competitive election ultimately undermined his ability to carry out his reform.

In the beginning, at least, Yeltsin proved to be a much smarter politician. Like the late Massachusetts congressman Thomas ("Tip") O'Neill, Yeltsin understood that all politics is local. Initially, Gorbachev sought to break out of the Kremlin and meet with ordinary Russians, but as criticism of his efforts began to grow, he became less willing to risk public criticism and as a consequence increasingly less accessible. In contrast Yeltsin periodically visited the provinces. During an August 1990 tour across the country, even though as chairman of the Russian Supreme Soviet he was entitled to state services, he intentionally traveled as a private passenger on Aeroflot. His ordinary-citizen approach was intended to contrast with the pomp of Gorbachev's traveling entourage.[50] Similarly, Yeltsin built and paid for his own dacha to highlight the penchant of Gorbachev and his wife, Raisa, for luxurious living in elegant and extravagant state villas. Eventually, however, Yeltsin also found it more convenient to use state facilities. Ironically, by 1992 he, too, was charged with being too imperial.

Yet Yeltsin's willingness to risk his power and prestige in competitive elections created something previously nonexistent in Russia. It gave him a legitimacy that no other government or party leader had. Anyone challenging his power, be it Gorbachev or coup conspirators, was at a considerable disadvantage. Consequently, people were willing to give their lives for Yeltsin during the August 1991 coup. By 1993, after two years of economic misadventure, that enthusiasm and support had waned, and Yeltsin had considerably more difficulty in winning overt support for his battle with his old Russian parliament, but in August 1991, a mere two months after his election, it was clear that Yeltsin, not party hard-liners, had the public's mandate. The putschists' lack of understanding of this unprecedented change in the political system was their greatest miscalculation.

3.

The Breakup of the Soviet Union

While Yeltsin seemed genuinely more interested in the well-being of the Russian people than Gorbachev was, his ego was no smaller. He was given to petty impetuous acts from which he sometimes had to retreat. His humiliation of Gorbachev at the meeting of the Russian Supreme Soviet on Friday, August 23, 1991, five days after the failed coup, when he forced Gorbachev to read the minutes of the Soviet cabinet meeting recorded at the time of the coup is one illustration. He wanted Gorbachev to acknowledge in public that Gorbachev's own appointees had been disloyal. In some sense this was Yeltsin's revenge for the time in 1987 when Yeltsin also had to confess to his failures as the party chief of Moscow.

Another example was the way Yeltsin behaved in October 1993 after he had finally dissolved both the Russian Supreme Soviet and Congress. To strengthen his position, he instituted censorship of all the country's papers, including those that normally supported him. He wanted no criticism of his leadership or indication that he had made mistakes. However, after widespread protests from both inside and outside the country, he revoked the decree, at least for those papers he deemed nonextremist (according to Yeltsin's definition of *nonextremist*).

Whether it was a matter of ego, health, or simple miscalculation, one of Yeltsin's more serious misjudgments came right after the 1991 putsch, when he was at the peak of his popularity.

There was a general sense of euphoria and accomplishment that the Russian people had put down an antidemocratic putsch for one of the first times, if not the first time, in the country's history. Given the heroic stance he took against the conspirators, Yeltsin probably commanded more genuine respect and affection than any previous Russian leader. This was the time for him to push through reform measures. As was true of President Lyndon Johnson in his push for civil rights and social reform immediately after President John F. Kennedy's assassination, it would have been unseemly to oppose him.

Admittedly, Yeltsin did not anticipate that he would be given such an opportunity, much less have it so quickly after his June election as president. Eventually, he did institute some reforms, such as transferring power from the Soviet Union to the various republics, but Yeltsin had no comprehensive, well-thought-out package of reforms ready to propose. Johnson was equally surprised by the Kennedy murder, but since the Kennedy people had already prepared a slate of reforms to present to Congress, Johnson had a blueprint on which he could elaborate as he went along.

But in a move that many now consider one of his most serious mistakes, Yeltsin disappeared from Moscow for two and a half weeks from September 24 to October 10, 1991. Some say he was writing a book; others say he was in poor health; still others insist he was drawing up plans for the months ahead. Perhaps it was a little of all three; in any case, he disappeared from Moscow at a critical juncture when his power was virtually unquestioned. This was to become a recurring pattern of behavior for him. Not only did he at the time enjoy the public's enthusiastic support; he also represented its desire to undo mistakes of the past and embark upon an active program of reforms. This was the moment when he could have created a new political party to help him push through his political agenda. It was also the ideal time to draw up a new Russian constitution to replace the 1978 Brezhnev version, intended for a very different era. (The Soviet constitution had been adopted somewhat earlier, in late 1977.)

Of course, even if he had stayed in town and poured out one reform edict after another, the reform process might have been blocked and stymied by the difficulties inherited from Gorbachev. Nevertheless, even his vice president, Aleksandr Rutskoi, who later turned against him, complained about having tried to reach Yeltsin twelve times without luck. The delay resulted in a loss of valuable momentum.

When Yeltsin finally returned to Moscow to embark on his reforms, he introduced several that compounded rather than alleviated the country's economic difficulties. Take, for example, his determination to break away from the Soviet Union. Others had attacked the Union earlier, but his attacks, coming from the head of the largest and richest republic, were the most destructive.

Actually, an effort to transfer economic and political power from the center to the republics had been under way for some time. We saw earlier that in Yeltsin's campaign to become chairman of the Russian Supreme Soviet in 1990, he had insisted that the republics have veto power over all Union legislation. He had also demanded that ownership rights over raw materials be transferred to the republics. While such attacks on the center reflected the desire of several of the republics' leaders to gain more power for themselves, in Yeltsin's case they also reflected a quest for revenge against Gorbachev. It is sometimes forgotten that Yeltsin had openly called on Gorbachev to resign as early as February 19, 1991.[1] (This was an exercise of glasnost that Gorbachev certainly never intended.) But since Gorbachev seemed to have no intention of resigning either during or after the coup, Yeltsin evidently concluded that the best way to rid himself of Gorbachev was to destroy his operating base—the Soviet Union itself.

It is hard to see how, even without a Yeltsin-Gorbachev feud, the Soviet Union as an operating body could have long endured once glasnost with its democratization and free election process began to have an impact. As elections in the outlying regions became more meaningful, they intensified the pressures to devolve controls to the various localities. For personal and patriotic reasons, Gorbachev struggled against such pressures. He not only wanted to hold on to his job; he also realized that a united Soviet Union would be a stronger international power than Russia alone. In an effort to keep the country together, he initiated a referendum on March 17, 1991, which while vague and boycotted in places like the Baltic states, asked people to declare themselves for or against the continued existence of the Soviet Union. For many, a vote against the continued existence of the Union was equivalent to being opposed to motherhood. Hence 70 percent of those participating voted yes. Such a one-sided vote convinced Gorbachev that he had the support of the people in holding the Union together.

Gorbachev also understood, however, that the referendum in no way eliminated the growing centrifugal forces. Consequently, he tried to mollify the secessionists through compromise. His idea was to turn over enough power to the republics to allow them to have control over their economic resources while retaining central control over national politics, foreign policy, the army, and security matters. Through a series of meetings, he hoped to work with the various republic leaders in order to devise a new, federal-type political structure. As part of that effort, he convened a meeting, on April 23, 1991, of republic leaders at Novo-Ogarevo, a country estate outside Moscow.[2] It was attended by nine of the fifteen republic leaders invited to participate. The treaty they signed came to be known as the "nine plus one agreement." However, the Baltic states, along with Moldava (formerly Moldovia), Georgia, and Armenia, refused to sign. They wanted even more power than Gorbachev was prepared to yield.

Meanwhile, the demands to decentralize authority became more insistent. Ukrainian authorities, for instance, had a year earlier, in October 1990, promised striking students in Kiev that they would approve a new Ukrainian constitution before agreeing to a new Union constitution.[3] This situation was unique not only because it marked a growing assertiveness by Ukrainian authorities but as we saw, because until this demonstration students in the Soviet Union, unlike those in many other countries in the world, had been relatively passive, if not apolitical. Ukrainian officials feared that a failure to adhere to their promises might unleash uncontrollable unrest.

For his part, Yeltsin had a strategy that was simple but that when implemented would emasculate the center. As was mentioned earlier, his tactic was to demand that the republics take control over taxation within their borders. Without the power to tax and without control over valuable raw materials, the Soviet Union would become a weak confederation, much like the United States prior to 1789. The republics agreed to reassign a portion of their tax revenues to the Soviet Union. It was a form of reverse revenue sharing, and given the prevailing mood, the odds were that the republics would keep the bulk of the money for themselves. The text of a treaty spelling out the relationship between the republics and the center was finally agreed to in late July. A formal signing ceremony was set to take place on August 20, 1991.[4]

However, once some of the republic leaders perceived that the center and Gorbachev were reluctant to use brute force to enforce their authority and prerogatives, the Soviet Union as a political entity was doomed. At the same time, thanks to Gorbachev, glasnost, and increasing democratization, a growing number of leaders and activists in the various republics began to lose their sense of fear. Whether because he might jeopardize his standing in the West or because he truly believed in glasnost, they realized that Gorbachev was unlikely to revive the policy of Stalinist-like terror. Taking a leaf from Eastern Europe in 1989, they decided this was their opportunity to attempt to gain their independence.

True, some military or police officials periodically tried to reassert the authority of the center. Thus Soviet government troops killed nationalist demonstrators in Georgia in April 1989 (when the soldiers used toxic gas), in Azerbaijan in January 1990, and in Lithuania on January 13, 1991. In each instance the violence was enough to provoke local shock, but not enough to subdue demands for more local autonomy. If anything, these violent episodes invariably intensified secessionist pressure in the areas where they occurred. The failure to follow up with massive repression caused disarray among the Soviet Union's police and military authorities. One of them told me, " Now in the aftermath of glasnost and perestroika—we can't even mount an effective crackdown."

The August 19, 1991, coup attempt marks yet one more, if an extreme, effort to prevent the unraveling of the Soviet Union. (The ill-fated October 1993 bid by Aleksandr Rutskoi, the vice president, and Ruslan Khasbulatov, the speaker of the Supreme Soviet, was an even more extreme effort, by like-minded and in some cases the same individuals and groups, to put at least part of the Soviet Union back together again. Undoubtedly, these were just the beginning of a series of such efforts.) However, the plotters' goal to prevent the formal signing on August 20, 1991, of the new "confederation" treaty, if anything, accelerated the collapse of the center. Its failure not only resolved whatever question there might have been about acknowledging the independence of Lithuania and the other Baltic states; in the immediate aftermath, it also permitted Yeltsin to ban the Soviet Union's Communist Party on August 23, 1991, and on September 5 to ban the Congress of the People's Deputies of the Soviet Union.

Neither measure, however, completely did away with the Soviet Union or the All Union president. Consequently, Yeltsin and Leonid Kravchuk, president of Ukraine, decided to create an alternative to the Union, in effect making the Union superfluous. Their idea was to create what in Europe would be called a commonwealth. Initially, this entity was to consist only of the major Slav republics—Belarus (previously called Belorussia), Ukraine, and Russia. The signing was set for December 8, 1991.

That Belarus participated in this effort was a bit of a surprise, because nationalism was not a major force there. Ukraine was a different story. A thousand years ago Kiev was the capital of Rus, but the Moscow princes and czars subsequently relegated the region to a secondary role and regarded the Ukrainians as "little brothers." During the years of Soviet power, this attitude was even embodied in the heroic statues dominating the Dnieper River in Kiev, depicting the comradely relationship between Ukraine and Russia. The Ukrainian figures were several feet smaller than those of the Russian workers. The Ukrainians deeply resented this treatment.

Ukrainians who complained about being treated as inferiors were brutally suppressed in the communist era and were labeled "bourgeois nationalists." The current president of Ukraine, Leonid Kravchuk, was a loyal Communist Party functionary and supported such suppression until late in his career. But his growing realization that the Ukrainian people were intent on seeking their independence, plus Russian insensitivity, eventually led Kravchuk to become a prime mover in the effort to create the Ukrainian Republic and the new commonwealth. Reportedly, he was particularly incensed by Gorbachev's repeated failure to take Ukrainian special interests into account in the new August federal treaty, despite promises to do so.

At first glance, Kravchuk seemed an unlikely candidate to be the first president of a new and independent Ukraine. He seldom took the lead on new initiatives. Moreover, unlike Yeltsin, Kravchuk appeared to show initial support for the coup. But once it became clear that it would fail, he managed to switch sides quickly. He was politician enough to shift his stance in time to retain his power. Despite his record as a party apparatchik, he won a close race in the election for president of Ukraine on December 1, 1991. He defeated Vyacheslav Chornovil, a well-respected nationalist who had been put in prison for his views. This time around, however, Kravchuk also backed Ukrainian independence in a referendum held simultaneously with the election.

The new commonwealth agreement signed in Minsk by Russia, Ukraine, and Belarus on December 8, 1991, was joined on December 20 by a majority of the other republics (the Baltic states and Georgia did not participate). The commonwealth agreement and the way it was reached represented a major embarrassment for Gorbachev.[5] Phoning him the following day, Stanislav Shushkevich, the president of Belarus, officially informed Gorbachev about the December 8 Minsk session. Shushkevich reported, "We had reached an agreement."

Caught off guard, Gorbachev asked, "About what?"

"It's already gaining support. We have had a conversation with George Bush."

"You have been speaking with the President of the U.S.A., and the President of this country knows nothing about it? Shame on you!"[6]

Actually, Gorbachev had been notified the preceding week, on December 1, 1991, that his salary would henceforth be paid by the Russian Republic because the Soviet Union could no longer do so.

As intended, the creation of what was called the Commonwealth of Independent States (CIS) precipitated the collapse of the Soviet Union. Effectively, the Soviet Union had a president and a few bureaucrats, but no legislature and no source of income. But the CIS itself was also more a concept than an operating entity. Indeed, this was exactly what some of the republic leaders wanted. There was no point in destroying the intrusive and all-encompassing Soviet Union only to replace it with an equally strong commonwealth. Kravchuk, in particular, fearful that an effort would be made to reconstitute the Soviet Union in some other guise, wanted as ineffective an institution as possible. For that reason he solidly supported the idea of establishing CIS headquarters in Minsk. Not only would this diminish Moscow's and, by extension, Russian nationalist and Soviet influence, but locating the headquarters in Belarus would help win Shushkevich's support.

Kravchuk knew full well that situating the center in Minsk demonstrated the participating republic leaders' slight regard for the CIS. It was like moving the capital of the United States to Peoria; both Minsk and Peoria are pleasant enough cities, but they both lack the stature, infrastructure, and communication and transportation facilities needed to govern complex modern industrial societies.

The exclusion of the Central Asians from the initial design of the CIS caused resentment among the Central Asians. Restricting the participants to the predominantly Slavic part of the country may have been a response to Aleksandr Solzhenitsyn, the famous Russian novelist, nationalist, and Nobel Prize winner, who earlier had called on the Slavic republics to secede from the Union. It also reflected racial and religious differences between Muslim-dominated republics and Slavs. Furthermore, most of the Muslim republics were still very much in the hands of the old-line communists. No doubt there was also some consideration of the reality that, except for Kazakhstan, most of these republics produced relatively little that was wanted in the outside world. Turkmenistan has valuable petroleum and gas deposits, Uzbekistan has gold, and almost all grow cotton, but on the whole the region had been treated as an economic burden by its more richly endowed northern neighbors. Many Slavs would have been happy to do without them. Such a separation would also have eliminated the need for further grants and loans to support their poor southern neighbors.

The breakup of the Soviet Union was not a wholly positive happening, even for those republics achieving independence. It encouraged other nationality groups to break away from the republics. For the Russians this is potentially explosive. Threatening and stifling as Soviet control was, it served a useful purpose by restraining and, if necessary, suppressing the more unpleasant aspects of Russian and the other nationalisms, and the ethnic and religious conflicts that have haunted Eastern Europe and parts of the former Soviet Union, such as Azerbaijan, Armenia, Moldava, Georgia, and Tajikistan.

It is unclear just what role nationalism will play in Russia itself. Yeltsin gives off confusing signals about the extent of his own nationalism. When he sought to win influence in the Russian Supreme Soviet in 1990, he argued strongly for a nationalistic approach. Indeed, his emphasis on seeking the presidency of the Russian Supreme Soviet rather than of the Soviet Supreme Soviet strengthened those advocating Russia for Russians at the expense of Russians as Soviets. Yet, at a crucial juncture, Yeltsin downplayed Russian nationalism and appealed for a more universal approach to the country's problems. In January 1991, after the formation of the Committee on National Salvation in Lithuania, which demanded that Soviet troops protect Russians living in Lithuania as well as other Soviet interests, Yeltsin sought to dampen nationalistic emotions. When Soviet troops fired on Lithuanian civilians, Yeltsin, to prevent further bloodshed and to show that he, not Gorbachev, could handle such matters, set off for Lithuania to urge calm. He pleaded with the Russian young men in the Soviet military units, the predominant ethnic group, not to fire on Lithuanians, who were, after all, fellow Soviet citizens. "Yours is the choice of a lifetime," he told them. "Are you on the side of freedom and truth . . . —or are you on the side of jails and lies? Are you with your generation or not? Answer! DO NOT SHOOT!"[7]

The Russian commander of the military units in Lithuania saw this as treachery to Russia as well as to the Soviet army. Yeltsin was warned, for his own safety, not to set foot in Lithuania itself. So he got only as far as Estonia.[8] But for a time this statesmanlike outspokenness worked. Unsure of how their troops would respond, the Soviet military leaders opted for a more cautious approach than might otherwise have been chosen.

Gradually, however, Yeltsin returned to the more outspoken Russian nationalist line. Before long, in fact, he joined with the nationalists. He promised to become the protector of the twenty-five million Russians living outside Russia's borders and warned of retaliatory steps if the rights of those Russians were abused.

Just as he was prepared to be nationalist when necessary, so his commitment to democracy was also changeable. Yeltsin was not a natural-born democrat. Admittedly, he had moved far beyond his days as the unchallenged Sverdlovsk Communist Party head. Yet, in October 1991, after the August coup, he showed no hesitation in sending his hand-picked representatives throughout the country to take over control of the local governments. This was done even though most of Yeltsin's men replaced leaders who had been democratically elected.[9] Similarly, in October 1993 he closed down the democratically elected local and regional Russian Supreme Soviet as well as hard-line parties and newspapers. Moreover, like Gorbachev before him, Yeltsin demanded the temporary power to issue decrees without the concurrence of the Supreme Soviet.[10] The Fifth Congress of People's Deputies, on October 28, 1991, did as requested and authorized Yeltsin to issue unilateral decrees for a one-year period. On November 6 he appointed himself prime minister. It raised even more concern when Yeltsin in June 1994 decreed that the time during which those arrested can be held without charges should be extended from two days to thirty. He also suggested that elections for the parliament be postponed for two years. These and other contraventions of Yeltsin's own constitution brought protests from members of parliament, some of whom argued that similar disregard for constitutional niceties in the 1930s had set the stage for the purge trials of 1937.

All these measures were intended to facilitate the implementation of his economic and political program. But Yeltsin should have been more realistic. Armed with similar powers, Gorbachev also found that he could issue decrees and yet nothing would happen. That was useful as long as the decrees were misconceived, but it meant that constructive decrees were also ignored. Having learned from Gorbachev's experience, Yeltsin was determined that the same thing would not happen to him, so he appointed emissaries throughout the country in the expectation they would be loyal to him. He reasoned that with his own administrators in place he could count on them to implement those decrees.

The tendency of Russian bureaucrats to ignore central decrees predates communism. As Russian authors like Gogol and Goncharov amply demonstrated, it was a curse of the czarist era as well. Moreover, by the time Yeltsin assumed control, the economic situation had deteriorated significantly from what it was when Gorbachev took over.

In addition, as a result of his own doing, Yeltsin was confronted with the sudden disintegration of the Soviet Union. Ultimately, the collapse of the Soviet empire should make possible a greater sense of local control and the enjoyment of one's own efforts in all the republics. However, in the short run this severing of long-established economic ties and interconnections was very disruptive to the economy. True, the unified, centrally planned Soviet economy was not a model of efficiency or a generator of personal wealth for the population at large. Still, however ineffectively the central-planning system may have operated, its collapse meant that there was no longer any coordination of important economic functions and no existing institutions to provide crucial interactive services.

The result was economic chaos. It was as if Illinois or a number of American states had suddenly declared themselves separate, independent countries with divisive tariffs, separate currencies, and economic protectionism that discouraged imports and exports.

Textile factories in Ivanovo, for example, were forced to close down when Uzbekistan refused to deliver the cotton they had routinely supplied for decades.[11] Even once-powerful ministries found themselves helpless in such an environment. After the breakup of the Soviet Union, the powerful and influential Ministry of Medium Machine Building, which was in charge of nuclear weapons, was unable to secure stocks of basic plastic compounds it had contracted to supply its joint venture molding factory in Estonia.

Yeltsin was in part responsible for this "every republic for itself" syndrome. Once he declared on November 16 and again on November 18 of 1991 that Russia, not the Soviet Union, was the rightful owner of the gold and oil located within Russian boundaries, he should have anticipated not only that the other republics would claim similar rights over minerals located on their territories but that various ethnic groups within Russia itself would do the same. It was just a matter of time before the Tatars, Bashkirs, Yakuts (Sakha), Chechens, and Ingush became more assertive about what they regarded as their political and economic prerogatives and property rights in Russia. Having been passive for decades, they insisted on controlling not only valuable commodities like gold and oil within their realms but also the levying of taxes.[12] And just as concessions by Gorbachev to such demands failed to satisfy the republics, similar concessions by Yeltsin were not sufficient for at least three of Russia's twenty autonomous republics. For that matter, even some of the predominantly Slavic regions in Russia began to toy with the notion of secession. In addition to a wish to assert greater control over what they deemed *their* resources, their demands expressed their dismay at the failure of the leadership in Moscow. In March 1992, for example, representatives from a number of regions in Siberia established an all-Siberian Congress of People's Deputies in Krasnoyarsk, where some of their representatives called for economic and political independence for their region.[13] Russia's Far East region headquartered in Vladivostok along with the Ural Republic centered in Sverdlovsk both declared themselves republics in June and July 1993.[14] These actions may have been more of a bargaining ploy for increased power within Russia than a move for actual independence; nevertheless, they intensified the centrifugal tendencies already in place.

For a time Yeltsin was tolerant of such initiatives, but occasionally he lost his temper and resorted to violence. For instance, in 1992, acting on the advice of his vice president, Aleksandr Rutskoi, he ordered Russian troops to put down what he saw as an insurrection among the Chechens. While his reactions including the sending of similar army troop enforcers into neighboring countries like the Dniester region of Moldava or Georgia or Tajikistan (former republics of the Soviet Union that the Russians now refer to ominously as "the near abroad") were often only short-term responses, Yeltsin eventually did move to reassert central control. This followed his October 1993 showdown with Rutskoi and Khasbulatov. In what was clearly a case of overkill, he met Rutskoi's and Khasbulatov's challenge to take away his power by proroguing the parliament and then sending in troops and tanks to implement his orders. Prior to that Yeltsin had found himself compelled to make one concession after another to the provinces in the hopes of winning their support in his battle with the parliament. Once he had effectively closed down the parliament, however, there was no longer any need to offer such concessions or engage in such gamesmanship. Consequently, Yeltsin once more began to reassert Moscow's control over the raw materials in the provinces and warned local leaders against any further moves to increase their autonomy, let alone to declare their independence from Russia. This did not eliminate all efforts at regional autonomy (many regions continued to withhold tax revenues), but it did temper some of the more strident rhetoric.

4. Economic Advice

Neither Gorbachev nor Yeltsin had come into the leadership with the background to deal with the urgent need for economic reform. To help them, both decided to call in outsiders for guidance. At the time that Gorbachev sought out his first economic advisers, this was a radical innovation. In fact, until Brezhnev died, in November 1982, it was not the practice to reach outside the walls of the Kremlin. Instead, Soviet leaders normally restricted their circle of advisers on economic and political matters to their subordinates, political peers, and members of the bureaucratic apparatus. While outsiders were consulted regularly for advice about military and space technology, pre-Gorbachev party leaders believed that officials dealing with day-to-day problems were in a better position to advise on economic and political issues than scholars from the Academy of Sciences, who spent most of their time in lecture halls and research institutes. The consensus among government officials was that the country's scholars may have had some theoretical knowledge but that, having spent most of their lives in an academic environment, they had little experience in dealing with the problems of daily life. Breaking with this pattern, Gorbachev and Yeltsin consulted with a large number of the country's leading nongovernment specialists. In time both men appointed some of those scholars to important posts in their governments. In particular they drew extensively on economists and social scientists in the Academy of Sciences.[1]

There were some exceptions to this practice of relying only on insiders for advice on domestic matters. Stalin, for example, became infatuated with the ideas of the pseudo-botanist Trofim Lysenko, who emphasized the importance of the environment over genetic makeup.[2] Though Lysenko never became a government figure, his programs set Soviet biological science back several decades. On a more positive note, the economist Evsei Liberman proposed in 1964 some far-reaching and economically rational reforms. Nikita Khrushchev and Aleksei Kosygin, who took over as prime minister after Khrushchev was purged, both supported a few experiments based on Liberman's ideas—experiments unfortunately mangled in implementation. As we will soon see in more detail, Liberman was an early proponent of scrapping central-plan production targets for industry and replacing them with profits and return on investment. However, Liberman himself was never asked to join the government or even serve as an official adviser. With a leadership drawn from party ranks, most of whose members had limited education, it was not surprising that they looked to practical men of affairs (joined by a very occasional woman), rather than to academically oriented intellectuals and researchers in the social sciences.

To be fair, until the 1930s Western political leaders showed similar attitudes. Before the Roosevelt New Deal few of them drew on academic expertise to help shape government policies. The Soviet cult of the personality, however, militated even more against expert counsel. For Stalin, Khrushchev, or Brezhnev all wisdom and new economic and ideological theories had to originate in the minds of the leaders themselves. To conclude anything else might suggest that someone else should be leader.

Andropov was the first party leader to seek out advice and guidance not only on foreign countries but also on economics. He did not go so far as to appoint academics to official government positions when he came to power in 1982. But in early

1983 he commissioned a study of the Soviet Union's long-run needs. One of the participants in the study was Tatiana Zaslavskaia, a sociologist and section head at the Institute of Economics and Organization of Industrial Production of the Siberian division of the Soviet Academy of Sciences. Her highly critical classified analysis of the prevailing Soviet economic system found its way into the hands of Dusko Doder, the Moscow bureau chief of the *Washington Post*. It was published in the *Post* on August 3, 1983.[3] Its revelation that all was not well in the Soviet economy provoked a great outcry as well as a search for the leakers. But after a brief flurry, intended to catch the leaker, Zaslavskaia returned to her research. The publication of her report, however, marked her as a bold, original thinker and increased her stature.

Actually, Zaslavskaia was one of the few researchers whose advice party leaders had drawn on earlier. Her fields of research included new experiments in agricultural organization. Some of her most innovative work dealt with a study of a brigade contract system established in a few of the country's collective farms. Peasants were divided up into smaller than normal work teams and given more control over their work practices and their pay.[4] Learning of her experiment, Mikhail Gorbachev, then chief of agriculture in the party's Central Committee, called in Zaslavskaia and five other specialists to comment on a ten-year food program that was to be introduced by Leonid Brezhnev in May 1982.[5] Gorbachev's openness to academic analysis probably owed more to his years at Moscow State University than to his peasant and bureaucratic days as an administrator of the Stavropol Oblast. Stavropol was one of the country's more successful agricultural regions, but it was still very much in the provinces. In any event, he must have been impressed with Zaslavskaia's advice, because the brigade contract system was subsequently incorporated into the country's food program.

Early in his career, therefore, Gorbachev, unlike all but a few of his party colleagues, showed an interest in meeting with academic experts. Even when Zaslavskaia a year later, in November

1983, was defending herself against criticisms that she had been leaking documents to the West, Gorbachev invited her and the director of her institute in Akademgorodok, the economist Abel Aganbegyan, to join several other economists for a discussion in Moscow.[6] Aganbegyan had been director of the institute since 1966 and had established a reputation for candor and insight into the shortcomings of the Soviet economy. On at least one occasion, the authorities retaliated by denying him permission to lecture abroad.[7]

Clearly impressed with Aganbegyan, Gorbachev made him his unofficial economic adviser. Aganbegyan worked closely with Gorbachev in the summer of 1984 on a speech scheduled to be given in January 1985 by Konstantin Chernenko, the successor to Andropov as general secretary. By late 1984, however, Chernenko had fallen ill, and the conference was called off.[8] When Chernenko died shortly thereafter, in March 1985, Gorbachev delivered the speech himself. The speech called for an intensification of machine tool production, which was to become a major focus of Gorbachev's initial reform. This old-line Stalinist emphasis directly conflicted with the public's long-denied demand for more consumer goods. Improvement in the population's material well-being, not more machinery, would have generated more popular support for his reform effort and perhaps given Gorbachev more time to work his way out of the mess he had inherited. By 1987 he had come to recognize the folly of the machine tool approach, and he dismissed Aganbegyan, but considerable damage had already been done. By emphasizing machine tools, Gorbachev destroyed the credibility of the reform effort and dissipated the momentum for reform.

Nevertheless, Gorbachev's desire for expert advice (faulty or not) did not diminish with his dismissal of Aganbegyan. He sought out other academic economists to replace him. He was, after all, the first general secretary to have graduated from a university. His immediate predecessors at best had a more narrow technical education. Gorbachev may also have been responding to the suggestions of his wife, Raisa. Also a graduate of Moscow State University, she pushed for more expert advice on affairs of state.

I

Those called in by Gorbachev served in a variety of capacities. Some served as consultants; others were asked to draw up comprehensive plans for reform. One of the first to be brought in to succeed Aganbegyan was Leonid Abalkin. In 1986 Abalkin was named director of the Institute of Economics of the Academy of Sciences. Prior to his appointment the Institute of Economics was known for its conservatism and resistance to reform.[9] Abalkin, a decent and thoughtful man, immediately began to restructure the institute and to explore reform possibilities. What made his subsequent appointment to positions in the government so unusual was that at the Nineteenth Communist Party Conference, in late June 1988, Abalkin on national television criticized Gorbachev's proposal to allow the general secretary of the Communist Party (Gorbachev) also to serve as the chairman of the Supreme Soviet, at the time the country's highest parliamentary body. He pointed out that the Soviet Union could never become a democracy as long as the general secretary held both posts and the Communist Party was the only authorized party.[10] Gorbachev responded by ridiculing Abalkin. In a low blow he complained that Abalkin "reeked of economic determinism."

In an earlier era such a put-down by the general secretary would automatically have meant the loss of one's professional career and even one's life. But unlike his predecessors, Gorbachev allowed his critics to continue their criticisms. In an even more atypical gesture, Nikolai Ryzhkov, Gorbachev's prime minister, invited Abalkin to give a series of briefings on the state of the economy to the Council of Ministers. In late 1988 Abalkin's Institute of Economics was asked to design an economic reform program for the Soviet economy.[11] Shortly thereafter Ryzhkov appointed Abalkin his deputy prime minister.[12]

Whatever Gorbachev's initial reactions to Abalkin, he came to appreciate his insights. In mid-1989 he made Abalkin the chairman of a new state commission on economic reform.[13] Thus Abalkin became the first academic, nonpolitical, nonapparatchik appointee to hold a major and influential post.

Even though Gorbachev had trouble in implementing the proposed reforms, he displayed good taste in choosing advisers. Almost without exception, they were intelligent and committed to reforming their country. Before Gorbachev was forced from office, in 1991, he had brought in and contemplated as many as twelve different programs of economic reform that attempted to move the country from a centrally planned command economy to a market-oriented economy. Given that almost all of these economists had been indoctrinated to believe in the superiority of central planning and that few, if any, had had formal schooling in market economics, their commitment to the market was impressive. Yet it was also clear that most of them did not fully understand what was involved in introducing the market. Most of their support for it derived from their misadventures with the central planning system and their being impressed by the plethora of goods they had seen on their visits to the market economies of the West.

But, like Gorbachev, most of them still believed that with some fine-tuning and minor adjustments the Soviet Union could move to a market economy within the framework of the existing planning system. They argued that an abrupt and premature switch to the market when there was still a shortage of consumer goods would lead rapidly to inflation and intolerable profits for the new private businesses. Only after the Soviet planners had managed to increase the availability of goods in the shops could the Soviet Union fully move to a market system. Thus, although Abalkin was more supportive of the market than any previous Soviet official, once in power he too began to back off. He postponed any radical changes for four years, until 1993, when he believed the state planners would be able to provide enough goods to create a semblance of market equilibrium.[14]

Abalkin, as well as Gorbachev and Ryzhkov, failed to understand that it was the planning system itself that caused the disequilibrium—that is, the shortages. Abalkin and most of his peers were still beguiled by "planning," which implies the ability to deal rationally and directly with economic problems and imbalances. If there is a queue for a particular item, it means there is an insufficiency and should signal the planner to order increased production. In practice, however, the desired increase in supplies seldom seemed to materialize. By the time the goods finally arrived, consumers had often gone off in search of some other product. In many cases the planners simply considered the good too unimportant for increased production. For example, the manufacture of women's sanitary products was deemed nonessential. Likewise, by the time more black-and-white television sets were produced, consumers had moved on to color television sets.

Lacking experience with the flexibility of the price system, which automatically balances off buyers and sellers, most officials and even some of the economists did not understand how a market could create an equilibrium condition. Those who did understand the concept usually feared that freeing prices to find their own equilibrium would lead initially to high prices, which might become permanent. Even if they were not permanent, a sudden increase in prices in the early stages of the process might spark political unrest. After three decades of price stability, even some of the more radical reformers were troubled by this possibility.[15] They did not comprehend that higher prices act not only to drive away former customers but also, if there is freedom of entry, to attract more suppliers and more goods and, thereby, gradually bring down the size of price increases. In other words, the market, not the planning system, offers the best chance for increasing the supply of goods and ultimately reducing inflation.

In October 1989, a mere four months after Abalkin had assumed office, his State Commission on Economic Reform produced a proposal for an overhaul of the whole economy.[16] Not unexpectedly, the plan failed to produce concrete results.

Abalkin found himself defending the shortcomings of the government and the remnants of the planning system. Since responsibility produces caution, Abalkin was to some extent co-opted by the system. Perhaps that was inevitable.

As the official responsible for the economy, Abalkin, to his surprise, suddenly found himself being treated as part of the problem. The fact that he had earlier been a bona fide critic of the Soviet reform effort afforded him no special protection. He was attacked for not moving boldly enough just as he had previously attacked others in the same way. Among his critics were several well-respected economists who were particularly agitated about the Gorbachev government's failure to introduce far-reaching reform. One was Oleg Bogomolov, who headed the Institute for the Economics of the World's Socialist Countries.[17] Through his study of Eastern Europe, Bogomolov was one of the first in the Soviet Union to track the early reform efforts in the neighboring satellites. This was an important avenue for learning about the outside world and the reform process, particularly because exposure to market economies was considerably greater in Eastern Europe than in the Soviet Union.

Another outspoken critic was Nikolai Shmelev, an economist at the Institute for the United States and Canada, who was especially critical of the Soviet government and Gorbachev's failure to improve the livelihood of the general public. As someone who did not abstain, he was especially critical of the crackdown on the sale of vodka.[18] This, he said, created needless alienation of the Russian work force. The essence of his reform program, however, was to increase substantially the purchase of foreign consumer goods.[19] To finance this he urged that the government use some of its gold reserves and increase its borrowing. With access to more consumer goods, the Soviet people would find they had something to gain from the Gorbachev reform effort. With this incentive the public would supposedly work hard for the reforms.

Shmelev's comments about the inadequacies of the reform process and the inevitability of unemployment were among the most perceptive and penetrating. It was no wonder that on occasion they also provoked Gorbachev's ire.[20] However, without changes in the law as well as in practices that frustrated efforts to develop new and more rational work practices and institutions, large-scale drawdowns of the country's gold reserves would not in themselves make much sense.

While Gorbachev was aware of Bogomolov's and Shmelev's proposals, he did not include these outspoken critics in his government. Nevertheless, he appointed other reformers. In January 1990, for example, only three months after Abalkin presented his official reform proposal, Gorbachev appointed Nikolai Petrakov his full-time economic adviser. Because of Petrakov's strong support of the market, many in the West believed that this appointment would lead to an immediate shift to market processes. Indeed, the Sovietologist Ed Hewett commented on National Public Radio that this appointment was a signal that there would be a significant shift to market reform, and he thought it just possible that by the year 2000 the Soviet Union might bear a strong resemblance to Sweden. Petrakov had been the deputy director and a senior member of the Central Economic and Mathematical Institute (TsEMI), long considered one of the more innovative centers of economic analysis. In the same quest for quick answers, Petrakov was charged with drawing up yet another version of a comprehensive reform program, for presentation on May 1, 1990. For a time Gorbachev took a serious interest in Petrakov's work but, as with Abalkin's plan, before long postponed action on Petrakov's proposal. Much as Gorbachev professed to believe in market reform, he could never bring himself to abandon central planning.

As Gorbachev kept shifting his advisers, economic conditions began to deteriorate. For the first time in decades, prices began to rise and, as in the late Brezhnev era, production began to stagnate or, as in the case of oil, decline. Feeling pressure to take some concrete steps immediately, Gorbachev announced on May 22, 1990, that he intended to introduce another five-year plan, a three-stage effort, that would result in an oxymoron called a "regulated market economy."[21] As an indication of what was to come, the government announced that prices on basic commodities such as bread and utilities would double or triple on July 1, 1990, and go up again on January 1, 1991.

As we noted earlier, a price increase in basic commodities had long been advocated by many, though not all, economists. However, even those who supported a series of gradual price hikes rather than a sudden freeing of all prices were critical of Gorbachev's decree because it called for a one-time-only event that was to be determined not by the market but by the central planners, just as in the old days. Close to 85 percent of the country's prices would continue to be determined centrally. Gorbachev's plan was definitely not comparable to the January 1990 shock therapy processes that had just begun in Poland, where this was accompanied by a whole series of liberalizing measures freeing up prices to increase production. Nothing of the sort took place in Russia. In fact, the advance notice that prices were to be increased within a month set off a panic, as the public rushed to buy as much as possible before the higher prices went into effect. In a few days the shelves were empty. Out of self-defense, the government reversed itself and canceled the price increases. Oleg Bogomolov and another economist, Pavel Bunich, described what happened: "We got the shock without the therapy."[22]

As if four different reforms in the space of eight months had not been confusing enough, several other economists decided to offer their own reform proposals. Gregory Yavlinsky, an energetic and imaginative thirty-eight-year-old economist who was a department head in Albakin's reform commission, drew up his own comprehensive economic overhaul of the Soviet economy. In February 1990, along with two other economists—Mikhail Zadornov, of the Institute of Economics, and Aleksei Mikhaylov, of the State Committee on Prices (Goskomtsen)—he presented their proposal as a 400-day program of reform.[23] Unlike earlier efforts, this one was patterned on the Polish shock therapy. Yavlinsky noted, "The time for gradual transformation has passed."

Initially, Abalkin and some of the other leaders encouraged

Yavlinsky in his efforts. Even Gorbachev seemed interested. In April 1990, however, Gorbachev's newly created Presidential Council rejected the idea, and Ryzhkov opted instead for his own five-year plan and the already announced price increases on bread and utilities. Disenchanted, Yavlinsky resigned his position and joined Boris Yeltsin, who as chairman of the Supreme Soviet of Russia since June 1990 decided to sponsor his own reform effort. Yavlinsky became Yeltsin's deputy prime minister for economic reform, in effect Abalkin's counterpart at the republic level.[24] Yeltsin also enlisted the services of Boris Fedorov. Though only thirty-three, Fedorov was one of the most intelligent and well-trained economists of the younger generation. Fedorov became the Russian Republic's minister of finance.

Yeltsin's hunt for more effective reforms forced Gorbachev to renew his quest. To maintain his role as national leader, Gorbachev had to keep ahead of the republic leaders. But committed as Yeltsin may have been to the reform effort, with Gorbachev controlling national fiscal and monetary policies, there was little Yeltsin could actually put into practice. Consequently, Yeltsin proposed to Gorbachev that they jointly draft a plan based on the Yavlinsky initiative.[25] Intrigued, Gorbachev, on August 2, 1990, formally accepted the idea of a joint effort. In the process Yavlinsky's 400-day program became a 500-day program. In August, Stanislav Shatalin, a deputy director of a new offshoot of TsEMI called the Institute of National Economic Forecasting and Scientific-Technical Progress, was made head of the study group and given but a month to come up with a proposal that combined the reforms of Gorbachev's and Yeltsin's economic advisers. Along with Petrakov and Yavlinsky, he presided over representatives from both the Yeltsin and the Gorbachev reform teams. Among the thirteen who joined in the study group were Zadornov and Mikhaylov, the original coauthors with Yavlinsky of the 400-day plan, and Boris Fedorov. They were Yeltsin's delegates. Shatalin, Petrakov, and, for a time, Abalkin represented Gorbachev.

At meetings around the clock in a government dacha in Arkhangelskoe, outside of Moscow, a difference of opinion developed over how far-ranging the reforms should be, and Abalkin left the group to organize his own study effort.[26] He was joined by Ryzhkov, the prime minister, and Valentin Pavlov, then the minister of finance and soon Ryzhkov's replacement as prime minister.[27] Their plan drew heavily on Ryzhkov's program of December 1989, as well as on Abalkin's.

The Shatalin effort, which came to be known as the 500-day plan, was sabotaged by bureaucrats fearful of the market and private property. The Shatalin team charged that Yuri Maslyukov, the chief of Gosplan, and Pavlov, in the Ministry of Finance, plus Vneshekonombank, the foreign-trade bank, as well as the Defense Ministry and the Foreign Economic Commission all withheld economic data that was essential for designing the plan and that Gorbachev had promised would be made available.[28]

Despite such impediments, it looked for a time as if Gorbachev had finally found a plan he could accept. As Table 4-1 indicates, he certainly had enough to choose from. But as the details of the Shatalin plan became public, Gorbachev, as usual, began to have second thoughts. He was worried the reforms would be too far-reaching. For example, one of the measures called for the sale of state property such as factories and trucks to the general public. That would help balance the budget and absorb the ruble overhang, which would clear the way for price flexibility. But was this necessarily good? In addition, the peasants would be allowed to withdraw from the collective farms and set up their own, private farms. As its critics emphasized, the Shatalin 500-day plan, if implemented with such provisions, would mean the effective end not only of central planning but of a strong centralized Soviet Union.

The decentralization of power was what most disturbed Gorbachev. Under the Shatalin plan the republics would in effect become economically autonomous. If it were adopted, the power of the Union would derive from the authority delegated to it by the republics.[29] The republics, not the Union, would have the power to tax and determine ownership of the raw materials located within its borders. The Union would be limited to coordi-

Table 4-1 Economic Plans Proposed to and Abandoned by Gorbachev

Plan	Economist	Date
1. Intensification & Acceleration	Abel Aganbegyan	March 1985
2. Overall Economic Plan	Leonid Abalkin & Institute of Economics	Late 1988
3. Overhaul Economy & Move to Market	Abalkin & Commission on Economic Reform	October 1989
4. Plan & Market	Nikolai Ryzhkov	December 1989
5. Support for Market	Nikolai Petrakov	May 1990
6. Five-Year Plan	Gorbachev	May 1990
7. 400-Day Plan	Gregory Yavlinsky Mikhail Zadornov Aleksei Mikhaylov	February 1990
8. 500-Day Plan	Stanislav Shatalin	August 1990
9. Plan & Market	Abalkin & Ryzhkov	Fall 1990
10. Integrate Shatalin & Abalkin & Ryzhkov	Aganbegyan	November 1990
11. Referendum on Property & Market Reform	Gorbachev	September 1990
12. Compromise	Aganbegyan	October 1990

nating defense, monetary and financial policies, customs, foreign trade, social welfare, and environmental control. This would mean the end both of the Soviet Union as it had existed for over seventy years and of Gorbachev's job. Not surprisingly, when he came to understand the implications of what was being proposed, he decided that the less sweeping Abalkin-Ryzhkov plan warranted another look.

To help him decide which way to turn, Gorbachev created still another study group. On November 4, 1990, he resurrected the recently discredited Abel Aganbegyan and asked him to integrate the Shatalin and Abalkin-Ryzhkov versions of reform. But both camps felt that such a compromise would destroy the essence of each of their plans. Yeltsin explained that merging the two plans was impossible: "It was like mating a snake and a hedgehog."[30] Determined to do something, Yeltsin asked the Supreme Soviet of the Russian Republic to adopt the Shatalin plan, and it did so.

Even though it was impossible at that point for Yeltsin to implement such a change for Russia without the Soviet Union's also making such a change, Yeltsin's act infuriated Gorbachev, who viewed it as a blatant grasp for power. Furthermore, his prime minister, Ryzhkov, threatened that he would resign if Gorbachev adopted the Shatalin plan.[31] Out of desperation, Gorbachev on September 17, 1990, declared he would hold a national referendum on introducing private property and the market reform.[32] In a short time he dropped that idea as well. In one last effort, Aganbegyan presented yet another compromise proposal.[33] Some of his proposals were adopted, at least on paper, but so much had been compromised away that little actual reform took place.[34] By late September, Gorbachev, having apparently had enough, turned his back on the reformers and moved to ally himself with antimarket hard-liners. By December 1990 not only Shatalin but even Ryzhkov had been fired and Pavlov had become prime minister.

II

With Gorbachev allying himself with the central planners, the prospect for any meaningful government reform seemed remote. The whole debate on reform turned into a economic talk show, not a serious discussion about the country's future. As so many different plans flashed by, there was little chance to examine any of them in a serious way, much less try them out. Besides, if Gorbachev was no longer interested, there was little likelihood that any proposals would be implemented.

Gorbachev's withdrawal, however, did not end the debates on the reform process either in the Soviet Union or in the West. After years of focusing only on their own economic problems, Western leaders suddenly realized the enormity of what was happening and became concerned by the growing political and economic anarchy that was overtaking the Soviet Union. They began to take a greater interest in the Soviet reform process. Most of them believed that because Gorbachev had made such important concessions on arms control, withdrawn Soviet troops from Afghanistan, and allowed the East European states to become independent, the West was obligated to help him reform and stabilize his power over the Soviet Union. The prospect of such an enlightened Soviet leader as Gorbachev being thrown out of office and his reforms countermanded was too horrible to contemplate.

Such reasoning led the Group of Seven (G-7), the leaders of the world's richest market economies, to invite Gorbachev to join them for their annual meeting, scheduled for London in June 1991. This was an unprecedented gesture on their part. The G-7 is an exclusive club made up of the presidents and prime ministers of the United States, Germany, Japan, the United Kingdom, France, Italy, and Canada. They and their ministers of finance and foreign relations meet at least once a year to discuss mutual concerns affecting the market economies of the world. Normally, their deliberations are on such intractable issues as tariff and nontariff barriers, inflation, the world's interest rates, and economic growth. Thus it was easy to predict that Gorbachev's presence at the conference would divert attention from such traditional and pressing concerns. Equally important, whatever the sincerity of Gorbachev's intentions, almost no one argued that the Soviet economy had much in common with the market economies. Gorbachev's concerns would result in a radical departure from the normal G-7 agenda, but the Western leaders invited him anyway.

To some extent the invitation was also the result of public pressure in the West, stemming in part from what came to be known as the "Grand Bargain," whose progenitors were a group of Western advisers and Soviet economic reformers. It marked the debut of Western experts in the Soviet debates on the nature of the transition process and the course of economic reform. After decades of officially ignoring Western economic advice and criticisms about the Soviet economic system, Soviet intellectuals and Soviet government officials alike suddenly became eager to learn more about Western analyses of their economy. Of course, unofficially and in some cases secretly, such interest had always existed. Why else would Soviet officials and academics give so much such attention to and direct so much criticism at Sovietologists and Sovietology? But the adoption of glasnost and the accompanying acknowledgment that the Soviet economy had fallen on hard times and was likely to deteriorate further provided an opportunity for at least the westward-looking Soviet intellectuals and officials to ask for Western advice.

A number of Western economists and analysts responded to this sudden overt interest in Western remedies for the Soviet economy with great enthusiasm. One after another they set off (some on their own, some invited) for Moscow to prescribe economic medicine. Nobel Prize winners like Wassily Leontief, with his input-output analysis, and Milton Friedman, with his emphasis on increasing the role of money and reducing economic fine-tuning by the government, arrived with their own brand of miracle remedies; a younger generation of highly respected economists also offered their particular remedies. Since much of the advice was contradictory and applicable only for already-existing market economies, the Soviets were often confused. It is not easy, for example, to reconcile the use of input-output procedures with the sharp curtailment of government spending and involvement and strict control over the issue of money and credit. Younger economists called for even more radical reforms than the Soviet experts had contemplated. Those advocating the institution of a gold standard or other instant cures only added to the confusion.

As a Sovietologist, I also experienced this switch in attitudes toward Western specialists. For over twenty years my writings had been the subject of continual criticism and attack within the Soviet Union. In fact, in 1979 and 1980 I was refused a visa to visit the Soviet Union. Shortly thereafter I was informed by two Soviet economists that if I went ahead with the publication of my forthcoming book, entitled *The USSR in Crisis: The Failure of an Economic System,*[35] I would never be allowed to visit the Soviet Union again. Then in January 1983, shortly after Brezhnev's death, I was permitted to return to the Soviet Union. But it was made clear to me by Soviet embassy officials in Washington that this was a special exception and a personal favor to Arthur Hartman, the U.S. ambassador to Moscow at the time. Ambassador Hartman had just arranged for a visit to the United States by a Soviet scholar who had at first also been denied permission to visit. But issuing me a visa as part of a quid pro quo did not obligate the Soviet Union to welcome me. In Moscow, I was detained at the airport for over an hour, and Soviet economists were directed to avoid all contact with me. Imagine my shock when in January 1986, not quite a year later, after Gorbachev became general secretary, I was welcomed to Moscow and suddenly many economists, including those who had shunned me three years earlier, wanted to hear my views on reform. This interest and openness accelerated so that by June 1989 over one hundred Russian specialists attended a lecture I gave on my prescription for Soviet economic reform. Like other Western specialists, I spelled out a strategy I urged the government to adopt.

However, the advice of various Western experts, while sometimes taken seriously within the Soviet Union, was for the most part ignored in the West until 1991 when two American political scientists, Graham Allison and Robert Blackwill, decided to support the Soviet reform effort.[36] As they accurately perceived, the Soviet Union was collapsing while Western officials, economists, and Sovietologists did little except cluck their tongues in dismay. For example, after the G-7 meeting in Houston, Texas, in 1990 the International Monetary Fund (IMF) and the World Bank became involved in analyzing Soviet needs and proposing solutions. They issued a very thorough report in December 1990, but neither the report nor the discussion that followed appeared likely to evolve into much more than an academic exercise.[37] Consequently, Allison and Blackwill decided it was time for some course of concrete action rather than endless reports.

Allison, a former dean of the J. F. Kennedy School of Government, at Harvard University, was very much a doer with an unusual feel for promotion and public relations. Although not a Sovietologist, he had been involved for many years with issues of nuclear disarmament. Once the United States and Soviet Union had come to terms on most arms control matters, Allison began to focus on questions of Soviet democratization, economic survival, and development. In April 1991 he contacted Gregory Yavlinsky, who was visiting the United States during one of the periodic meetings of the International Monetary Fund. Since Yavlinsky's had initiated the 400- and then the 500-day reform programs, he seemed an appropriate Soviet counterpart to involve in a joint effort to reform the Soviet economy.

At this point Yavlinsky was no longer a member of the government. In mid-1990, after Gorbachev had backed away from the 500-day plan, Yavlinsky joined Yeltsin's government as deputy prime minister of the Russian Republic. However, in November, after Yeltsin too appeared reluctant to embark on fundamental economic reforms, Yavlinsky also resigned from that post.[38] Although no longer officially associated with either Gorbachev or Yeltsin, he remained a source of very fruitful and imaginative ideas and had access to both leaders. Consequently, Allison began to work with Yavlinsky to design a reform scenario for the Soviet Union that would garner Western help in its implementation. It was initially entitled the Grand Bargain and later the Window of Opportunity, and its idea was to provide Western aid in order to help underwrite the enormous capital and technical needs of the transformation process. In exchange it was anticipated that the prospect of Western support would induce the Soviets to carry out sustained rather than erratic reform efforts.[39] Western help was to be extended step by step and only as the Soviet Union implemented economic and political reforms.

Allison and Yavlinsky were joined by a small group of American economists and political scientists. Among them was Stanley Fischer, an economist at MIT, who had earlier been asked by the U. S. secretary of state, George Shultz, to be an American adviser to Israel in its attempts to halt inflation and restore economic stability. He subsequently accepted a brief term as chief economist for the World Bank. In December 1990, under his guidance, the World Bank and the International Monetary Fund carried out a survey of Soviet economic conditions.

Also included in the group was Jeffrey Sachs, a young economist at Harvard. Although only thirty-seven, he had already had extensive experience working with countries beset by serious economic difficulties. His first success was in Bolivia in 1986, when he helped that country reduce its inflation from 40,000 percent a year to 15 percent.[40] To a lesser degree, he had also worked with Venezuela and Ecuador.

Sachs's involvement with the communist world had actually begun two years earlier, in 1989, in Poland, where he worked with the then reform minister of finance Leszek Balcerowicz to implement what became the model for shock therapy in the communist world. Allison brought in Sachs in the expectation he could contribute the insights gained from the Polish experiment, which in the spring of 1991 seemed to be achieving some degree of success.

Fischer and Sachs worked intensively with Yavlinsky to revise his plan to encompass the fiscal and monetary methods used in shock therapy. This meant a retreat from the gradual reform approach. As Fischer explained, though, the Soviet economy was collapsing so quickly that it could not afford the luxury of a gradual approach. Before long, however, tension developed between Allison and Sachs. Sensing that the American public and Congress were hesitant about setting aside large sums of aid money for reforming the economy of a former enemy, Allison did his best to avoid indicating how much the Grand Bargain would cost the West and, especially, the United States. By contrast, when Sachs was asked, he indicated that the cost could be as much as thirty to fifty billion dollars a year over five years.[41] As the media began to focus on the huge sum and asked whether the United States alone and/or the G-7 would bear the cost, the Grand Bargain began to lose its allure.

Despite the controversy over the cost, Allison and Yavlinsky did not abandon their effort. With missionary zeal they lobbied the main financial centers of the world, from Washington to Tokyo to Europe, and also sought Gorbachev's support for their program. At the same time they kept working out the details of their plan, which was finally released on June 29, 1991, only days before the mid-July G-7 London meeting. With world attention on aid for Gorbachev at its peak, there was great interest in Gorbachev's encounter with the leaders of the industrialized world.

Notwithstanding Allison's best efforts, however, Western leaders did not back the Grand Bargain or, for that matter, go beyond offers of good wishes and concern about "the deterioration of the Soviet economy."[42] Their hesitation reflected not only their reluctance to tax themselves to provide the large sums needed in the middle of a recession but also their concern that the Soviet Union at the time would not be able to use effectively the sums proposed by the Grand Bargain. Western officials as well as Sovietologists believed that the Soviet Union had to undergo some fundamental institutional change before large grants or loans could be productively utilized. For example, there had been little privatization of land or business; it had not even been determined that the collectivized agricultural land could be subdivided. There were also few wholesale and other market-creating entities.[43] Very little had been done to re-create the pre-communist market infrastructure. In addition, the state industrial enterprises were unaccustomed to responding to price and profit incentives. If anything, for six decades or more they had been conditioned to ignore them. Such market signals as sharply higher prices and profits would therefore have little impact.

Most important of all, there was virtually no acknowledgment that the Soviet official who would ultimately be responsible for implementing the reform process and utilizing the desired credits was not Gorbachev but the current prime minister, Valentin Pavlov, a man decidedly cool, if not occasionally hostile, to the concept of the market and even the West. As one example, a few months earlier, in January 1991, Pavlov had warned of a conspiracy by Western investors to destroy the Soviet monetary system.* That in part may have explained why he was not allowed to accompany Gorbachev to London. Had he been there, his views would certainly have made the Western leaders even more cautious than they already were. Finally, the Grand Bargain did not deal with the sharply deteriorating ethnic relations and demands for republic independence. Within a week of the conclusion of the G-7 meeting, even Yavlinsky apparently had come to have some second thoughts. He admitted openly that it was not the right time for the West to provide assistance to the Soviet Union.[44]

We will never know whether, despite all these reasons for not providing financial support, the G-7 leaders would have acted any differently if they had known that within a month a group of hard-line conservatives (including Pavlov) would attempt to overthrow Gorbachev. Equally intriguing is the question whether the coup makers would have aborted their efforts and whether Gorbachev and the Soviet Union would have survived if Gorbachev had returned home with tangible evidence of billions of dollars worth of loans and grants.

III

Gorbachev survived the putsch at least temporarily and was able to return to Moscow after four days under house arrest. He

* Subsequent information suggests that there may well have been such a conspiracy involving the mafia and that Pavlov was not being unduly alarmist. Claire Sterling, *Thieves' World* (New York: Simon and Schuster, 1994), pp. 177–83.

retained his post as president of the Soviet Union, but by then his time as leader and, for that matter, the time of the Soviet Union had passed. Some continued to treat Gorbachev as if he had not lost legitimacy. His friend and supporter Eduard Shevardnadze returned from voluntary retirement and again took over the Soviet Ministry of Foreign Affairs. For a time right after the London meeting, Yavlinsky also held out the hope that Gorbachev might yet move ahead with reform. But after the coup Yavlinsky and most of the other unrequited reformers began to shift their attention to Yeltsin and his reform effort. Thus in September 1991, Yeltsin's prime minister, Ivan Silayev, appointed Yavlinsky to be the deputy head of the Committee for the Operational Management of the National Economy of Russia.[45] Although working for Yeltsin and the Russian Republic, Yavlinsky's group operated on the assumption that Yeltsin should continue to stress the importance of the larger but economically centralized Soviet Union, although under Yeltsin's control.

At the same time other teams of reformers began to prepare alternative packages of reforms. One loosely structured group centered around Yuri Skokov.[46] Skokov had been a deputy prime minister under Prime Minister Silayev and had headed the economic policy side of Yeltsin's 1990 campaign for president. It was generally assumed that Yeltsin would probably continue to rely on Skokov as his economic adviser and implementer.

Yeltsin surprised everyone, however, and opted for advice from a group of inexperienced young theorists headed by a bright, but untested, thirty-five-year-old economist, Yegor Gaidar. Gaidar had received his doctorate from Moscow State University in 1978 and been a research analyst on its economics faculty from 1981 to 1987.[47] He then worked as a senior researcher at the Institute for Systems Research. His first monograph was a joint effort with V. Koshkin and F. Kovalev called *Evaluation Indicators in the System of Enterprise Economic Accounting*.[48] In the same vein his next book, also with V. Koshkin, was entitled *Economic Accountability and the Development of Economically Accountable Autonomy for Enterprises*. These were both studies of how to operate Soviet enterprises more rationally and efficiently.

By 1989 he had broadened his focus and begun to consider systemwide reform, and he coauthored *Economic Reform: Reasons, Directions, and Problems.* It is a measure of his increased credibility and prestige that his coauthor was his former teacher and mentor Stanislav Shatalin. Finally, in 1990 Gaidar became the sole author of *Economic Reforms and Hierarchical Structures.*[49]

Gaidar's early research was very much influenced by Shatalin and Shatalin's colleague Nikolai Petrakov. Both impressed on their students the need for reform and then mentored them and brought them into contact with one another. This reflected the Soviet practice of housing leading scholars in various research institutes rather than in universities, as is common in the United States, where universities are more preeminent. Thus not only Gaidar but a large number of the economists who would become his assistants ended up working with Shatalin at his Institute of National Economic Forecasting and Scientific-Technical Progress and with Nikolai Petrakov at TsEMI (the Central Economic and Mathematical Institute).[50] It is also noteworthy that as far back as 1983–84, during the Andropov regime, Shatalin had asked some at his institute to draw up proposals for reform.[51]

Although for the most part these younger economists at the time held no policy-making positions, it was during the Gorbachev years that the group began to coalesce. Gorbachev's call for glasnost and perestroika made it possible for economists to experiment with possibilities and options for economic reform that would earlier have been impossible and in many cases unthinkable. Through increased contact with reformers in Eastern Europe and visits there, as well as contact with Western economists, some of the more daring economists in Moscow and St. Petersburg came to learn more about other economic systems. While most of our attention in the West has focused on the role of Moscow economists, Leningrad economists also played a very important role. As far back as the late 1970s, a small group of economists in Leningrad began to discuss reform alternatives.[52] Led by Anatoly Chubais, subsequently the deputy prime minister in charge of privatization, but then a young assistant professor at the Tolyatti Engineering and Economic Institute, the group included Gregor Glazkov, subsequently an adviser to Konstantin Kagalovsky at the World Bank in Washington, and Yuri V. Yarmogaev, later a specialist on the budget in the Supreme Soviet. Initially, the three limited themselves to a consideration of possible micro reforms. Given that the Leningrad intellectual climate at the time was tightly ruled by Grigori Romanov, one of the more dogmatic members of the Politburo, this was a daring, even dangerous, thing to do. In fact, as the group of economic reformers began to expand, the KGB forced one of its members to spy and report on the group's activity. But the informer immediately reported what had happened to Chubais, and the reluctant KGB agent then agreed to mislead the KGB about the group's activity.

With Brezhnev's death, in November 1982, some of these reformers thought that for the first time there might be some possibility of real economic change. However, the intellectual climate remained relatively closed. Shortly after January 1983, as part of the U.S. cultural exchange with the Soviet Union, I delivered a lecture to some economists at the Academy of Sciences in Leningrad and was fiercely attacked for even daring to suggest that the Soviet Union might benefit from some economic reforms. The reaction was so intense that my escort from the U.S. consulate in Leningrad was worried that the Leningrad branch of the Academy of Sciences might suspend the cultural exchange program with the United States.

Despite the oppressive intellectual environment, the Leningrad group under Chubais continued to focus on micro reforms and began to attract other reformers such as Sergei Vasilyev, who joined Chubais in 1982.[53] Subsequently, Vasilyev organized the Center for Research into Economic Transformation, with branches in Moscow and Leningrad, in order to broaden and systematize their discussions. Konstantin Kagalovsky became director of the institute and Sergei Glaziev its deputy director. As for Chubais, he continued to advocate reform and became a deputy mayor of Leningrad under Anatoly Sobchak, the new reform mayor.

The Leningrad reformers, particularly Chubais and Vasilyev, were drawn into contact with Gaidar at Shatalin's institute in Moscow. Glazkov also went to Moscow in 1984 as a member of TsEMI under Petrakov. As for Gaidar himself, in 1983 he was made a member of Gherman Gvishiani's Commission on Economic Reform in Moscow. Gvishiani was the son-in-law of Aleksei Kosygin, who had been prime minister under Brezhnev. With such significant protection, Gvishiani arranged for wide-ranging contacts with economists in Eastern Europe, where there was considerably more economic ferment than in Moscow. In addition Gvishiani helped create a research center in Vienna called the International Institute for Applied Systems Analysis (IIASA) under the partial auspices of the American Academy of Arts and Sciences. One of its purposes was to bring together economists and engineers from the United States and the Soviet Union.

The Moscow and Leningrad groups began to interact more frequently in 1986. They met in 1987 and 1988 at a conference organized by the Voznesensky Economic Institute, in Leningrad at a rural resort called Snake Hill. Their circle expanded further in 1988 when Chubais went to study in Hungary. In the spring of that year, Hungary hosted an economic conference where a large number of the reform-minded economists from Moscow and Leningrad met with East European reform economists. Those attending included Leszek Balcerowicz, later the reformist finance minister in Poland, and Václav Klaus, an outspoken devotee of the market, who would become the prime minister of Czechoslovakia. Similar sessions were held in the fall and the spring of 1989. These interactions with East European economists intensified the drive for economic reform at home.

While Gaidar himself did not participate in these East European meetings, many of the Russians there had already come to look to him for intellectual leadership. In addition to the various monographs of which he was author or coauthor, he began to attract notice through his work as economic editor of the official communist journal *Kommunist*. Under Gorbachev a reformer, Otto Latsis, was made editor, and in 1987 he brought Gaidar in as part of his new editorial team.[54] In 1990 Gaidar was appointed to a similar post at *Pravda*, but *Pravda* proved less open to reform proposals, and in late 1990 he left to establish the Institute for Economic Policy.[55]

Sensing that the Soviet Union was becoming politically unstable, Gaidar began to focus his reform proposals on just the Russian Republic. Consequently, in the aftermath of the August 1991 coup, Gaidar was in a position to present a program of economic growth for a Russia separate from the Soviet Union, which of course was the Yeltsin approach. What makes Gaidar's subsequent rise to power so fascinating is that prior to the August putsch, Yeltsin and Gaidar had not met each other.

In retrospect Gaidar owes his role in the government to an insightful emphasis on policy as much as to circumstance, particularly his decision to join the initial few thousand who rallied to Yeltsin at the Russian White House on the first day of the attempted coup. While helping to protect Yeltsin, he was introduced to Gennady Burbulis, a trusted Yeltsin aide. After three days of talks Burbulis found himself in agreement with Gaidar's reform plans and his "Russia first" concept. Shortly after the coup failed, Burbulis arranged for Gaidar and his team to seclude themselves in the Russian government's official dacha, in the exclusive suburb of Arkhangelskoe, to formulate a reform plan for Russia.[56] Gaidar immediately called for reinforcements and began to draw upon his earlier studies and colleagues. Among others he added Chubais and several of his fellow Leningraders to his team.[57]

While Yavlinsky stuck to his Union approach for economic reform, Gaidar and Burbulis perceived that the Union was doomed. Ultimately, Yeltsin found their economic plan most appealing for Russia and incorporated it into a state-of-the-republic speech that he delivered on October 28.

But while incorporating Gaidar's concepts, Yeltsin continued with his pre-coup deputy prime ministers Yuri Skokov, Oleg Lobov, and Mikhail Maley. To avoid political wrangling, he decided to make himself his own prime minister, but as economic conditions continued to deteriorate, a group of Yeltsin's political supporters warned him in early November that he had to act quickly and vigorously to address his economic difficulties.[58] They recommended appointing Gaidar a deputy prime minister so that there would be someone who could focus on the economy. They also wanted Yeltsin to appoint the other twenty members of the Gaidar team to assist him. They would all become part of the government. At first Yeltsin hesitated to make such a far-reaching decision. After all, Yeltsin had met Gaidar only in August, a mere three months before. Admittedly, Yeltsin had included some of their ideas in his October speech, but that was very different from turning over responsibility for the economy to a group of young, untested theorists. Intelligent and eager as they were, none of them had ever had any administrative or managerial experience. In a word, this group of thirty-five-year-olds had never met a payroll.

Yeltsin's decision was a surprise to Gaidar as much as it was to Yeltsin.[59] Gaidar certainly wanted to participate in economic policy-making. That, after all, was why he had formed his study group and presented its recommendations to Yeltsin. He probably was hoping that he would be put in charge of a body with a role similar to that of the U.S. Council of Economic Advisers, with no day-to-day administrative responsibility. Gaidar was thus incredulous when he was informed in early November 1991 that he was to become minister of finance of Russia. After all, he had virtually no administrative experience. Although there had been rumors that he was being considered for a promotion, Gaidar himself said, "I didn't believe it. I didn't think I was going to get the job. I thought it would go to Skokov."[60] When he and his associates moved into their spacious offices on Staria Ploshchad, in what used to be the headquarters building of the Communist Party's Central Committee, it was a heady experience. As Andrei Nechayev, also just appointed minister of economics, put it, "For all of us to sit in those chairs, it was a bit—not fantastic, exactly, but phantasmagoric."[61]

I had occasion at the time to see Gaidar in a public meeting. It almost seemed his eyes were bulging from the pressures suddenly put on this academic economist. While preparing himself as an economic adviser, he clearly had not anticipated this enormous range of responsibilities. Giving economic advice was one thing; becoming finance minister with immense responsibilities was quite another. Like Admiral William Stockdale, Ross Perot's running mate for vice president, Gaidar seemed to be saying to himself, "Who am I? What am I doing here?"

Despite the sudden imposition of enormous responsibilities, however, Gaidar immediately began to implement his theories. He admitted that he fully expected to last no more than five months in office, if he was lucky.[62] Gaidar was not far off the mark; he lasted about thirteen months.

Although poorly equipped for the job, he did begin to learn quickly once in office. Moreover, in that short time he was transferred from his post as finance minister and appointed deputy prime minister, and then, even more unexpectedly, on June 15, 1992, only a week after Yeltsin said he did not plan to appoint a prime minister for several months, he was made acting prime minister. The appointment had to be submitted to and ratified by the Congress of People's Deputies. Ultimately, Yeltsin would decide to abandon Gaidar. For the time being, however, Gaidar's promotions were signs of renewed confidence not only in Gaidar but in the reform process itself.

While Gaidar's appointment signaled support for economic reform, that support went only so far. Yielding to criticism from state enterprise managers and members of the Supreme Soviet regarding the Gaidar team's lack of experienced leadership, Yeltsin on May 30, 1992, brought in three officials who were products of central planning and appointed them deputy prime ministers.[63] As their former positions suggest, it would have been hard to find better examples of the old industrial apparatchiks. Viktor Chernomyrdin had been the minister of the gas industry and had just been named head of the newly created Gazprom Corporation, a privatized version of the former Ministry of Gas. He was joined by Vladimir Shumeiko, a deputy leader of the Supreme Soviet and a former plant manager of state industry, and Georgi Khizha, the manager of a large military-industrial complex in Leningrad. Until Gaidar's promotion two weeks later, it was unclear where these new appointees stood in the hierarchy relative to Gaidar. According to official announcements, for example, Shumeiko as first deputy prime minister was supposedly ranked as equal if not superior to Gaidar. These appointments seemed at the time to run counter to the reform effort.[64]

Gaidar remained as acting prime minister until December 14, 1992, when Yeltsin once again met with resistance from the Russian Congress of People's Deputies. Although Yeltsin actually had the authority to retain Gaidar without the full approval of the Supreme Soviet (for that matter, he insisted until the last minute that Gaidar would be his man), he decided for reasons of political expediency to replace him with one of his recently appointed deputy prime ministers, Viktor Chernomyrdin. Yeltsin had known Chernomyrdin from their days together in Siberia—Yeltsin in Sverdlovsk and Chernomyrdin in Orsk.[65] Chernomyrdin was more attractive to the Russian Congress of People's Deputies, because the delegates viewed him as both older and more experienced. Like many of the representatives to the Russian Congress, he had worked in state industry and the Central Committee of the party, and thus had managerial and bureaucratic experience.[66] Through a correspondence course he had also graduated from a technical institute and, in common with many others of his generation, had on-the-job training. Chernomyrdin presented the prototypical, almost obligatory profile of the traditional Soviet manager cum prime minister who had preceded Gaidar. Before being brought into the government, he had actually worked at an oil refinery.[67] His jobs in a refinery, in the Ministry of Gas, and at Gazprom made him stand in sharp contrast to the purely academic Gaidar group. Gaidar did in time become more politically sophisticated and in late 1993 formed his own political party, Russia's Choice; he even had the benefit of regular weekly coaching from a master politician, Robert S. Strauss, the U.S. ambassador to Russia. But his youth, lack of practical experience and empathy for the elderly and poor, his occasional mistakes, along with his reluctance to seek political support from others outside his reformist circle, especially those in the parliament, and, most important, his failure to improve economic conditions led to his dismissal in December 1992. At the urging of Yeltsin, Gaidar rejoined the government in mid-September 1993, this time as Deputy prime minister to Chernomyrdin. In mid-1992 it had been just the reverse. But after Russia's Choice, the political party created by Gaidar, received so few votes in the December 1993 elections, Gaidar was again excluded from the new government formed by Chernomyrdin in January 1994.

It may have been harsh and unfair, but Aleksandr Rutskoi, Yeltsin's vice president, was certainly not alone when he characterized Gaidar and his team as "urchins in pink shorts and yellow sneakers."[68] Daring as they were, the Gaidar reforms did seem to many to be little more than classroom exercises. It came as no surprise, therefore, when they resulted in widespread economic hardship.

5.

Shock Therapy

Boris Yeltsin, like so many other world leaders, needed advice from his economists because he had virtually no training in economics himself, especially not in market economics. His strength was politics. And when his health and drinking were under control, Yeltsin was a superb politician. Unlike his predecessors, Yeltsin was more than a behind-the-scenes operator; he also went out to mix with the people. When it came to campaigning for political office, Yeltsin instinctively worked the crowd, touched the flesh, and racked up votes as efficiently as any of the best politicians in the world. Given that prior to the semi-open elections in 1988, virtually no one in the Soviet Union had to, or was even allowed to, run for office, Yeltsin's transformation into a man of the people was all the more remarkable. In his Sverdlovsk days he had, it is true, interacted with his constituents far more than had most of his Central Committee peers in charge of other regions of the country. But considering that until 1988 and 1989 he never had to woo voters or experience the give-and-take of election campaigning, his transformation was striking.

Impressive as Yeltsin's emergence as a democratic politician may have been, his embrace of the market was even more so and in many ways as unexpected. Gorbachev, for example, had no trouble accepting the concept of elections—that is, as long as his seat was guaranteed and he did not have to subject himself to popular elections. At the same time Gorbachev had very mixed emotions about the market and especially about private property. For the most part, support for far-reaching economic reforms came from the younger generation; Yeltsin was a major exception among his generation.

Some argue that Yeltsin's attitude toward both democracy and the market reflected, at least in part, his effort to distinguish himself from Gorbachev and at the same time to twit him. Indeed, although Yeltsin mixed with his constituents in Sverdlovsk, he gave almost no indication that he was interested in or even contemplated any democratic or market experiments. Yeltsin's transformation into a supporter of the market may be explained by his growing realization that central planning had outlived its usefulness, as was becoming increasingly clear in the 1980s. In any case, unlike his fellow bureaucrats, Yeltsin began to work with some of the economists who rose to prominence in the Gorbachev era, particularly Yavlinsky, Shatalin, and, later, Gaidar. He became a staunch supporter of the Yavlinsky 400-day cum Shatalin 500-day plan in mid-1990. These plans later served as a model, at least in part, for Gaidar's proposals.

Nevertheless, while Yeltsin was considerably more willing than Gorbachev to move from discussion to actual implementation of economic reforms, it is unclear just how deep his understanding of or commitment to the market was. In that respect Yeltsin seems to resemble Ronald Reagan, who governed more by instinct than by intellect. During the intense meetings in the late summer of 1990 between representatives of Yeltsin and Gorbachev to work out a compromise on Shatalin's 500-day plan, Yeltsin was off in Siberia meeting his constituents. Upon his return to Moscow he immediately moved to push the Shatalin plan forward, if need be in Russia alone. However, some of the participants in the discussions suspected that Yeltsin had not even bothered to read much of the program.[1]

I

However imperfect his understanding of the full implications for Russia of replacing central planning with a market economy, Yeltsin called for just such a transformation of the Russian economy. In a speech to the Fifth Russian Congress of People's Deputies, on October 28, 1991, prepared in large part by Yegor Gaidar and his team, Yeltsin put forth what ultimately became the Yeltsin-Gaidar reforms. Nevertheless, despite Yeltsin's hearty endorsement of the market, the speech laid out general intentions, not specific actions. This added to the widespread sense of confusion following the August coup attempt. Moreover, how could Yeltsin carry out such a far-reaching reform package in Russia when neither the Soviet Union nor the neighboring republics had shown any intention of introducing similar reforms? It was as if the state of New York were to declare that it intended to introduce central planning while the rest of the United States continued to operate as a market system.

As though that had not been disruptive enough, because of Gorbachev's faulty economic stewardship Yeltsin and Russia were confronted with an ever-increasing rate of inflation (as high as 1,100 percent), a collapsing GNP (down as much as 20 percent), and an increasingly distorted disarray of incentives and economic institutions. At the same time the collapse of the Soviet Union itself seemed imminent. For their own reasons Yeltsin and Leonid Kravchuk, the leader of Ukraine, were doing their best to bring that collapse about—Kravchuk, as we saw, because he wanted independence for Ukraine from Russia and Yeltsin because the only way to rid himself of Gorbachev was to dismember the Soviet Union.

II

On December 25, 1991, Yeltsin had his revenge. With virtually no way to hold the Union together nonviolently, Gorbachev closed down the Soviet Union and resigned his office. Exhilarating as this must have been for Yeltsin, the disappearance of the Soviet Union exacerbated Russia's already serious economic and political problems. The impact was the same in the other fourteen now independent states. Yeltsin and the other presidents not only had to build new political structures in their republics; they also had to deal with collapsed economies. In addition, Yeltsin needed to superintend a shift from central planning to the market, privatize state-owned businesses, industries, and farms and civilianize a bloated and powerful military-industrial complex. Any one of these challenges would have taxed the abilities of the best of leaders. To make matters worse, they had to be dealt with in an environment of suddenly assertive ethnic pride and grievances that emboldened their constituents, including local Russian chauvinists who along with many non-Russians began to insist on more control over their tax revenues and locally based raw materials. These demands gradually expanded to include more political autonomy and ultimately independence from Moscow. Throughout Russia local areas such as Chechenia decreed that henceforth local laws would take precedence over national laws.

The seriousness of the situation meant that Gaidar and his team lacked the leisure to move gradually. By November 1991, fueled by a widening budget deficit and the printing of money by the Central Bank, hyperinflation had sparked a run on those few consumer goods, such as canned products, that had not already disappeared. Rapidly rising inflationary pressures have a particularly disruptive impact on centrally planned economies, with their system of fixed and subsidized prices. When prices in the nonstate market sector begin to soar, they act like giant magnets and draw what goods there are out the back doors of state shops into the market, both legal and black. In the fall of 1991 there was a real possibility that the state bakeries in the major cities would even run out of bread.

Gaidar's measures were predicated on his often expressed notion that the transformation from central planning to the market was an enormous undertaking involving many disparate but interactive parts of the economy. Consequently, the reform stood the best chance of success only if the interactive parts were transformed simultaneously, as an ensemble. While such an approach complicated the reform process, Gaidar believed that moving piecemeal or step by step would not only be more time consuming but undermine the whole reform effort. Because the various reform measures impinged on and were impinged on by other parts of the economy, if any sectors of the economy were left to operate as they had under central planning, they would hinder the effectiveness of the new measures.

The old economic mantra "We will make possible a more rational and humane allocation of resources," which had been the premise for introducing central planning, had by 1991 become the very essence of the problem. Soviet planners had prided themselves on their efforts to protect Soviet consumers by keeping consumer prices low. For thirty years or more bread prices, for example, had remained the same. This seemed to be much more humane than the situation in the West, where despite some relatively modest subsidization consumers had to deal with constantly rising prices. The problem was that because of the rising costs of agricultural inputs, the cost of producing bread increased annually. Consequently, to prevent increases in retail bread prices, the government had to provide subsidies to farmers. This appeared to be a small price to pay—at least in the beginning.

By the mid-1980s, however, the subsidies had become an enormous expense. Approximately a hundred billion pre-inflation rubles were needed to sustain low consumer goods prices. The ever-increasing budget subsidies not only helped create a budget deficit; they also warped the economy. For example, to finance this deficit, the government printed increasing quantities of money. By 1990 this had intensified inflationary pressures to such a point that the dangers could no longer be ignored or suppressed. At the same time the low bread prices proved disruptive because they increasingly distorted the allocation of resources and led to periodic bread shortages. With the price so low, peasants found it advantageous to feed bread rather than grain to their livestock. Roughly 15 percent of the country's bread was diverted and fed to peasant livestock. Similarly, urban dwellers treated bread almost like a free good. Because it cost so little, no one worried about wasting it.

III

Against this background Gaidar concluded that his first task was to stop inflation and restore the value of the ruble. This became the essence of shock therapy. To check inflation the government had to stop printing money, and that meant the budget had to be balanced or at least the deficit reduced. For example, with the Cold War at an end, there was no need to continue to spend so much on the military. Indeed, budget expenditures for military equipment purchases were cut by at least half, some say more.[2] Equally far-reaching, to end state subsidies and the printing of money, it was necessary to stop setting low prices and instead allow market pressures to determine retail prices. This would mean an across-the-board, one-day massive increase in prices of at least 200 to 300 percent. This was the shock. Yet, even then, the reformers realized that wasteful usage of resources was so ingrained that a one-step elimination of all subsidies and military expenditures would not be feasible. It would thus be impossible to reduce the budget deficit altogether. Therefore, Gaidar and his team sought to reduce the budget deficit to 3 percent and, when that failed, to 5 percent of the GNP.

Shock therapy was put into effect on January 2, 1992. Subsidies to farms and factories were cut and consumer prices decontrolled. Except for fifteen basic commodities such as bread, milk, and gasoline, this meant that retail prices were allowed to find their own equilibrium level on the basis of supply and demand. At the same time an effort was made to restrain the Central Bank from issuing large credits. But since the Central Bank was under the jurisdiction of the Supreme Soviet, not the prime minister or president, this was very difficult to do. Other steps taken as part of the reform process eventually included an effort to privatize land and state enterprises, both service and industrial. The state also sought at least partial convertibility of the ruble. Integrating Russian prices and manufacturing potential with world markets was intended to facilitate the rational allocation of goods, which was the ultimate goal of shock therapy.

IV

Bold and even revolutionary as the Gaidar reform package seemed, it was not too different from the strategy that groups such as the International Monetary Fund (IMF) typically recommended to developing countries. The key was an assumption that higher prices or market-determined prices are a panacea for a basic economic malaise. In that sense, shock therapy was like an over-the-counter drug—good for any ailment regardless of preconditions, ideology, or institutions. There was no need for a fancy prescription—brand X would do as well.

To be sure, Gaidar's reform efforts contrasted favorably in scope with those introduced during the Gorbachev era. But while the Yeltsin reforms were more far-reaching, it seems reasonably certain that the initiative for their extreme nature came from Gaidar and not Yeltsin. That conclusion is warranted in part because a year and a half earlier (and before Gaidar's association with Yeltsin), Yeltsin had insisted that his transition program to a market economy would involve a grace period of two to three years and would avoid any decline in living standards.[3]

Whatever Yeltsin's involvement in designing and implementing the reforms, Gaidar and his team moved boldly and comprehensively, without hesitation and self-doubt. Gaidar's approach, like Gorbachev's, however, was a top-down imposition of a reform program. It was the opposite of the reform in China (discussed in Chapter 9), where spontaneous reform efforts emanated from below.

Equally serious was the fact that Gaidar and his advisers, both Russian and foreign, neglected to consider the institutional framework within which their reforms were to take place. They were correct in their argument that, theoretically, higher prices will drive some consumers from the market and attract new sources of supply, which will ultimately diminish the rate of inflation. They did not understand, however, that in order for their reforms to be carried out, it was necessary also to change the existing institutions, such as the collectivized farms, monopolized industry, and weak service sector. These changes were essential because the shock therapy approach was predicated on the presence of supply flexibility within the system and mobility among the factors of production. But the existence of virtual monopolies in important industries made it unlikely that these industries would respond to market signals.

In retrospect it is clear that the reforms were doomed to fail as long as nothing was done to replace the marketing and production infrastructure destroyed by Stalin in the late 1920s and the 1930s. It was bad enough that he outlawed private ownership. But, as the privatization effort has demonstrated, enterprises can be reprivatized. Unfortunately, Stalin did not stop at confiscation and nationalization. In search of those elusive economies of scale that he and others insisted would make communism superior to capitalism, Stalin shuttered small as well as big businesses and amalgamated many into larger units. Consequently, even though the present-day reformers have privatized a large number of small shops, not only do many of them continue to operate as if they were still part of a central-planning regime, but large portions of the retailing, not to mention the wholesaling, network were destroyed and never rebuilt.

The Soviets prided themselves on the fact that such a small portion of their GNP was wasted on services like marketing. It is no wonder that the post-Brezhnev market sector has been slow to respond to price incentives and that when it tries, more often than not, it finds itself stifled by the mafia. As an example of the mafia's growing control of most of the newly developing private sector, the economist Oleg Bogomolov described what happened to a larger than anticipated watermelon crop in the Moscow area. When a group of peasants decided to lower their prices in the hope of selling more, the mafia torched their trucks, destroyed their melons, and beat them up.[4] They did the same thing to kiosk owners who tried to cut the retail prices of cigarettes in St. Petersburg. Through such intimidating tactics, the mafia not only took over virtual control of private trade but also intimidated the government sector through bribes and the outright hiring of government officials, especially police. Its funds were obtained through extortion and a quasi tax imposed on all private traders. Even street vendors with folding cardtables were expected to pay fifty dollars (in dollars) a month to sell their wares. The fee for kiosks and shops was higher.

Reflecting the pervasiveness of their control, the Russian mafia extended its operations to Beijing. Since the late 1980s thousands of enterprising Russians have flocked across the border to buy cheap Chinese consumer goods for resale in Russian kiosks. By 1993 these traders were no longer restricting themselves to hand luggage; they were filling buses to the ceiling with their purchases. On arriving in Beijing, however, these Russian traders were "taxed" one hundred dollars a visit by the resident members of the Russian mafia. Failure to pay in either Moscow or Beijing was sure to bring the threat of physical violence, including death or firebombing.

In an effort to fend off the mafia, some private businessmen hired their own protective forces, but, as might have been anticipated, these "guards" often were nothing more than another cheaper variation of the mafia. In either case the mafia acts as a restraint on private enterprise. The end result is fewer goods and fewer suppliers than would appear in a free market.

V

In any about-face of this political and economic magnitude, there is bound to be large-scale disruption as ministries are eliminated or merged. Thus the abolition of Gosplan and Gossnab, which set production targets, coordinated resources, and carried out the wholesaling function of moving goods between producers and retailers, left a vacuum. While Western advisers to the Gaidar government did understand the importance of markets and wholesaling, they were not overly concerned with this missing market factor. Because it is so basic to the functioning of Western economics, many took its existence for granted and never bothered to ask if the Russians needed markets and wholesalers. Their advice focused instead on achieving fiscal stability and monetary restraint in order to restore some semblance of macro control. This strategy had worked in "similar" rescue efforts, and Russia was clearly in need of similar controls. But with no wholesaling infrastructure, domestic as well as foreign businessmen did not know where to turn. They could not even find phone books or industry guides. Such materials had generally been regarded as classified documents, and Standard and Poor–type directories were nonexistent, at least in the initial stages of the reform. In other words, new businessmen without connections to the old system were hard-pressed to find sources of supply or customers. Until recently there was no infrastructure in place to help them. Only gradually are entrepreneurs begining to create a new one.[5]

Reform in Russia was also hampered by the near-collapse of government authority and effectiveness. After seventy years of excessive government control and abuse, this was not entirely bad news. But, as so often in Russia today, there is a tendency to go from one extreme to another—in this case, from authoritarianism to anarchy. In dismantling the Leninist political structure, both the government under Gorbachev and, at least for the first two years, the government under Yeltsin became too weak to maintain economic and political order. This weakness, more than anything else, explains the current government's inability to bring inflation under control, stop the decay of what marketing infrastructure there was, and limit mafia expansion. In this instance, the sudden collapse of a centralized bureaucracy worsened rather than alleviated many of Russia's economic problems.

The reformers did not seem to understand that institutional change should have priority or that there must be continued assertion of governmental control over market behavior. It was not enough to focus only on price deregulation, budget balancing, and monetary control. Shock therapy, when it works, requires flexibility in the system and factor of production mobility. But in the Russia of 1992 the farms were still collectivized, industry monopolized, and services in the thrall of the mafia. Thus the usual fiscal and monetary controls that in noncommunist economies work to halt inflation and market disruption worked imperfectly or not at all in the Soviet economy. In a more normal market economy such fiscal and monetary measures create higher prices that drive some consumers from the market and simultaneously generate new sources of supply. A few months after the raising of prices in January 1992, more consumer goods slowly reappeared in Russian shops. But that was a consequence more of the higher prices driving consumers out of the market, particularly pensioners and those on fixed incomes, than of an increase in the production of goods. At least the demand portion of the equation worked. What did not work, at any rate in the short run, was the supply side of the equation. Given the monopolistic control of state industries, the existence of the mafia, and the resulting absence of a significant number of independent enterprises, higher prices alone were not enough to stimulate a meaningful increase in supply, at least in the short term. Until micro changes in the form of the large-scale creation of private or nonstate manufacturing, retail, service, and wholesale institutions take place, no reform effort in Russia is likely to succeed. Unfortunately, such changes will take many years to bring about.

Undaunted, Gaidar and his team decided that the dire circumstances demanded drastic and quick action. Their far-reaching measures, particularly the overnight threefold increase in retail prices, fell especially hard on the elderly and others on fixed or relatively stable incomes. It appeared that the inexperience and the youth of the reformers made it hard for them to anticipate and empathize with the suffering resulting from their reforms. One instance of this came in the interview Jeffrey Sachs gave the *Financial Times*. "Professor Sachs dismissed the tide of complaints against the vastly increased prices and taxes levied on enterprise as 'yak yak yak.' "[6]

The Gaidar team was evidently aware of what it was up against. According to the Israeli economist Gur Ofer, the economic crisis was so serious in late 1991, and his ability to implement effective change so limited, that Gaidar consciously did what he did in the hope that at least a few of his reforms might take effect and be enough to prevent further collapse. Almost as an afterthought Gaidar allowed that perhaps some of the reforms might generate positive change as well. It was almost as if he decided to announce his reforms and then stand back and see whether anything happened.

VI

Poland had been Gaidar's principal model. But the underlying situation in Poland, though also serious, produced a far more favorable response. That was because of the very different Polish institutional framework. Higher prices in Poland sparked the anticipated response because, while state-owned enterprises dominated the economy, there were enough small but well-established private retailers to make a difference. There were even some private, if small, wholesalers and manufacturers. Most important, 80 percent of the country's farmers had never succumbed to the campaign to collectivize agriculture. When prices were unleashed in January 1990, there were thus decision makers, both independent farmers and private owners (even if dulled by years of state-mandated central planning), who eventually responded to material incentives.

The reformers around Gaidar were very much impressed by the Polish reforms. Reasoning that Polish conditions in 1990 were not all that different from what they faced in Russia in late 1991, they decided to follow much the same strategy. Unfortunately, they and their advisers like Jeffrey Sachs all tended to disregard the important distinctions between Poland and Russia. In fact, Peter Aven, at the time Russian minister of foreign economic relations, criticized those who insist that "economies of all countries in equal measure are special. . . . That is wrong. There are no special countries from the point of view of economists. If economics is a science, with its own laws—all countries and all economic stabilization plans are the same."[7] In other words, those who insist that Russia is not Poland are wrong. "That is an illusion." Arguments to the contrary were repeatedly rejected.

It took several months and enormous and in many ways needless human suffering, but by 1993, just a year later, a few advisers had come to acknowledge that Russia might after all be different from Poland. The institutional differences created by the rigid central-planning process over sixty years differentiated the Russian economy from that of most other countries. Relatively unfamiliar with Soviet practices and culture as well as institutions, most of the foreign advisers and, for that matter, many of their Russian counterparts did not fully appreciate the degree to which Russian market institutions and market behavior had been destroyed. They did not fully understand that the gigantic state industrial enterprises and the underdeveloped distribution network that were both structured to facilitate central planning were also designed to inhibit the development of a market economy and booby-trapped in such a way that anyone attempting to re-institute a market system would cause enormous chaos. This difference in structures explains the threefold immediate increase in Russian prices in January 1992 and the twenty-four-fold increase for the whole year. This stands in sharp contrast to the sixfold increase for the whole of 1990 in Poland.

The biggest obstacle to reform was that few of the institutions created by the system of central planning were willing or able to take advantage of the increased prices. On the contrary, the response of the bulk of Russian enterprises was simply to sell at the higher prices, without changing the quantity offered. Soviet managers who for seventy years had been ordered to produce set amounts were conditioned to be oblivious to changes in market conditions. In fact, in some instances Russian economists reported that the quantity offered actually diminished.[8]

Yet, even if a marketing and wholesaling infrastructure had been in place and the mafia not been a problem, Gaidar and his colleagues would still have had difficulties. Although they did initially have substantial control over government expenditures, they lacked control over the Central Bank. The problem became especially difficult in July 1992 after Gaidar, yielding to the Supreme Soviet, appointed Viktor Gerashchenko acting director of the Central Bank.[9] Subordinate to the Supreme Soviet, the Central Bank chairman adopted an increasingly independent and at times deliberately antagonistic stance toward the reform economists appointed by Yeltsin. As in Western countries, the bank's separation from the executive branch was presumably intended to ensure that there would be an independent proponent of price stability. Typically, presidents and prime ministers desire a booming economy and full employment even if it means excessive money creation and subsequent inflation, and thus there is a need for an independent central bank to rein them in. In Russia, paradoxically, it was the prime minister (or at least Gaidar as long as he was the acting prime minister) who fought for monetary restraint, while the Central Bank director was determined to print up hoards of money. The concept of separation of fiscal stimulus from monetary restraint apparently did not anticipate a situation in which the institution supervising the bank, the Supreme Soviet, would be dominated by factory directors whose primary interest was to keep their factories operating and therefore fully funded.

It was essential to the reform process to control not only the Russian Central Bank but also most of the central banks of the other republics. These banks continued to operate as before and issued ruble credits to enterprises in their republic that requested them. For the most part, this credit was to buy products from suppliers located in Russia. But since the Russian ruble was initially used as a local currency in Ukraine and several of the other republics, the ruble credits also funded local economic activities. Therefore, even when the Russian Central Bank agreed to some monetary restraint, it had little impact, because of a lack of restraint in neighboring republics. Consequently, in the summer of 1992, the Russian government complained bitterly that its efforts at restraint were frustrated by Ukrainian bank officials who provided Ukrainian enterprises with a credit of five hundred billion Russian rubles.[10] (At the same time, of course, Ukrainian officials blamed Russia for their inflation. How, I was asked during a visit to Kiev in June 1992, could Ukraine control its inflation when Russia had the sole power to print money?) In the end Ukraine agreed to cease issuing ruble credits without permission of the Russian Central Bank, but by then the inflationary damage to Russia had been done.

VII

Closer Russian control of ruble credits issued by non-Russian governments and the appointment of a more cooperative and tighter-fisted director of the Russian Central Bank would have facilitated the economic reform process, but it is misleading to imply that their absence spelled the difference between success and failure of the reforms. Actually, for a time under Gaidar the Central Bank adopted the fiscal and monetary discipline the IMF required. Table 5-1 indicates that, following a doubling of the country's money supply in 1991, the government and the bank

Table 5-1 Money Supply and Credit to the Russian Economy, January 1992–June 1993 (in billion rubles)

Month	Money Supply	% Change	Gov't Credit to State Enterprises	% Change	Consumer Price % Change
1/92	951.4	12%	439.4	17%	345%
2/92	1,069.5	12%	516.6	35%	38%
3/92	1,194.2	14%	697.3	32%	30%
4/92	1,359	10%	918.1	12%	22%
5/92	1,495.2	9%	1,025.3	2%	12%
6/92	1,630.6	28%	1,041.8	34%	19%
7/92	2,082.3	25%	1,393	34%	11%
8/92	2,609.5	32%	1,860	16%	9%
9/92	3,435.8	28%	2,153.2	27%	12%
10/92	4,381.6		2,731		23%
11/92					26%
12/92					25%
1/93					27%
2/93		10%			26%
3/93		17%			21%
4/93		23%			25%
5/93					19%
6/93					20%

SOURCE: *Ekonomika i zhizn*, no. 46 (Nov. 1992): no. 51 (Dec. 1992): 1; *FBIS*, Feb. 16, 1993, p. 21.

took heroic steps to bring inflation under control in early 1992.[11] When Yeltsin assumed power, the Central Bank was creating new money each month at a double-digit rate, 12 to 14 percent of the existing money supply. By May the rate of increase fell to 9 percent a month.[12] Similarly, in the first quarter of 1992, the government slashed government expenditures from approximately 50 percent of the country's GNP to 20 percent. The expenditures on military equipment were especially hard hit. Some commentators have claimed that such radical cuts made it possible, at least for a time, to balance the budget in early 1992.[13]

However imperfect such measures may have been, there were promising signs that the monetary and fiscal restraints might be working after all. Following a two- or three-month lag, price increases formerly as high as 20 to 30 percent a month responded to the cutbacks in credit and expenditures and dropped to as little as 9 percent a month in August 1992. These efforts, however, were comparable to placing a granite wall in front of a 200-mile-an-hour Japanese bullet train. The impact was too much to absorb. Without government loans and bank credits, substantial portions of the country's government-owned industries (at the time about 90 percent or more of all industrial production) would have been unable to pay either their suppliers or their workers. Faced with the prospect of layoffs and factory closings in a system without welfare and unemployment support, the factory managers feared the consequences of massive plant closings. As if reaching a spontaneous consensus, most factory managers decided to keep producing even where there was no demand for their output. I frequently saw the streets near big factories jammed with items such as farm combines and trucks that no one wanted or was able to buy.

After a time these managers encountered severe financial problems. Without customers for their goods there was no money to pay wages and bills to other factories. Factories simply stopped paying for delivery of components. At one point Russian enterprises were in arrears for 220 billion rubles just for wages. Many of my friends complained that they had not been paid their salaries for three months. If there had been a bankruptcy law, many of these defaulting enterprises would presumably have been declared bankrupt. It did not help, either, that the transfer of funds between banks usually required three weeks or more. In a time of near-hyperinflation this added to the economic malaise, because the funds when finally received were worth considerably less than originally intended. It is a measure of how severe the problem grew to be that enterprise accounts payable, which totaled 37 billion rubles in January 1992, exploded to 3.2 trillion rubles in August 1992 and 25 trillion rubles in early 1994.*[14] This was obviously more than inflation. Denied credit and money from the government and the Central Bank, Russian factories created their own credit lines simply by not demanding repayment.

This example illustrates why the IMF prescription of price hikes and the cutbacks in credit and government expenditure did not evoke the same response they tended to do in other countries. Because Russia lacked the independent farmers and businessmen who could have responded to the newly introduced economic stimuli by producing more goods and providing jobs, these reforms proved counterproductive. Thus, when the Russian government and the Central Bank finally did adhere to the IMF prescriptions, the impact was potentially so far-reaching and dangerous that factory managers took matters into their own hands and created their own money and credit equivalents. Recognizing what was happening, the banks and the government in mid-July again began to increase credits and expenditures. Government credit rose from 440 billion rubles in January 1992 to 1.4 trillion rubles in July.[15] Simultaneously, increases in the money supply rose from 9 percent in May to 28 percent in June. This undermined the fight to hold price increases to the single-digit level, and by October and November 1992 prices were again rising by more than 20 percent a month.

It is unfair to place blame for what happened solely on the Central Bank or on factory managers. Yeltsin was also to blame. To ensure support before the April 1993 referendum on his stewardship, he promised to double pensions, student stipends and the minimum wage. (He did much the same thing before the December 1993 election.) To win support from automobile owners, he introduced a decree freezing gasoline prices. Some econo-

*This enterprise form of credit creation was not unique to Russia. It has occured in other countries, such as China and Rumania, when state and bank credits were tightened.

mists estimated these concessions would cost as much as three trillion rubles. Like politicians everywhere, Yeltsin reversed himself after his victory on the referendum and allowed gasoline prices to rise, restricted increases in the amount of student stipends, and also cut back on budget expenditures for social problems. But he did not abandon all his promises. That is why, in responding to pressure to control the money supply, Viktor Gerashchenko, the acting chairman of the Central Bank, sarcastically noted that the bank would cut back on the issuance of credit when the government curbed its appetite for increasing expenditures.

Nevertheless, the actions of the banks greatly undermined the country's economic recovery. In the spring of 1991, for instance, Vneshekonombank, the bank designated by the Central Bank to handle foreign-currency transactions, began to default on payments in hard currency *(valuta)* to some of the bank's private depositors.[16] By the fall the funds of state enterprises were also frozen. In a clearly illegal move, the bank withdrew four billion dollars in private depositors' hard-currency deposits and used the funds to repay the overdue national debt.[17] By December 1991, when Russia took over control of the bank from the no longer existing Soviet Union, the bank was already in default and froze about six to eight billion dollars worth of customer deposits.

Once a bank freezes or diverts deposits this way, its credibility is destroyed. To prevent any further loss of their money, depositors instinctively did all they could to smuggle existing assets, both *valuta* and commodities like oil, out of the country and to ensure that future earnings were sent to bank accounts abroad. Consequently, Russia also began to experience capital flight, or *ottoke*. Even the official news agency Itar-Tass began to require that its foreign customers in Moscow deposit payments for its services in Tass's West European bank account. To halt further outflow of *valuta*, Russian authorities declared it illegal to open accounts outside of Russian territory. Since they did not have the legal facilities to enforce this ruling, such decrees did little to stop the flight.

I have been a firsthand witness to the process. One of my Moscow acquaintances asked me to help him open an account in the United States. He wanted to buy some video equipment and books for his business. For convenience' sake I arranged for a new joint account with both our names in my bank. He deposited a thousand dollars or so and wrote checks periodically, and the monthly statements were forwarded to me. In early 1993 I received a notice from the bank that a deposit of $60,000 had been made to my account from Deutsche Bank in Frankfurt, Germany. I spent the weekend trying to determine what I had done to warrant such beneficence. I planned to call the bank to tell them it had been a mistake, when I realized the money was not for me but for the joint account. That $60,000, needed at home, had been diverted from Moscow to Massachusetts for safekeeping from confiscation and inflation. Estimates of the amount diverted this way range from a billion dollars or so to fifteen to thirty billion dollars.[18] Vice President Aleksandr Rutskoi suggested a figure of seventeen billion dollars.[19] In most cases it exceeds the inflow of capital investment and grants sent in by Western investors and governments.

Like financial authorities in other countries that react in much the same way when faced with capital flight, the Russians reverted to their old methods and reintroduced tightened administrative controls. In addition to banning overseas bank accounts, Russian officials in late 1990 ordered that 50 percent of all dollar export earnings be converted into rubles at what for a time was a disadvantageous rate of exchange.[20] Ten percent of those proceeds were to be set aside for the Russian Central Bank. About a year later, in December 1991, a more favorable rate closer to the market rate was permitted on 10 percent of the export proceeds, but the need to swap *valuta* for rubles was still a form of confiscation and served as a significant disincentive to export.[21] Adding to these disincentives, Gerashchenko, at the Central Bank, acknowledged that if he could have his way, exporters would have to give up 100 percent of their export earnings for rubles.[22] Moreover, the authorities sought to impose an export tax of 30 percent in an effort to ensure a source of *valuta* for the government.[23] This was also intended to compensate for the fact that domestic prices, particularly on sought-after raw materials, were often no more than 25 to 30 percent of the world price. This disparity created an enormous incentive to gain access to products like oil and export them. Presumably, if domestic prices more closely approximated world prices, there would be less of a windfall and less need for the export tax. In addition to the export tax and the requirement to swap *valuta* for rubles, the authorities in June 1992 threatened to impose an income tax on foreigners as high as 60 percent. Even more discouraging, Russian authorities set the stage for a 23 percent investment tax on foreign investment inside Russia in the spring of 1994. Some in the government denied there was any such tax, but just the confusion was unsettling. These measures and threats discouraged foreign investment in the Russian economy.[24] Admittedly, many of these measures, such as the ban on unauthorized foreign bank accounts, were poorly enforced, if at all, and by mid-1993 some were rescinded or eased, but they acted as a restraint on Western investment. The Economic Commission for Europe estimated that the net inflow of foreign direct investment into Russia in 1992 totaled only $200 million.[25] According to the Ministry of Finance, the sum increased somewhat in 1993, to an estimated $700 million.

Some of these restrictive measures were in response to Russian nationalists, who have historically been opposed to foreign investment or any foreign involvement in Russian domestic affairs. These expressions of suspicion, even paranoia, reached a peak during the effort of the Supreme Soviet to impeach Yeltsin in March 1993 and again in the fall, shortly before Yeltsin's troops assaulted the White House.[26] Just how widespread such sentiments were was dramatically demonstrated by the more than 23 percent share of the vote in December 1993 that went for the nationalistic Liberal Democratic party of Zhirinovsky. Hardliners charged Yeltsin with attempting to impose "primitive, savage and predatory capitalism" on a poor Russia. One critic even accused Yeltsin of "derailing Russia as instructed by western intelligence sources."

Upsetting to all Russians, not merely to the nationalists, was the rapid collapse in the value of the ruble. The illegal but operative street rate for the ruble had hovered at 3 to 4 rubles for a dollar for many years, but in 1990 it began to fall. By July 1992 it had fallen to 140 rubles per dollar and continued to fall and hit 2,000 rubles per dollar in June 1994. This collapse came despite the considerable efforts of the Russian Central Bank to stop it. The bank spent some one billion dollars in *valuta* to prevent an even sharper drop.[27] At times the bank was supplying up to 60 percent of the *valuta* available for purchase with rubles. Since it had to be diverted from repaying the country's international debt service, this was money the bank could ill afford. The expectation had been that creating a stronger ruble would attract more foreign capital and that therefore the problem would more or less resolve itself. Instead, most of the *valuta* exchanged for rubles was moved outside the country, either as part of the capital flight or as cash to finance the purchases of foreign consumer goods beginning to pour into the country in the early 1990s. Thus, other countries, especially those that manufactured cheap consumer goods, such as China and India, benefited by providing goods that had long been absent from Russian shelves.

These various measures, some of them misguided, resulted in further default in the payment of Russia's international debt. In 1993 its foreign debt was estimated to have reached about eighty billion dollars. The minimal cost of servicing this debt (interest and repayment of principal) in 1994 was expected to reach fifteen billion dollars.[28] The Russians were even unable to repay the vital U.S. credits that had been set aside for the purchase of U.S. grain exports. By fall 1993 they had defaulted on a billion dollars in payments.[29] These defaults were particularly significant because, under existing U.S. law, once the Russian government fell behind, the U.S. government was obligated to cut off future credit and halt additional grain deliveries, at least until the arrears could be repaid or the U.S. Department of Agriculture could find some new way to interpret the law.

VIII

Some of these monetary and financial problems could probably have been avoided if the Gaidar group had begun by introducing a currency reform. As Stalin did in 1947, Gaidar should have decreed that on the first day of the reform all Russian citizens would have one week to convert ten existing rubles into one new ruble. This would have wiped out the bulk of the country's monetary overhang, thereby shrinking the inflationary potential that was sure to follow when prices were set free. Because no such reform was ordered, the holders of the billions of rubles that had been set aside for the day when price controls were abolished did as should have been expected: on January 2, 1992, they bought out their rubles and overnight drove up prices threefold.

Admittedly, a currency reform, because it would have wiped out a substantial share of the population's savings, would have penalized those who had previously been induced to accept ruble payments and thus would have undercut the credibility and future trust in the ruble. Moreover, a currency reform in late 1991 might already have been too late to penalize speculators like the mafia. Anticipating a currency reform, the more sophisticated members of the mafia had already converted their rubles into *valuta* to protect themselves against just such an act.

Imperfect as it might have been, an across-the-board currency reform like the one in West Germany (not one that targeted only rubles of a specific denomination, as happened in 1991, or specific years, as happened in the summer of 1993) would have made the subsequent reforms much less traumatic in their impact. Price increases and adjustments would have been much less extreme and prevented some of the public shock and anger that followed. Moreover, such a currency exchange could have been designed to have a progressive impact. Thus, even though the overall rate of exchange would have been ten to one, the authorities could have decreed that everyone could first exchange a maximum of three thousand rubles at a more favorable rate of one old ruble to one new ruble. This step would have protected pensioners and others with fixed incomes.

Equally important, with less of a money overhang, there would have been less inflationary pressure, and so the government could also have extended the range of commodities freed from price controls. In particular, it might have been able to allow more price flexibility on energy products, especially petroleum. Instead, aware of how central petroleum was to the economy, they decided to retain price controls on petroleum. Since world prices for petroleum were generally five times higher than domestic prices, smuggling of petroleum out of the country was sure to follow. Russian traders were up to the challenge. They managed to ship out millions of tons of petroleum across the unpoliced border to Latvia from Russia and from there to Western Europe, where they deposited the hard-currency earnings in Western banks. As a consequence the government lost five billion dollars a year or more in hard-currency earnings that previously had gone into government accounts. Since petroleum exports have traditionally been the Soviet Union's largest source of hard-currency earnings, the loss of all this *valuta* curbed the import of Western technology and consumer goods that would have helped cushion the blow of the reform process.[30]

IX

Nonetheless, whatever the shortcomings in the actual reforms, it is likely that even if Gaidar's group had decided to opt for a broader reform that included a currency reform as well as institutional changes such as decollectivization of agriculture and encouragement of the establishment of brand-new businesses, manufacturing, and services, a successful implementation of the economic reforms would still have taken decades, not just a few months. Nor did it help that Yeltsin promised many of these institutional changes in his October 28, 1991, speech and then settled for much less. The privatization of land, for example, was postponed until a landownership provision could be included in a new constitution. That process dragged out for over a year and a half, and in October 1993, after he had abolished the parliament, Yeltsin simply issued a ukase, or decree, declaring the peasants could become owners of the land. (This, by the way, was something he could also have done in 1991 or early 1992, when he was still on good terms with the parliament and it had granted him extraordinary powers to take such steps.) Even then, however, the October 1993 decree was neutered with all kinds of qualifications.

Against all these odds Yeltsin and Gaidar held to their promise to introduce price flexibility. On December 3, 1991, Deputy Prime Minister Gaidar declared that price controls would be removed on December 16.[31] This announcement of an end to price controls two weeks in advance, much like Pavlov's earlier in 1991 under Gorbachev, sparked another panic-buying spree, after which little was left to buy. Most everything not subject to spoiling had already been purchased in anticipation of just such a possibility.

Decisions regarding price increases should be implemented as quickly as possible. However, Gaidar was forced to wait even longer when officials in Ukraine and Belarus protested the suddenness of the decision. They complained that since they still used the ruble and were not involved in the initial decision, they needed more time to prepare.[32] Somewhat reluctantly, Gaidar postponed price decontrol to January 2, 1992.

Walking the streets of Moscow that week, I was overwhelmed by how desperate conditions had become. I had never seen the shops so empty. They had never been very full, but in the immediate aftermath of the decree some shops simply closed their doors, because there was nothing to sell. Other shops could offer only some small bags of rice and barley.

Gradually, however, the economic medicine of shock therapy did seem to be taking hold. Before the price reform, prices of goods sold at state stores were kept substantially below those of the private shops. The state shop managers quickly came to appreciate that they could earn more money by taking kickbacks from backdoor private buyers who would then resell those goods. Alternatively, they could hoard their goods and wait until the government allowed price increases or the market determined prices. That was why there were no goods on state store shelves. Once sellers were allowed to charge higher prices, shop managers no longer had any incentive to divert their price-controlled products out the back door to a black-market buyer and goods began to reappear.

The difference I found between January 1992 and June 1992, when I returned, was stunning. It was not that all Russian shop shelves had become fully stocked. Nonetheless, many products, such as cheese, which for most consumers had become exotic and had not been seen since the early Gorbachev era, suddenly reappeared in the shops. Even imported bananas were being offered for sale, items most Russians have never seen, much less tasted. This was a deserved source of satisfaction to the reformers.

But this success was in part merely apparent. The problem was that there was no significant impulse by manufacturers to increase output. As we noted, the economic medicine did not work fully, because the production and distribution infrastructure remained much as it had been in the central-planning era. There was basically no elasticity on the supply side. The directors of state enterprises went about their business as usual. Since, as state employees, they stood to gain little from any increased sale of government produced goods, they saw no reason to respond to the stimulus of higher prices and potentially higher profits. In the still-small private sector, the mafia, as we saw, could act as a monopolist and did all it could to prevent any increase in production.

Consequently, unlike economies in the West or even Poland, the Russian economy did not respond. Goods reappeared on the shelves primarily because the higher prices deterred many of those who formerly would have stood in a queue for highly subsidized products. Very little of the new abundance was due to new manufacturing within the country. The state authorities could essentially choke off demand, but they were powerless to force manufacturers to increase their output. Thus, as we noted earlier, only half of the demand/supply equation worked. And because there was little if any supply response to the higher prices, there was little to offset the pressure for higher prices as additional money kept rolling off the printing presses. By the end of 1992, prices had risen about twenty-four-fold.

This uncontrolled inflation was enormously disruptive. Paradoxical as it might seem, one of the by-products was a shortage of cash. Prices rose faster than the printing presses could print money, at least until they decided to increase the denominations of money being printed. Moreover, much of the money expansion that was occurring took the form not of paper money *(nalichnye)*, which made up only 15 percent of the total money supply, but of bank credits *(beznalichaya)*. True, these bank credits could be used only to pay debts to other enterprises and could not be converted to cash, but they still had an inflationary impact.[33] Throughout 1992, enterprise managers periodically were short of money to pay their employees' wages. During one of his visits to the provinces, Yeltsin won over local officials by promising them that he would arrange for a special plane to follow after him loaded with cash.

In addition to the runaway inflation, the situation was made even more complex by the growing separation of ethnic regions in the Soviet Union. For example, 80 percent of the equipment used to extract petroleum was manufactured in Azerbaijan.[34] Since it was prerevolutionary Russia's first major oil-producing region, it was natural that extraction equipment would be manufactured there. When new and larger fields were discovered in Tiumen, in West Siberia, Azerbaijan supplied extraction equipment to that area as well. Beginning in January 1992, however, supplies of this equipment were disrupted not only because Azerbaijan was now at war with Armenia but also because Tiumen was now in another country, Russia. By July 1993 more than 30,000, or 20 percent, of the oil fields had become inoperative.[35] The shortage of equipment, along with the increasing disruption of other basic deliveries from all over the former Soviet Union, was a major reason why petroleum output declined by 14 percent in 1992.[36] Similarly, automobile and appliance output, and as we saw, cotton textile mills in Ivanovo were affected when the flow of components and parts to factories in Russia suddenly had to come from foreign countries.

With so much going wrong, it is easy to understand why so many were discouraged about Russia's prospects and why, despite the best of intentions, few foreign investors were able to operate profitably. There were some positive signs, but these stemmed not so much from fiscal and monetary policy as from new institution building. Even here the result was not flawless, but in an effort of historic proportions, the Russians came to recognize the need to broaden and diversify the ownership profile of the country's enterprises and move away from state ownership of virtually all economic activity. This is a necessary but not sufficient step if the reforms are to succeed. As we shall see, the task has not been easy.

6. Privatization

While their first priority was price liberalization and fiscal control, the Gaidar reformers were not oblivious to the need for institutional change. Before long they came to realize that they also had to begin privatizing state-owned enterprises, both service and manufacturing. Thus, a few months after the decontrol of prices on January 2, 1992, the government officially announced that it would start the privatization process. Some of the reformers even agreed with critics of their strategy like me that the privatization process should have preceded price decontrol and fiscal control, or at least have begun simultaneously with the other reforms. Even more important an equal if not greater emphasis should have been placed on creating an extensive and viable base of brand-new private and nonstate decision-making enterprises in both agriculture and industry. In any event, once begun, privatization was increasingly viewed as one way to create the market-oriented and responsive institutions needed to complement the shock therapy process. It was also seen as a means of eventually creating a middle class whose interests lay in supporting economic reforms and democracy. This would have to be implemented in both the agricultural and the nonagricultural sectors.

I

Like everything else in postcommunist Russia, however, the process was more easily conceived than implemented. The obstacles in agriculture stemmed from Russians' historical wariness of, if not aversion toward, private property. After all, Russia has had a relatively short-lived experience with private entrepreneurship and private family farming.[1] The bulk of Russian peasants were serfs on large estates until 1861. As was mentioned earlier, for the rest of the nineteenth century they were beholden to the village commune, or *mir* or *obshchina*, which it was very difficult to leave. That was because the *mir* was saddled with the burden of financing the peasant's new freedom from the landlord. This form of collective redemption meant that if a resident of the *mir* appealed to leave the commune, those who remained had to work that much harder, because the size of the redemption payment remained the same. This discouraged peasants not only from migrating to the city but even from engaging in private farming.

The liability of the *mir* for collective redemption was abolished in 1903, and the redemption debt itself was nullified in 1905.[2] Beginning in November 1906 the Stolypin reforms, named after the prime minister of the time, authorized peasants to split off strips of the *mir*'s land and consolidate them and form a private farm. Only then were large numbers of peasants able to own their own land. By 1915 some 14 percent of the land of the communes had been set aside to form such farms.[3]

Although this move to private farming coincided with the time of the highest annual grain production in Russia, the beginning of World War I, the subsequent Bolshevik Revolution, the redivision of some of the newly created farms, and, most critical, Stalin's collectivization of farmland in 1928 put an end to this brief experience with private farming. Most peasants have thus not lived and farmed on their own. Given the option by Gorbachev in December of 1987 to set up their own private farms, very few took advantage of the opportunity. Admittedly, the state did not do much to encourage such initiatives, but at least until 1993 most rural residents preferred the security of remaining in collectives or on state farms.[4] This spared them the entrepreneurial risk inherent in running their own farms. At the same time they could continue to use their small private gardens to boost their incomes. This arrangement was particularly attractive to the elderly and female members of a farm, and by the late twentieth century they made up the majority of the rural population. It also spared these peasants from having to engage in the large-scale financial borrowing that would otherwise have been required for them to buy the equipment and facilities needed to establish a private farm.[5] Although the existing collectives were being reconfigured as "associations," joint stock companies, or cooperatives, they continued to operate as collective and state farms. Consequently, those who initially sought land for private farms under Gorbachev's policies were mostly urban residents. Only in 1992 did more peasants seek to engage in private farming. As late as March 1994 only 270,000 private farms had been created, representing a mere 5 to 6 percent of the cultivated land.[6] The minister of agriculture, Viktor N. Khlystun, estimated that, at its peak, the number of private farms would reach 500,000 to 600,000, representing about 7 to 8 percent of the arable land. This estimate was made before Yeltsin's October 27, 1993, decree establishing private landownership. Presumably, the number of farms will be considerably higher as a result, but even with the 1993 decree and the revocation of the ten-year ban on land sales, the idea of private farming continues to inspire less than complete enthusiasm.[7]

Given fifty years or more of collectivization, as well as the prerevolutionary heritage of serfdom and the *mir,* it is not surprising that there was so little enthusiasm for private farming. With little experience with private farming, the antiproperty attitude was widely shared. The first pioneers to set up their own farms often encountered enormous resentment and sometimes outright violence. Arson was common.[8] Even though it was Gorbachev who first allowed for the possibility of private farming, he personally always came out against the idea. He explained, "I have always supported the market and still do. But while I favor the market, I do not accept for example the private ownership of land; do with me what you will. I do not accept it. A lease—even for a hundred years, even with the right to sell the lease rights and with inheritance—is all right. But private ownership with the right to sell the land that I do not accept." Reflecting on his own childhood as a member of a collective farm, he added, "That, incidentally, is the tradition of the rural community, our rural community."[9]

Yet Yeltsin, who also came from a collective-farm background, expressed considerably more support for the idea. Unlike Gorbachev, who proposed the idea of a referendum on private ownership and then never did anything about it, Yeltsin sought to have it included in his April 11, 1993, referendum. The Congress of People's Deputies ultimately overruled him and omitted it from the referendum that took place on April 25, 1993. This reflected the lobbying of the big farm directors, or "Red landlords," who came to realize that decollectivization and the breakup of the state farms into smaller private farms would mean an end to their power and prerequisites. In some ways their authority differed little from that of the nineteenth-century landlords before emancipation.

Yet, for all his public support of the concept of private farming, as often as not, Yeltsin's support in practice, at least until October 1993, was ineffective or actually counterproductive. Although he issued a decree calling for the privatization of land, it was signed December 28, 1991, somewhat after the December 3 announcement about price reforms.[10] The delay was not great, but it nonetheless created the impression that privatization was of secondary importance. Moreover, reflecting his lukewarm enthusiasm he assigned his vice president, Aleksandr Rutskoi, in mid-1992, to superintend agricultural reform.[11] Rutskoi had by this time already become an overt critic of Yeltsin and the Gaidar government. His assignment was regarded as a form of punishment for having become openly critical, just as the equally critical Yegor Ligachev had received a similar assignment from Gorbachev.[12] Like Ligachev, Rutskoi expressed reservations about establishing private farms at the expense of the collective and state farms.[13] Since collectivization no Soviet leader had been able to resolve Russia's agricultural problems; thus such an assignment seemed to be a clever way to discredit one's opponent. What seemed to be forgotten, however, was that failure to improve conditions in agriculture not only undercut Ligachev and Rutskoi, it also hurt Gorbachev and Yeltsin, who were ultimately responsible for such failures.

Certainly, Yeltsin could have done more to promote private landownership than he did. Until December 1992 he had the power to issue presidential decrees, which had the force of law. Admittedly, his decrees were often amended or set aside by the increasingly contentious Congress of People's Deputies.[14] But even when he finally did act, with his far-reaching October 1993 decree on landownership, Yeltsin himself continued to encumber the land privatization effort with all kinds of regulations, procedures, and committees, presumably to prevent corruption and to promote equity.[15] As a result the privatization process became a tangle of red tape and bureaucracy resembling Alexander II's ill-fated 1861 decree emancipating the peasants. And not surprisingly these measures failed to prevent corruption and inequities, because local leaders simply allocated the best lands to themselves and their children.[16]

With such diverse views on whether or not to encourage private landownership, the laws that were passed were confusing and contradictory.[17] The hard-liners opposed even the leasing of land; the moderates agreed to the leasing of land for various lengths of time and the private ownership of buildings on the land; the reformists supported outright ownership and the right to sell and resell land, as well as the buildings on it. The concept of leasing was approved in March 1989 at Gorbachev's initiative.[18] In 1990 the Russian parliament agreed to recognize the constitutional right of Russians to own land, but then to deter speculation it imposed a ten-year ban on any land sales.[19] Later the prohibition against land sales was reduced to five years. Steps were also taken to broaden the definition of leasing. Eventually, leasing was extended to mean lifetime leasing of the land with the right to pass the land on to one's heirs. And though the Russian Supreme Soviet adopted a series of laws in late 1990 and 1991 that allowed in principle for the breakup of unprofitable collective and state farms and the transfer and sale of their land to the former members of those farms, the legislators also decreed that the new peasant owners must use the land only for farming.[20]

On December 7, 1992, Yeltsin made an effort to clarify the situation by declaring that Russians had the unconditional right "to own land and use it at their own discretion."[21] The Congress of People's Deputies, however, refused to go along and continued the ban on the sale of land used for communal farming.[22] Nevertheless, it authorized the limited sale and purchase of the relatively small, 600-square-meter garden plots planted by most peasants and many city dwellers for their own use. It also allowed the sale of the land used for dachas or summer homes, but only if purchasers continued to use the land in the same way as before the purchase. Presumably, this condition, like the ban on selling land for ten years, was meant to prevent land speculation, but it did nothing to clarify a very complex and seemingly contradictory legal situation.

In addition, the "Red landlord" directors of the collective and state farms, along with a large number of local authorities, continued to frustrate private farming by obstructing access to credit, machinery, seeds, and pesticides and by ruling that the new private farmers could not hire labor. These various obstacles may explain why one-half of the new private farms were unprofitable (in 1993 some 14,000 private farms were abandoned), and why many peasants hesitated to set off on their own.[23]

One way that Yeltsin, and Gorbachev before him, could have maneuvered around these ideological and bureaucratic roadblocks would have been to allow the peasants to double the size of their 32.6 million individual garden plots.[24] Although they constitute only 2 to 3 percent of the country's land area, these gardens have accounted for 20 to 30 percent of the agricultural crop. As I proposed as early as 1987 in my book *Gorbachev's Challenge*, the authorities should simply announce a doubling in the size of the garden plots.[25] Then, after a few months' time, they should announce a further doubling. In this way they could finesse the ideological hang-up about private farming and allow the peasants to do what they already do well. The Ukrainian government announced such a policy on December 22, 1992.[26] It distributed 13 million garden plots to individuals, who were then allowed to buy and sell them to anyone except foreigners. Production on these small plots rose 50 percent in 1992.[27]

II

Not burdened by the deep emotions associated with the privatization of land, the task of legalizing private enterprise and creating new private shops and other commercial and manufacturing enterprises met with much less resistance. Indeed, it was unfortunate that the Gaidar team did not make encouraging the establishment of brand-new enterprises—the "green field" approach—its number one priority. This is where the preponderant share of growth came from in China, Hungary, and Poland.

The decision to allow the opening of brand-new businesses originated with Gorbachev in 1987. He was the first general secretary since Lenin to permit the establishment of new private and cooperative enterprises. But, as we saw, Gorbachev had very mixed feelings about the whole process. In fact, in 1986 he launched a widespread crackdown on private trade. He reversed himself a year later and ended the ban, but he could never quite bring himself to endorse an all-out campaign to promote the private sector. That explains why initially he restricted entry into the private sector to students and pensioners; he was afraid that if there was no restriction on entry, people would leave their jobs in the state sector. However, by restricting entry this way, he all but guaranteed that those who were able to open up their own businesses would become millionaires. The country had been deprived of consumer goods and services for too long, and there was an eager population waiting to pay high prices for them. But these newly earned monopoly profits attracted the attention of the mafia and other racketeers, and they began to strong-arm their way to control of almost all private semipermanent and permanent business activities.

Consequently, when Yeltsin took over, the private retail network was rather modest. Only about 2 to 3 percent of it was operated by newly organized private owners, and almost all of them were under the control of the mafia. It would have been much better if the private share had been larger and the mafia share smaller. Yet, modest as the private sector was, the Gaidar people should have done more to nourish this activity, since the capital requirements in retailing and the service industry were usually quite modest and thus more affordable and the payback in terms of benefits for the public much more readily realized. In addition, the likelihood of stimulating new ways of thinking and behaving is often greater in a smaller firm.

For a time Yeltsin and Gaidar did seem to support new-business formation. As early as January 29, 1992, Yeltsin decreed that henceforth anyone could open a new business and sell anything, so long as the products were not detrimental, such as drugs.[28] Almost overnight, all over the country, the streets were packed with individuals seeking to sell anything that was portable—handicraft products, resold state store goods, imported goods. Some, out of desperation, sold their most valuable household possessions.

Given that the country's shelves had been virtually empty just a few weeks earlier, this was a remarkable turnabout. With so many people on the street, it was impossible for the mafia to control what was happening. The fact that anyone could join in the process meant that thousands became acquainted with the market. Recognizing the potential of such a development, Yeltsin on October 19, 1992, declared, "The prosperity of the state is above all else the prosperity of its citizens. Our ideal is not equality in poverty, asceticism and envy, but that people should have more opportunities to show initiative and enhance the quality of their lives. I have already said and I will repeat it—that we need millions of property owners, not a handful of millionaires."[29] This seemed to echo the early stages of the Chinese economic reform when Deng Xiaoping acknowledged that it was good to be rich and that what mattered was not the cat's color but its ability to catch mice. After such a clear signal the Chinese peasants and urban residents took to the streets, as the Russians were to do thirteen years later. Following the Chinese model, there was every reason to anticipate that, as a next step, at least some of those Russian street vendors might also begin a gradual move up to kiosks, shops, and then wholesaling and manufacturing.

Unfortunately, a substantial group in the leadership in Russia regarded this embrace of the market as degrading and uncultured. Whereas Deng Xiaoping never permitted more than a temporary slowdown in the move to the market in China, Yeltsin eventually yielded to his former comrades who opposed the market. Admittedly, lines of old women selling a single bottle of shampoo, a plastic bag, a pack of cigarettes, a liter of vodka, or an heirloom silverware fork revealed to the world the desperate situation of many Russians. Moreover, daily gatherings of these sidewalk vendors made an undignified and unhealthy mess. For Russians who had always prided themselves on the cleanliness of their streets, not to mention law and order, this was a degrading and humiliating sight. Consequently, in January 1993, members of the Congress of People's Deputies lashed out at this breakdown in culture and tradition. The newly appointed prime minister, Viktor Chernomyrdin, reflected these sentiments when he asserted, "Russia is not a country of shopkeepers." For Chernomyrdin, a former Soviet minister of the natural-gas industry, the "industrial sectors," as in the days of Stalin, Khrushchev, and Brezhnev, were the priority sectors. He emphasized that Russia was not meant to be "a bazaar."[30] But it was the bazaar in China that quickly gave birth to the private service and industrial sectors. The bazaar was a step on the road to these other sectors. Whereas in China, Deng Xiaoping's approval of the "bazaars" set the tone for the whole country, in Russia the national leadership did not seem to be willing to override the local authorities throughout the country who began to reinstitute some controls.[31] Yuri Luzhkov, Moscow's vice mayor and soon its mayor, decreed, for example, that as of May 2, 1992, vendors would have to have permits and be restricted to certain locations.[32]

Their insistence on better sanitation and control masked their effort to restrict the private sector. There was no doubt that the streets had become filthy. But the mess left by similar outdoor markets on Moscow's old Arbat Street was promptly cleared up each night. The vendors at the Arbat were under the control of the mafia, to whom they made a fifty-dollar payoff each month.[33] At the more popular markets near the Bolshoi Theater, there was no such control. Since these vendors had no tables to sell from, they were more mobile and less subject to control and intimidation by the mafia. But by requiring that all such vendors register with the municipal authorities, the city and criminal authorities would be able to gain access to their names and addresses and thus to reinstitute mafia control, not to mention payoffs to the city and criminal authorities.[34]

By early 1993 the attitude to private trade and the mafia had become so negative that even the stands on the old Arbat were closed down. New entrepreneurs across the country reported that, despite Yeltsin's verbal commitment to creating new enterprise, it was in fact more difficult to open brand-new businesses in 1993 than it had been in 1992. This was a result of increased taxation, municipal regulation, and harassment by the mafia and mafia-controlled banks.

III

Conceivably, the process of "green-fieldization" would have been somewhat more successful if Yeltsin and Gaidar had made it their chief priority. Instead, they devoted most of their emphasis as well as their best talent to privatizing the existing state sector. Privatizing the state sector was indeed essential for a successful reform, but given the inefficiency and cumbersomeness of the state sector, the results were bound to be slower in coming than an equal effort applied to new-business formation.

The privatization campaign had two separate aspects: the selling off of small shops to private groups and the conversion of medium-size and large state enterprises into private joint stock companies with the ownership divided among the workers, the management, the public, and the state. It must be said that, in view of the scale of what was being attempted, the privatization process was remarkably successful. Even if after a closer look the success turns out to be less than initially advertised, the fact is that the Russians attempted privatization on a scale unmatched anywhere else in the world.

Most of the credit for what has happened since, 1992 when the process began, belongs to Anatoly Chubais from St. Petersburg. As we noted earlier, he was one of the early reformers involved in his own and in Gaidar's study groups. Chubais was aided and advised in his privatization efforts by a young Russian émigré who is now a Harvard professor, Andrei Shleifer. Starting with a nearly blank slate, Chubais supervised the privatization of 46,815 enterprises in 1992. That included 27,132 small businesses, or 35 percent of the 77,004 known to exist.[35] About 5,613 large entities, each with one thousand or more employees, were converted into "open joint stock companies," whose shares were held primarily by private industries or private enterprises.[36] Altogether they accounted for 19 percent of all Russian enterprises existing at the time. The announced goal to privatize 50 percent of all Russian firms the first year turned out to be unrealistic. Nevertheless, by mid-1993 about 30 percent of all the country's enterprises, or 60,000, had been privatized, including 56 percent of all the country's small shops.[37] The goal was to privatize 80 percent of the country's industrial capacity by July 1994.[38] The transformation of such a large proportion of enterprises in such a short time was unprecedented.

Actually, the privatization of state enterprise began before Chubais was put in charge, but most of this effort was decentralized at the local level and resulted in considerable corruption and self-dealing. Chubais's countrywide effort, which began in November 1991, during the early days of the Yeltsin administration when Gorbachev was still in charge of the Soviet Union, sought to prevent such abuses. One advantage he had was that the bulk of his staff consisted of his highly motivated fellow reformers from St. Petersburg. They were more likely to be honest than the ordinary career officials. However, there were no precedents for an effort of the scale that Chubais had in mind. Eager to produce results as quickly as possible, Chubais and his team had to devote enormous amounts of intellectual and administrative energy to come up with operational guidelines. They managed to draw up legislation that was adopted in June 1992, and in a few days privatization offices were opened all over the country.

The economic rationale the Chubais group presented for privatization was that it would give managers and workers alike a new incentive to increase their productivity and the profits of their enterprises. Consequently, they were more likely to produce goods the consumer rather than the state wanted and to do it more effectively by reducing the work force and raising capital more effectively. To the extent that such an approach increased the profitability of the enterprise, it would help free the enterprise from its dependence on state subsidies and central planning. Such measures would also give more importance to the role of prices and the market in general.

The political motivation for privatization was that widespread ownership would evoke more support for other economic reforms and greater resistance to bureaucratic and authoritarian obstruction.[39] In time privatization could lead to the creation of a middle class. To some extent the Chubais approach was patterned after the Stolypin agricultural reforms of 1906, which sought to encourage peasants to set up their own private farms. Just as Stolypin sought to generate democratic stability and economic growth by relying on the "steady and the sober," who for Stolypin were independent peasants, Chubais sought to achieve the same effect among Russian managers and workers.

Given the economic chaos and the many years of communism, however, there were very few potential investors, other than members of the mafia or party-appointed managers, with the necessary capital to buy the enterprises from the state. Consequently, it was decided to issue each citizen a voucher with a face value of 10,000 rubles. This was an attempt to create instant people's capitalism. It was not quite the same as issuing money, but the effect was to create a new national semiliquid investment fund. The backing for these vouchers was the country's economic assets. As of October 1, 1992, every Russian citizen, including infants, was authorized to pick up (for a fee of 20 rubles or so) a minute claim to Russia's economic patrimony. This excited some but dismayed others. As one of my economist friends complained, "Imagine! After seventy years of communism and all those years of blood and toil when the wealth of the country is divided up, all I get is 10,000 rubles, or about twenty dollars [at the time], for all my family's efforts."

Because of the newness of the system and some uncertainty just how it was to work, there was some initial hesitation by the public about using the vouchers. However, within several months, almost all those entitled to do so picked up their vouchers. With voucher in hand, the new owners could do one of three things. They could sit with the vouchers until December 31, 1993 (a deadline subsequently extended to June 30, 1994), when the vouchers would become invalid. Holding the vouchers this way meant they would have lost their value. Alternatively, they could sell their vouchers to other investors at the market price fixed on the commodity exchanges established in many of the major cities. In February 1993 the price fell sharply, to a low of about 3,900 rubles. However, after the April 1993 referendum the price began to rise gradually and by June 1993 was again close to the 10,000-ruble face value. In October, after Yeltsin's victory over the parliament, the voucher price rose to 34,000 rubles. However, reflecting the inflation, the dollar value of the vouchers was not much higher than it had been at first.

The third and most common option was to use the vouchers in order to swap them for 10,000 rubles worth of shares of some of the joint stock companies being privatized by the government. The vouchers in other cases could be used to pay for other forms of state property, such as trucks or buildings. The vouchers needed were sometimes gathered from those issued to family members or purchased on the exchanges.

Recognizing the potential, some entrepreneurs established mutual investment funds in the hope of persuading the private-voucher holders to swap their vouchers for shares in their mutual fund. The vouchers obtained by the mutual fund would then be used to obtain shares in the newly privatized enterprise. According to the Brandeis University economist Barney Schwalberg, the enterprise managers did this, even if at first it might look as if they were yielding control, because they were fearful that otherwise a substantial portion of the enterprise stock would end up in the hands of the mafia. These managers deemed it better to have a friendly takeover by a mutual fund (which sometimes the enterprise managers controlled) than one that would put them at the mercy of the mafia.

One way or another, the mutual fund concept became very popular. As of mid-1994, 657 mutual funds had already been established.[40] In exchange for their state-issued vouchers, individual investors received shares in the mutual investment funds. These funds claimed to have research staffs that would enable them to come up with more profitable joint stock companies to invest in than the ordinary unsophisticated investor might be able to find. Ordinary investors would also be able to diversify their investments, something they would not be able to do if they converted their vouchers for stock in only one enterprise. The funds also argued that by taking a substantial share of stock in the companies they selected, they would be able to keep tighter control over management. So confident were they of their ability to find undervalued and potentially profitable opportunities that some investment funds offered extraordinarily high returns on their investments. In St. Petersburg, for example, mutual funds promised investors that they would receive a 12,000-ruble bonus, or more than the market value of the original voucher, in less than two months' time.[41]

While the vouchers were intended to make all the people in the country feel they had a part in the privatization effort, there were special arrangements for the workers and managers of each factory, which in most cases allowed them, especially the managers, to end up with a dominant share of ownership as well as effective control of the enterprise. Just as the peasants took it for granted that if the land was to become privatized, they should become the owners, so the factory workers and managers took it for granted that once the assets of the factory were privatized, it should be theirs.

IV

There were at least three alternative routes to the privatization of state enterprises. In most cases the publicly issued vouchers played a role. For example, according to the first privatization variant, the workers and managers are to be given 25 percent of a company's nonvoting shares free of charge. The management can buy another 5 percent of the voting shares, and the workers and managers together are allowed to buy an additional 10 percent at a 30 percent discount.[42] These share purchases can be made with either rubles or vouchers. The remaining 60 percent of the stock can then be sold to the public, also for cash or vouchers. About 17 percent of the privatizations in the country opted for this variant.

The most popular variant was the second. Over three-quarters chose this approach. In this second scenario 51 percent of the shares can be sold to the workers at 1.7 times the book value of the enterprise as recorded in January 1992.[43] The workers can use vouchers to cover one-half of their purchase. As for the stock not set aside for the plant staff, the public can bid for those enterprise shares at an auction. Payment can also be made in both vouchers and rubles. Given the inflation since January 1992, the real cost to the worker of making such purchases in rubles has become very low.

In the third case, which applies mainly to the somewhat smaller enterprises, the managers and workers are given 20 percent of the enterprise shares and are allowed to buy another 20 percent at a discounted value of 30 percent from par value. They can pay in either cash or vouchers. Again inflation makes this a bargain for those who buy the shares.

In an effort to constrain the managers and prevent the blatant seizing of resources, the State Committee for State Property (the GKI) established certain procedures and controls. Upon receiving a request to privatize, the state committee set up a privatization committee to oversee the process.[44] These commissions consisted of representatives from the state committee itself, as well as the antimonopoly committee, and the management of the enterprise. After consulting with the unions of the enterprise and taking a vote of its membership, the privatization committee is to decide which option to choose. If two-thirds of the work force decides it wants to buy a controlling stake in the firm, it exercises option two and purchases 51 percent of the firm's shares.

Impressive as the speed and the magnitude of the privatization process were, it was not free of controversy. There was anger at what some considered the trivial share of their proceeds, and there was resentment that so often the director of an enterprise ended up as the effective owner of all that wealth. That would occur even when the managers held no more than 5 percent of the enterprise's shares and the workers held 50 percent. As in the United States, this is because the nonmanagerial shares of the stock are usually so widely dispersed that no one is able to organize any check on managerial prerogatives and a challenge to the existing managers or directors. That seemed to be the case at the Lutch Engineers Joint Stock Company, which I visited in Podolisk, outside Moscow. One half of the shares were owned by the workers and 35 percent had been purchased by some Greek investors. But effective operating control resided in the 15 percent share owned by eleven members of the senior management team. Reflecting its power relative to that of the employees, management had reduced the work force from 2,500 employees to 1,500 after privatization. In some cases the mangers were aided in gaining control by local government authorities who ended up sharing the loot. This process came to be called "grabitization."[45] Moreover, the managers began to act as if they were the sole owners of the enterprise, and frequently they began to sell off assets of the enterprise. The sales were generally made at low prices to friends or relatives of the manager. This "stripping of assets," as it is known in similar cases in the United States, offers a convenient way to convert public into private wealth. Vice President Rutskoi called this outright corruption and theft. He also singled out Chubais for a whole variety of sins that he likened to thievery.[46]

V

Given what seemed to be the ever more serious economic problems the country faced in the wake of Yeltsin's economic reform, the amazing thing was not the corruption, frustration, and backtracking but the continuing support, even if reduced, for economic reform. There was plenty of reason to feel discouraged: the appointment in May 1992 of old-guard industrial managers like Viktor Shumeiko, Georgi Khizha, and Viktor Chernomyrdin as deputy prime ministers; the replacement of Gaidar as prime minister by Chernomyrdin in December 1992; the selection in April 1993 of Oleg Lobov as the first deputy prime minister in charge of economics, over the reform-minded Boris Fedorov; and the irrational and apparently intentionally nonsensical currency reform of July 1993, and periodic attempts to restrict what free economic activity that did develop. For that matter, Gaidar's and Fedorov's replacement by Chernomyrdin despite the most wishful of thinking and Gaidar's dismal showing in the December 1993 election reflected the political reality that, unable to obtain economic success that he could point to, Yeltsin had to make concessions to the country's political conservatives. It was also discouraging to see that some of the earlier market achievements, such as the growth of commodity markets, had been set back. By mid-1993 many of the six hundred or so commodity markets that had existed at one time had closed down. In some cases it was because of the continuing drop in production; there were fewer goods to trade. In other cases it was because of the imposition of taxes like the VAT (the value-added tax) and the unwillingness to fight the mafia and excessive regulation.

Yet, amid all the gloom, there have been some positive signs. Despite many complaints about how unfair it has been, the process of privatization is moving rapidly. There are also signs that some privatization has reached the countryside, even if it is only a move by peasants and city dwellers to seize fallow parcels of land in order to expand their own gardens. The creation of biweekly and, eventually, daily currency auctions and de facto convertibility of the ruble was also a good omen. It was a way of restoring value to the ruble, even if in the process the ruble kept losing value because of the still uncontrolled printing of money. For that reason it was quite encouraging when, in June and July 1993, the ruble began to gain value against the dollar, from its low point of twelve hundred rubles to the dollar. Consequently, the July 24, 1993, currency reform, which called for the invalidation of all money printed before January 1, 1993, marked a very serious step backward. It revived memories of the Pavlov currency reform on January 23, 1991. Indeed, both reforms were the work of Viktor Gerashchenko, the president of the Central

Bank. That only rubles printed in 1992 and earlier should be eliminated made no sense. If the aim was to penalize speculators, it was unrealistic, because the speculators were most likely to be holding large quantities of the 1993 rubles, which after all were printed in larger denominations. Yeltsin eventually watered down some of the more extreme conditions of the 1993 currency reform, but much of the damage had already been done, and it inevitably dealt a blow to the reform process.

Still, it was encouraging to see that in various parts of the country local authorities were attempting to conduct more and more of their own reform experiments. Frustrated by the lack of systematic reform in Moscow, the local authorities in Nizhni Novgorod, abetted by the International Finance Corporation of the World Bank, set off on their own to support privatization and the opening of brand-new businesses. All too often in Russian history, change has come from above. The changes exemplified by Nizhni Novgorod were coming from below, and in the most exciting sign of where it might go, Boris Nemtsov, the governor and chief activist in this effort, has pointed out that as a result of the competition in his city, prices in the newly opened private stores are lower than those in the traditional government shops and the quality of their goods is better.[47] That is the reverse of the typical Russian pattern.

Equally impressive are signs throughout the country that more and more individuals are beginning to create their own businesses. There is a danger in highlighting isolated instances of such efforts, because it may inadvertently convey the impression that more than just a few are involved. But, difficult as it is to obtain permits and dodge the mafia, each day a few more Russians nonetheless try, and some succeed—some in a way reminiscent of nineteenth-century American entrepreneurs. For example, Konstantin Borovoi, a longtime student at Moscow State University, started out as assistant professor of mathematics. Born in 1948, he specialized in the teaching of mathematics and computing. His father was also an academic.[48] In what was a radical decision, he decided in 1988 to leave teaching and set up a cooperative, a year after it became legal to do so. At the time giving up a prestigious teaching post to go into business was considered an unorthodox and risky thing to do. Becoming ever more adventuresome, he set up a trading company in 1989. Then, in April 1990, in a move unprecedented since at least the 1917 revolution, Borovoi decided to establish the first postcommunist exchange in Russia. Called simply enough the Russian Commodity and Raw Material Exchange, it was located in the former central post office building at 26 Myasnitskaia, in downtown Moscow. Borovoi became its first president.

Once outside academic boundaries, he continued to create new businesses. His next step was to organize and head a financial group, which began by opening up the Russian National Commercial Bank. He followed through by establishing the Economic News Agency and a communications company, VKT. This led to the opening of the Moscow Convention of Entrepreneurs, a sort of trade association.

Having become one of Russia's richest men, he decided to move into politics. On May 15, 1992, he cofounded the Party of Economic Freedom for Business. Among its main tasks has been resisting encroachments of the mafia (an attempt was made to assassinate him in March 1994) and government bureaucrats on business, as well as lobbying against the imposition of excessive taxes. In one instance members of Borovoi's group threatened to move many of Moscow's most important businesses to St. Petersburg. They were protesting a plan to impose what Borovoi considered to be exorbitant municipal taxes. The party has also served as a nucleus for a broader-based attempt to influence the elections, and it ran candidates, for the most part unsuccessfully, for the new parliament in December 1993.

Very few have come close to what Borovoi has accomplished, at least very few not associated with the mafia. It is necessary to remember that upward of 30 percent of the population has fallen below the poverty line (some say as much as 80 percent was below it in 1993).[49] It was distressing that so many members of what were the old professional classes found that not only did their status in society no longer command the respect it once did but that inflation had also wiped out their savings. One of my close friends in Moscow, Ivan Petrov (not his real name), and his wife lamented in mid-1993 that they no longer saw a future for themselves and, most important, for their son, a bright thirteen-year-old who was fluent in French and learning English. Ivan had given up his university post at the Plekhanov Institute many years ago and had become a member of various commissions, including some dealing with economic reform. Because those commissions were closed down or because the salary they paid fell behind inflation, he decided to take an administrative position in an organization created to help settle Russians fleeing from the non-Russian regions of what was once the Soviet Union. Neither his new position nor his wife's job gave them enough income to do much more than obtain the food they needed. Fortunately, they were able to supplement their salaries with food grown at their country dacha. It had been in the family for many years and become an important part of their day-to-day survival. Their greatest fear, however, was that they would not be able to provide for the schooling of their son. They bitterly resented the fact that some of his classmates, especially the children of the mafia, would have much better opportunities, including the ability to study overseas, something they clearly would never be able to afford. It was not that before Yeltsin they could afford such opportunities; but then no one else could either. The reality that now some could and they could not made them quite upset.

Driven by such anxieties, both husband and wife found themselves contemplating setting up businesses on the side. Though not daring to leave their full-time and official jobs, both have begun to moonlight, one organizing an investment firm for rich Russians eager to invest their money overseas (capital flight) and the other selling herbal medicines. It is too early to tell at this writing how successful my friends will be, but in a sense their decision in late 1993 to set up private ventures is what should happen if the reform is ever to succeed. Again, both Borovoi and the Petrovs were involved in the opening of new businesses, not the privatization of existing enterprises.

VI

So far it is unclear whether there are enough Borovois and Petrovs to make the reforms a success. More than that, while the privatization effort has been a success in terms of the number of large-scale enterprises and mom-and-pop shops run by private owners, the vast majority of them continue to operate much as they did before the government's name was taken off the door and the stationery.[50] They are still overstaffed, and the large enterprises especially rely on easy-to-obtain nonrepayable loans from the Central Bank and the government.

For many, especially in the West, these continuing problems come as a deep disappointment. It is difficult for outsiders to understand that under the best of circumstances economic difficulties are likely to continue. Moreover, until the economic problems are resolved, the odds are that political turmoil will persist. Thus, even with a functioning constitution and a cooperative parliament, Yeltsin or whoever assumes the leadership of the country will still have problems. But without some show of economic success, there will always be a disproportionate number of Russians who cherish the old—communist and czarist—way of doing things. As a consequence we should expect to see recurrent struggles between those committed to reform and those opposed to it—those supportive of such measures as land reform and those determined to push through counterreform monetary measures like Gerashchenko's July 24, 1993, currency exchange decree. The struggle between the parliament and Yeltsin in October 1993 and the protest vote for Zhirinovsky and his neofascist party in December 1993 provide other examples. The lesson to be learned from this is that such steps backward are not anomalies or random events, as they often appear to be to those of us in the West who continue to be optimistic; they are instead part of the normal response of those opposed to or skeptical of the reforms—a series of conflicts likely to persist for years if not decades.

VII

Unfortunately, the instances of failures as exemplified by the 1993 currency reform far outnumber the success stories. In fairness it is important to repeat that the reform process would have been slow to produce results no matter what strategy was ultimately adopted. Under the best of circumstances the reform would still have required decades to undo all the damage inherited from the decades of central planning. Nonetheless, Yeltsin and Gaidar and their associates and Western advisers can and should be faulted for concentrating so much on monetary, fiscal, and price reforms and not enough on institution and infrastructure building. Had they done the latter, there would still have been difficulties, but there might also have been a few more success stories.

The failure to provide Russia with new farms and businesses suggests the story of the patient who found himself with cancer. The doctor told him that he would surely die in the next month unless he agreed to a very dangerous and painful operation, which would have to be done without anesthesia. Even then there was only a 20 percent chance of recovery. The patient decided to see another doctor, who disputed the first diagnosis. If the patient was also willing to undergo chemotherapy, he was told, the chances of survival would increase to 40 percent. There was still no anesthesia, the operation was still painful, and the chances of recovery would be better but still less than fifty-fifty. Similarly, if the Russian reformists had done more to stress privatization, along with all their monetary and fiscal reforms, the reforms would still have been painful and the chances of success would have increased somewhat, but still have been less than fifty-fifty.

7.

Lessons of History: Postwar West Germany and Japan

Just as there is danger in arguing that Russia's economic problems are not different from those experienced by other countries, so there is danger in insisting that the economic upheaval that Gorbachev's perestroika set in motion and Yeltsin compounded is unique. In fact, many countries, not only Third World and communist but West European as well, have been afflicted with similar bouts of hyperinflation, the destruction of economic institutions, and a sharp fall in GNP. West Germany and Japan suffered similar economic crises in the wake of military defeat and political upheaval. After World War II a dozen or so currency reforms were adopted throughout Western Europe in the hope of restoring economic stability and subsequent growth.[1] We will examine the efforts of West Germany and Japan to deal with these crises to see whether their experience can provide some additional insight for Russian economic reformers. Subsequently, we will look at the different models of reform used in Hungary, Poland, and China to see whether Russia might have done better with a model of reform different from the one it followed.

I

In some sense Germany's post–World War II recovery was facilitated by echoes of World War I and premonitions of World War III. As punishment for having launched World War I, the victorious Allies exacted onerous reparations from the defeated Germany. This in turn evoked demands for revenge that were exploited by Hitler at enormous cost to the rest of the world. Because of the extraordinary cruelty of Hitler and the Nazis, some argued for the reimposition of harsh conditions, but eventually a policy of swiftly returning Germany to economic normalcy won out. This policy was accelerated in the late 1940s by the impending Cold War. As Stalin imposed communist regimes in the countries of Eastern Europe, including East Germany, the fear arose that if economic difficulties in other European countries became serious enough, they along with West Germany might opt for communism. Thus, the Western Allies, rather than suppress Germany's economic revitalization, sought to help restore its economic well-being. This approach gave rise to the Marshall Plan, which provided aid not just to Germany but to all of Western Europe. Some aspects of the process of rehabilitating the West German economy, even without the Marshall Plan, have relevance for Russia and other countries of the Commonwealth of Independent States.

The damage inflicted on Germany during World War II left the German economy in much worse shape than Russia was in after the end of the communist era. The widespread Allied bombing destroyed Germany's industrial base. The populace was without adequate housing and jobs. Production in 1948 was approximately one-half of what it had been in 1936.[2] At the same time inflation was heightened by the tenfold outpouring of currency that had been used to finance the war. To make matters worse, a 1936 Hitler decree ordering a freeze on prices was still in force.[3] Like that in the Soviet Union, this freeze caused a massive diversion of goods to the black market, where more realistic barter arrangements could be made. The resulting empty shelves and hyperinflation all but destroyed the viability of the reichsmark, the prewar German currency. Because of inflation, it was in 1948 being used for less than one-half of the country's daily transactions. In its place cigarettes became the most widely accepted money substitute for the purchase and sale of most consumer goods.[4] Similarly, manufacturers had to barter in order to obtain supplies and, on occasion, even to hire labor.[5]

With American guidance West German officials launched far-reaching economic reforms. On June 20, 1948, the West German government instituted a ten-for-one currency reform and substituted a new currency, the deutsche mark, for the reichsmark, at least in West Germany. This was combined with a decree decontrolling the prices of four hundred products immediately.[6] Within a month 90 percent of the country's price controls were removed and the 1936 price freeze abolished. Simultaneously, tax rates were cut by an average of one-third.[7]

Until then German factory directors, along with the public in general, had been hoarding goods. They considered this to be the best hedge against inflation. Once price controls were lifted, goods immediately reappeared.[8] This was very different from what happened in Moscow in January 1992 when price controls were lifted. Unfortunately, the Russians did not precede their price decontrol with a ten-to-one currency reform. Moreover, the absence of a large body of nonstate independent suppliers in Russia meant that an increase in the flow of goods to the market took much longer to kick in, and even then supplies were spotty. Equally if not more important, West German production increased almost immediately. Within six months output had risen by an estimated 50 percent.[9] Again, this stands in sharp contrast to developments in Russia, where production, including consumer goods production, declined approximately 20 percent after the 1992 price decontrol. The existence of a large number of private German businessmen who, if they increased production, stood to benefit from higher prices and profits, uninhibited by a mafia, was a crucial difference.

Although the German economy responded immediately, at

the time there was little to suggest that its recovery would one day come to be regarded as an "economic miracle." In the spring of 1948, before the reforms were introduced, it was hard to see how the German economy would ever recover. Out of desperation the U.S. military occupation forces decided to call in some outside advice. They sent for Joseph Dodge, a conventional commercial banker from Detroit. He and Ludwig Erhard, recently appointed director for economic administration in the American and British occupation zones, became the architects of the reform. Dodge was made financial adviser to General Lucius Clay, the commander of the American occupation forces. When the British, French, and American zones split off from the Russian zone to become the Federal Republic of Germany, Erhard became its first minister of economic affairs and later succeeded Konrad Adenauer, the first West German chancellor, when Adenauer died in 1963.

Dodge and Erhard were fervent advocates of the classical economic approach, associated with the University of Chicago school: free up prices, slash subsidies, and balance budgets—an early version of the shock therapy approach. There were others, particularly among the German Social Democrats, who favored the use of more controls and social policy. They seemed to gather support when unemployment began to increase and there were calls for a "return to a controlled economy."[10] However, the increase in the value of the new deutsche mark brought with it a more rational utilization of resources. That meant less need for barter, lower transaction costs, and less labor time wasted on finding goods to barter. Because workers no longer had to leave work at midday to stand in line for scarce consumer goods, there was also a sharp drop in absenteeism.[11]

Offsetting these positive developments, however, the effort to balance the state budget resulted in a cut of subsidies, which led to the closing of many factories and shops. In addition, the West German/East German exchange rate turned out to be too generous to East Germans, who began to purchase more West German goods, which caused prices to rise again. In protest against both high prices and growing unemployment, the West German labor unions called a one-day general strike for November 12, 1948.[12] It was a clear sign of disquiet over the unemployment, income inequality, and social disruption that accompanied the marketization process. The presence of the U.S. occupation army, however, ensured that order was maintained.

Fortunately, in mid-1949 the first installment of $600 million of Marshall Plan aid was sent and immediately put to work. In time the Germans received about $1.5 billion. At today's prices that would amount to approximately $9 to $10 billion. That provided an immediate stimulant. But important as the money was, a key to the Marshall Plan success was the fact that receipt of the money was contingent on the German government's formulating a plan that spelled out how the aid money would be utilized. The German government was also required to explain how it would use the deutsche marks that it was to receive from the sale of American equipment and commodities that were also to be supplied as part of the new aid plan. These deutsche marks were to be put aside in a special account, called counterpart funds, for use by the German government.[13] The Marshall Plan thus not only helped the government reconstruct the country's infrastructure but also forced it to specify a list of domestic priorities open to domestic and foreign investors. To date the Russians have not been able to do any of this. The polarization of public opinion has so far made it impossible for the government to agree about Russian investment priorities and whether the Russian government should encourage or even allow foreign investment and, if so, where. It would have been useful if U.S. aid to Russia had been made contingent on Russia's working out a set of priorities similar to that required of the West Germans.

Unlike Russia's after communism, much of Germany's prewar industry was destroyed during the war. This offered the Germans a chance to upgrade their technology and direct their capital and foreign aid into building brand-new factories. In contrast the Russians have had to devote themselves to maintaining existing factories whose prime purpose was military production and whose machinery is obsolete and to converting and privatizing an outdated industrial plant. To make matters worse, it is very difficult for the Russians to close their factories or even reduce production, because these factories not only provide jobs for thousands of workers but also operate hospitals and supply the majority of housing and schooling facilities for the entire community. It is also worth noting that in Russia shock therapy has precipitated a continuing drop in industrial output and an increase in prices, whereas in West Germany industrial production was over two and a half times higher in 1951 than it had been in 1948, and prices were actually lower in early 1951 than in late 1948.[14]

II

Like postwar Germany, Japan may at first glance seem to present an inappropriate analogy for Russia. But even more than Germany, Japan offers the Horatio Alger economic success story of the twentieth century. In the course of four decades, this country has seen its per capita income rise from one of the lowest in the world to one of the highest. But what is the relevance for Russia? It is hard to find two more diverse cultures and two more different resource endowments than those of Japan and Russia. Certainly, there are enormous differences, but then no country quite resembles the former Soviet Union or Russia. Nevertheless, a country like Japan, which has gone through an economic transformation, holds important lessons for Russia—some to be copied, some to be avoided, and some that are not applicable.

The biggest difference between Japan and Russia is that Japan lost World War II and Russia won it. If most Russians could be guaranteed Japan's economic growth, they might well prefer to have lost—in a modern-day version of the movie *The Mouse That Roared*. But it is symptomatic of Russia's present economic and political difficulties that a substantial number of Russians would most probably opt for forty years of postwar military and political glory rather than for economic success. Superpower status, with its parades and military prowess, was to them preferable to the hard work and the prosaic routine of the workbench. Before World War II, however, some Japanese also thought along the same lines.

We sometimes forget that Japan was not economically insignificant before World War II. Reminiscent of Russian industrialization in the last half of the nineteenth century, Japan's economic transformation dates back to 1868 and the Meiji Restoration. Reflecting its economic potential, Japan in the 1930s and early 1940s was able to build up a credible modern military force. Like the Soviet Union, though, it was able to do that only by diverting a disproportionate amount of its wealth from consumption to the military.

After losing the war, Japan found itself with a new de facto emperor, General Douglas MacArthur. MacArthur was the supreme commander of Allied powers (SCAP), and he and his advisers became the architects of Japan's economic and political recovery.

Often regarded as a conservative, authoritarian figure in the United States, the Japanese MacArthur, to the surprise of many, introduced radical measures in Japan, including antitrust, land, and labor union reform. These initiatives were all designed to deny influence and power to Japan's wartime elite.[15] In industry the *zaibatsu* (large combines), which controlled about 40 percent of the prewar economy, were broken up (although not as completely and as finally as MacArthur had intended). Similarly, in agriculture after the 1946 and 1947 SCAP decrees on land reform, Japanese landlords were forced to sell off their land, and in the process landless tenants became landowners. The Japanese government had introduced its own version of land reform in December 1945, but it was a relatively weak decree, and since the landlords were not intimidated by the postwar Japanese government, they generally did not comply. But something had to be done to give more power to the peasants. MacArthur's land reform did it. Whereas in November 1946 tenants cultivated 46 percent of the land, by August 1950, after MacArthur's intervention, their share had fallen to 10 percent.[16] Landlord holdings were parceled out to tenants who were helped to purchase the land they formerly tilled for someone else. The Russians would have done well to duplicate these initiatives. In a similar manner the ban on Japanese trade unions was replaced with a series of labor laws. All of this strengthened the labor unions, legitimized collective bargaining, and mandated improved working conditions. The proportion of unionized workers in Japan rose from 3.2 percent of the work force in 1945 to 53 percent in 1948.[17]

Under normal circumstances such a transformation might have provoked opposition from the old power holders and demands for even more radical change from labor unions and leftists. They did protest, but the fact that MacArthur could impose his reforms under the umbrella of the American occupation army meant that their protests were easily contained. For example, as we saw, the landlords initially sabotaged the December 1945 Japanese Land Reform Act. They tried the same thing with MacArthur's land reform decrees until MacArthur directed the occupation troops to force compliance. From the other side of the political fence, the newly created Japanese trade unions decided to protest what they saw as their disadvantaged position by declaring a general strike for February 1, 1947. MacArthur had no qualms about applying authoritarian methods to ban the strike and in the name of democracy to enforce the reforms he wanted. There surely were times when Gorbachev and Yeltsin wished they could have used MacArthur's methods to suppress the opposition in order to facilitate and maintain their economic reforms. This was particularly important because in the short run reforms of this sort are almost certain to be painful and disruptive.

MacArthur and his staff quickly saw that their structural and institutional reforms by themselves did not suffice to rehabilitate the Japanese economy. Breaking up the *zaibatsu* and turning the land over to the peasants did lead to an increase in output, but it was not enough to halt the inflation set off by deficit financing during the war years. While the 365 percent inflation of 1946 seemed to have been the high point, prices nonetheless rose about 200 percent in 1947 and over 165 percent in 1948. Anticipating the inflation in Russia fifty years later, Japanese consumer prices rose almost eightyfold in four years.[18] The full effects of this hyperinflation were accompanied by a drop in GNP in both 1945 and 1946.[19] There was an increase in output in 1947 and 1948, but it was feared that unless inflation was curbed, further economic growth and, with it, democracy would be jeopardized.

Having seen Joseph Dodge's success in checking inflation in Germany, President Harry Truman decided he should also send Dodge to Japan.[20] Arriving in early 1949, Dodge ordered the Japanese government to cut its budget. In contrast to a budget deficit of 142 billion yen in 1948, there was a budget surplus of 157 billion yen in 1949.[21] Moreover, Dodge insisted that there be no more backdoor financing of special accounts by the issuance of government bonds and loans. This was also what Dodge's latter-day counterparts in Moscow tried to do in 1992. They lacked effective control over Russian bank credit, and, in any case, without the U.S. occupation army to maintain order, they were unwilling to face the consequences of widespread unemployment.

Equally important, Dodge took steps to ensure that the powers of the Reconversion Finance Bank would be sharply limited. This proved to be politically embarrassing because this bank had just been established in January 1947 by the finance minister, Tanzan Ishibashi. It was designed to provide funds to basic industries that the Japanese private banks were reluctant to finance.[22] The Reconversion Finance Bank provided the wherewithal for much of the growth and output that began to rebound in 1947. But while curbing the bank reflected badly on the Ministry of Finance and restricted output of key industrial sectors, failure to rein in the bank would have ensured continuing inflation. The bank's funds were provided in large part by the treasury and the sale of debentures that were sold to and purchased by the private bankers.[23] The treasury was in effect printing money. This was a direct cause of the resulting inflation. Until Dodge began to restrict its activities, the Reconversion Finance Bank, much like the Russian Central Bank forty-five years later, generated net loans equal to 3.5 percent of the GNP in 1947 and 2.5 percent of the GNP in 1948.[24] In 1949 the bank began to cut back and in 1952 was disbanded.

If anything, the Dodge plan worked too well. As intended, the government budget increased only 56 percent in 1949 and 1.2 percent in 1950, compared with 135 percent in 1948.[25] Similarly, the monetary base rose a mere 0.3 percent in 1949, compared with 61.5 percent the year before. These measures not only served to diminish annual price increases; they also began to curb economic growth. The GNP grew only 2.2 percent in 1949, and when Dodge returned to the United States in 1950, there was mounting concern that he had solved the inflation problem only by creating a recession.[26] Fortunately for Japan, the Korean War began in June 1950, and the United States decided to procure a large portion of its supplies from Japan. This provided an important economic stimulus, and because much of the financial and production excess had been eliminated by the Dodge plan, the economy was especially well positioned to respond to this opportunity.[27]

In a sense, the Germans and the Japanese benefited from having an alien undemocratic force (the U.S. occupation army) on hand to push the country toward economic and democratic reform. However, in the absence of some form of external or strict internal authority, it is difficult to impose basic structural economic and monetary reforms and expect compliance, at least in a short period of time. Invariably, such far-reaching changes disadvantage one segment of the population or another and give rise to resistance and disruption. The presence of an outside benevolent force also spares the local authorities from having to carry out undemocratic acts. This meant the Americans could be blamed rather than the German Christian Democratic Party or the Japanese Liberal Democratic Party. Thus local parties were less likely to end up with scars from the process. Yegor Gaidar and his foreign advisers would probably have welcomed a modern-day Joseph Dodge who could have reined in the Central Bank and its chairman, Viktor Gerashchenko, just as easily as Dodge closed down the Reconversion Financial Bank and introduced currency reform.

Another advantage Germany and Japan had over Russia in their postwar economic transformation was that they already had well-established capitalist institutions like private ownership, a market economy, and commercial laws. Some further refinements, such as land and currency reform, were necessary, but a marketing infrastructure and a broad base of commercial institutions already existed. The German and the Japanese experience highlights the importance of having these market institutions in place (even if dormant) and the handicap their absence was bound to create for the Russian reformers.

III

Although it had little to do with either West Germany's or Japan's recovery, the International Monetary Fund (IMF) has come to embrace as its own much of the same strategy that evolved in rehabilitating the German and the Japanese economies. To some extent the IMF has assumed the role in Russia that the United States played in Germany and Japan, although without the occupation armies. Established at the Bretton Woods Conference in the last days of World War II by the Allied powers, it initially focused most of its work on providing first-aid type of monetary relief for Europe's industrialized countries beset temporarily with nonstructural financial stringency and panic. However, as more and more colonies gained their independence and as Western Europe became economically more prosperous, the IMF began to concern itself increasingly with Third World economic problems. Then, under pressure from first Gorbachev and later Yeltsin, the leaders of the G-7 nations (the world's seven largest economies) in turn began to pressure the IMF and its sister institution the World Bank (the International Bank for Reconstruction and Development) to devote an increasing share of their resources to assisting the Soviet Union and its successor states. It was not an obvious evolution, particularly since the Soviet Union had historically taken a hostile attitude toward the work of the IMF and the World Bank. But, in a sense, the former Soviet Union's problems had come to resemble those of the Third World. Moreover, universalizing aid is politically safer than a strictly bilateral approach because it avoids the type of recrimination that often results when a borrower becomes too dependent on a lender. It is also true that it is easier to accept painful discipline and structural change if required by an international organization than if demanded by individual nations.

As the IMF's work has shifted from the developed world toward the developing and now the former communist nations, it has increasingly emphasized structural change and the adaptation of market-type institutions and the elimination of market restrictions. In many ways this is a classical economic approach. The IMF seeks to help countries make this transformation by offering not only advice but also loans. However, it offers loans only after certain conditions have been met—it calls this "conditionality." The ultimate aim of conditionality is the elimination or at least the restriction of the government's day-to-day influence on decision making in business enterprises. This means transferring decision-making power from government administrators who are motivated primarily by political pressure and favoritism to individuals whose actions are determined primarily by impersonal market forces. Prices are to be set not by price committees eager to shelter one group or another but by market forces and signals.

Once political considerations are no longer important, price subsidies can be eliminated and government programs can be abolished. This will make it possible to reduce, if not eliminate, budget deficits. As a result there will be less need to print money and to issue credit, actions that serve to fuel inflation. Without subsidies to ward off bankruptcy, enterprise managers will be forced to take cost reduction and profit maximization seriously. A more economically rational allocation of resources will follow. These are the hard budget constraints advocated by János Kornai, the Hungarian economist, and intended to make the economy more competitive.[28]

The IMF adds to these changes in the way the domestic economy operates with some measures that are essential in order for an economy to become integrated into the world economy. For example, the IMF also insists, particularly when countries seek to borrow money, that the prospective borrowers make their currencies convertible and reduce what is often an overdependence on and overindulgence in foreign luxury goods. Conditionality also tends to require a currency devaluation.[29] This helps to eliminate further trade deficits and to enhance the value of the currency. Acceptance of such IMF conditionality is not costless. The suspension of subsidies and slashing of expenditures usually hurts all segments of the population. It almost always affects the poor and elderly who are dependent on food and energy, two traditionally heavily subsidized products. The cutback in expenditures and the pursuit of profits are also likely to cause an increase in unemployment and its accompanying social costs, even for those who have always assumed they were productive, solid citizens. Only a few countries in the world have been able to absorb the full impact of such changes without some political reaction and social disruption.

Nevertheless, the IMF conditions have often produced positive, sometimes even excellent results, as seen in countries like Mexico, Argentina, Chile, and the Ivory Coast. Far less positive results have come in Nigeria, Peru, Brazil, and Egypt, where the political determination to resist popular opposition to such painful changes has often been absent. Yet even where successful, the imposition of hard budget constraints is likely to set off protests, if not outright violence, and on occasion government upheaval. Moreover, because the conditions are being imposed by outsiders, they evoke suspicions of ulterior motives and nationalist resentment. Local leaders are almost always accused of having sold out their country to the dictates of IMF or American bankers.

IV

Given the social upheaval that radical economic reform almost always causes, it is no wonder that so many countries that have tried it have failed. It helps, of course, when outside assistance in the form of financial aid and technical guidance is available. West Germany and Japan after World War II also benefited politically by the presence of U.S. military occupation troops. The U.S. Army took the blame for the administration of the necessarily bitter medicine. This not only cured the disease but also diverted blame for the resulting political and social upheaval from the domestic political parties that were in control. Of course, such an option is not possible or even desired today. The IMF can play a role, but it lacks the force to impose it. Moreover, as we saw, Germany and Japan already had institutions to absorb the kind of medicine the IMF is prescribing, but Russia does not. For it to be successful there must exist an institutional infrastructure waiting to be "reawakened." New institution building is possible, but only if the basic foundation of a market system and individuals and organizations susceptible to economic stimulus are already in place. Laws mandating fixed and low prices may have driven private businessmen out of business, lax monetary policy may have created hyperinflation, and tax policies may have suffocated the basic desire to produce; but that can all be repaired if the patient is willing to risk simultaneous and powerful doses of monetary and fiscal medicine. That will necessitate, among other measures, a reduction in government budget expenditures, an increase in taxes, a tightening of credit policy, and an end to subsidized prices. Since the pain can be severe, it helps if the finance minister or president has the clout to carry out these plans, as well as a strong commitment to the approach.

Reportedly, General Lucius Clay was worried enough about the prospects for Ludwig Erhard's plans that he called Erhard for reassurance.

"Herr Erhard, my advisers tell me you are making a terrible mistake."

"Don't listen to them, General," Erhard replied. "My advisers tell me the same thing."[30]

8. Gradualism or Shock Therapy: Hungary versus Poland

There is no one, uniform approach to reform in Eastern Europe. Since the economies of both Poland and Hungary were regarded as typical communist-run economies, the contrast between them is very instructive for Russia's reform. Hungary was one of the first to begin the process of reform and to modify successfully some of the more rigid aspects of the communist economic system. Starting as early as 1956, it utilized what has come to be called a gradualist approach. Poland, after several half-hearted and ill-fated efforts at reform, in January 1990 suddenly began an all-out effort that it called shock therapy and that resembles the International Monetary Fund model, including acceptance of some forms of conditionality. Although Poland and Hungary are much smaller, in area and population, than Russia and have few ethnic problems within their own boundaries, an analysis of the reform effort in these countries provides a good perspective on two contrasting approaches to reform.

I

The Hungarians were the first to move away from the Stalinist model of central planning. In the mid-1950s there had been protests and even violent demonstrations against the existing system in several of the East European countries, but once the protests had been quashed by Soviet troops, the Stalinist economic system continued to operate much as before.

Hungary was the exception. While the physical suppression of the democratically inspired uprising of October 1956 differed little from the heavy-handed suppression elsewhere in Eastern Europe, the resulting political process differed significantly. János Kádár, who became the head of the Hungarian Socialist Workers Party (a euphemism for the Communist Party) after the 1956 revolution, chose not to institute the typical repression against the protesters. Instead, he embarked on a policy of healing and reconciliation.[1]

His ability to maneuver between the hard-liners in the Soviet Union and Hungary, on the one hand, and the Hungarians seeking a relaxation of communist controls, on the other, was a testimony to Kádár's skill as a leader. Compromising as he did, Kádár was seldom able to satisfy everyone, but in the process Hungary became a more tolerant, more open country than the other countries of Eastern Europe. In 1989 he was forced from office and criticized for his complacency in confronting an evil system. To some extent this treatment was unjust because while he did bear responsibility for keeping the Communist Party in power, the fact that the Hungarian government loosened many of its controls and developed an economic system more responsive than that of any of the other members of the communist bloc was due primarily to his adroitness and guidance.

After the suppression of the uprising in 1956, Kádár and his supporters did not return to the rigid Stalinist model but sought to moderate and readjust the economic system. A number of Hungarian economists had been discussing just such a possibility for some time.[2] While they hardly expected that central planning or collective ownership would be abolished, they nonetheless sought to revitalize market forces. The reformers aimed to reduce the number of planned indicators assigned to a factory and limit the planners' responsibilities to basic macro criteria, including the allocation of investment.

This willingness to moderate the planning system was also

paralleled by the government's flexibility in the countryside. During the uprising some peasants broke off from the state collective farms. Rather than force the peasants to return to the state farms, Kádár allowed them to operate on their own for several years. As another concession, the state offered them higher prices for their grain in voluntary contracts with the state. Eventually, the government reasserted control in the countryside and carried out a new collectivization campaign from 1959 to 1962.[3] But learning from the mistakes of the original collectivization process of the 1950s, the Kádár regime allowed collective farms to operate more as cooperatives.[4] After 1956 the compulsory delivery system for the collective farms was replaced by a contractual system that decentralized more decision making to the farm units.[5] The peasants were also encouraged to do more on their private plots with considerably less hindrance from the state. An end to all mandatory plans, even for state farms, was instituted in 1966. Consequently, grain production from 1971 to 1980 rose 3.5 percent a year.[6] Hungary did not dispense with all bureaucratic interference or ideological obstructions, but unlike that of most of the countries of Eastern Europe at the time, the Hungarian economy became more responsive to its population's needs and more involved in communist international trade. Agricultural products were a major export; in the mid-1980s agricultural goods generated 25 percent of Hungary's total export earnings.[7]

Industrial reforms were introduced gradually after the changes in agriculture. But they were more erratic and were revoked periodically. Such doubling back and forth occurred in part because the reforms did not always accomplish what was promised. More important, the country's economic planners and state enterprise managers grew concerned about losing their power and becoming obsolete overnight.[8] Besides, some of them sincerely believed that central planning, with all its faults, was still a superior system. Thus the reforms came slowly.

II

While debate continued over whether the planning process should be broadened or narrowed and whether or not market forces should be relied on to set prices, the central planners proceeded to create facts. Following the Soviet economic model, Hungarian planners also began to combine and integrate industrial enterprises in search of economies of scale.[9] Being a small country of only 10.3 million people, prewar Hungary was not suited to the development of a highly competitive, broad-based mix of industrial activity. Consequently, in the 1950s, when the planners amalgamated the few competing firms that did exist, the result was a highly concentrated industrial profile. As in the Soviet Union, in Hungary most industries became monopolies.

Theoretically, monopolies in a well-run centrally planned system would not be as wasteful and inefficient as those in an unregulated market economy. The central planners would ensure that they functioned efficiently and rationally for the public good. It would have been wishful thinking, though, to describe Hungary as having a well-run centrally planned economy. Given the tendency to place political above economic criteria, its industrial monopolies did not function efficiently and were not economically rational. Moreover, since the mergers limited industrial competition, those opposed to moving to the market were able to argue that with such a high degree of monopoly domination of the Hungarian economy, an end to central price setting would give rise to unrestrained inflation.[10] In effect, those opposing a return to competition were at the same time strengthening their case for the continuation of central price setting. They were behaving like the boy who after murdering his parents sought money from the judge because now he was an orphan.

By 1964, however, as the shortcomings of central planning became ever more evident, some economists had resumed their efforts to draw up a more comprehensive reform.[11] The result was the New Economic Mechanism (NEM), put into effect in 1968.

Hungary's new policy had been preceded by the debate over the Liberman reforms four years earlier in the Soviet Union.[12] As we saw, those reforms called for a greater reliance on the market and the use of market signals to guide enterprise decision making. But though the debate over the Liberman reforms was vigorous and promising, the actual results in the Soviet Union were slight and disappointing. In addition, the 1968 Prague Spring, with its potential for a new, open society, ended abruptly when Russian tanks invaded the city's streets. Nonetheless, despite the failure of the Liberman reforms, the Prague Spring, and memories of similar scenes in Hungary twelve years earlier, the Hungarians under Kádár pushed ahead with their NEM.

Given the circumstances, it is not surprising that the NEM was limited by all kinds of compromises and self-restraints.[13] These limitations were to reassure party stalwarts and their Russian protectors that the impact of the market would be circumscribed and their jobs as managers and party bureaucrats would be protected. Consequently, there were continuing restraints on "investment allocation, price setting, wage formation and the distribution of enterprise profits" as well as on foreign trade.[14] Nevertheless, within broad limits the NEM allowed the enterprises to determine the volume and mix of production and to choose their customers and suppliers.[15] The enterprise managers were also to determine the size and makeup of their work force. A three-tier system of prices was established; the prices of one set could fluctuate freely, another set could move within limits, and the third set was fixed. But as long as the prices of a significant share were fixed, market guidance could not be economically rational. Still, the Hungarians were able to do what Liberman failed to accomplish in Russia—continue to delegate macroeconomic controls to the state, but let profit rather than the plan determine enterprise behavior.[16]

For a time the NEM worked reasonably well. A small private sector began to develop, and an effort was made to legalize economic activity that had previously been forced underground.

The Hungarians also began to develop export markets in the West for such products as textiles, leather wear, and bicycles.

But because the results were meager, the NEM reforms lasted a relatively short time. Moreover, throughout the reforms the government bureaucracy continued to exercise economic power. With their hostility and suspicion of the market, the rising resentment at the growing income inequalities, the emergence of a new class of rich peasants, price speculation, and increasing crime rate, these bureaucrats did their best to obstruct the reform process. In the end they succeeded.[17]

III

Even well-meaning bureaucrats hindered the reform process. That need not have been so. Government bureaucracies are not necessarily incompatible with the market system. After all, the countries of Western Europe, the United States, and particularly Japan have large bureaucracies and well-functioning markets. The difference between the former communist world and the West is that in the West the bureaucracies have operated historically within a market environment. In the communist world the underlying structure was bureaucratically determined, and the market was allowed only a marginal influence. Under those conditions the market lacks deep and pervasive roots. As a consequence managers of enterprises even in states that are trying to shed their central-planning apparatus tend to look first for guidance to their old bureaucratic mentors rather than to the market. The bureaucracy thus continues to retain much of its influence even when its size and powers have been sharply pruned. János Kornai describes this tendency as a shift from direct to indirect bureaucratic control. Even when several ministries were consolidated into one Ministry of Industry, Hungarian state enterprises still deferred to government preferences. Thus although central authorities were no longer authorized to issue written orders, they were usually able to accomplish much the same purpose by picking up the telephone and offering oral suggestions. This prevents the market from functioning. In Kornai's words,

> the frequency and intensity of bureaucratic intervention into market processes has certain critical values. Once these values are exceeded, the market becomes emasculated and dominated by bureaucratic regulations. . . . The market is not dead. It does some coordinating work but its influence is weak. The firm's manager watches the customer and supplier with one eye and his superiors and the bureaucracy with the other eye. Practice teaches him that . . . managerial careers, the firm's life and death, taxes, subsidies and credit, prices and wages, all financial "regulators" affecting the firm's prosperity, depend more on higher authority than on market performance.[18]

The biggest blow to the Hungarian reforms, however, came from the price shock of October 1973, caused by an embargo on oil shipments by the major OPEC nations.[19] Even if the reforms had been working perfectly, the Hungarian economy would have suffered. No non-oil-producing country was unaffected. For one year Hungary was partly protected because most of its energy came from the Soviet Union and the Soviets continued to export oil to Eastern Europe at pre-1973 prices until late 1974. Hungary suffered nonetheless because the higher oil prices in the non-communist world caused a recession, which in turn led to a decline in Hungary's newly developed export trade.[20]

As a result of these various internal and external forces, the Hungarian economy began to falter and, with it, the enthusiasm for continued reform.[21] More administrative controls were reintroduced to deal with the ensuing economic difficulties, among them increasing inflation.[22] But more industry consolidation, more centralized planning, and less integration with the outside world were not the way to cope with inflation. By establishing price controls on oil products and expensive raw materials, for example, the authorities inadvertently stimulated rather than discouraged the consumption and waste of energy products, leading to an increase in imports. At the same time, the drop in exports created a growing trade imbalance for Hungary. Hungarian products had already begun to encounter competition from lower-cost producers in Asian countries, especially South Korea and Taiwan.

The price controls not only wasted energy; they also lessened the profits of the domestic producers of energy products. But since those enterprise managers knew that the state and the central bank would come to their rescue with operating subsidies, they had no qualms about operating at a loss. These "soft budget constraints," as Kornai describes them, made the managers less concerned about the rational utilization of their resources.[23] Without managers' having to make hard decisions, the country began to experience some serious economic distortions.

IV

By 1979, with no sign that the return to controls had improved matters, a group of reformers decided they could no longer settle for half-measures, compromise, or retreat. Instead, they began to push to adopt bold, more comprehensive measures.[24] The "reform of reforms," as the Northwestern economist Michael Marrese calls it, has continued to the present day.[25] These changes include a series of price reforms in 1979, 1980, and 1992 and the decision in 1981 to increase the number and influence of small businesses and dismantle the monopolies created in the preceding decade.[26]

Although this revitalized reform effort was not smooth or consistent, the overall tendency was toward increased liberalization. In a renewed move to reduce the influence of the bureaucracy, on December 6, 1980, the three main ministries dealing with industry were consolidated into the single Ministry of Industry and the size of the staff was reduced by half.[27] Similarly, the range of prices set by the market was expanded. Beginning in June 1980 the number of commodities subject to domestic market and world prices was increased. By the mid-1980s the role of market forces was expanded to encompass a growing share of the country's capital and labor resources.[28] By 1984 the market, not the government, determined wage levels for a wide spectrum of enterprises, and taxes were used to offset income disparities.[29]

The banking system was also revitalized. The country's monopoly bank, the National Bank of Hungary, which served as a central bank and a financing arm of the government central plan, was in 1986 split up into a central bank and three commercial banking groups.[30] Though they remained either wholly or partially owned by the state, by the end of the year the commercial banking groups plus some existing specialized banks were transformed into individual commercial banks.[31] Because they remained burdened with a portfolio of basically bad debts, some viewed this as a mixed blessing.[32] These bad loans were a legacy of the noncommercial way the National Bank of Hungary had extended credit. Before 1987 the National Bank issued loans determined more by the national economic plan than by commercial loan criteria. Consequently, a substantial portion of the loans went to the large industrial monopolies, most of which were in need of annual subsidies to keep operating. Recognizing that reform would never be meaningful as long as the country's ten largest commercial banks had a negative capital base of about 15 percent of their risk-weighted assets, the Hungarian government decided in December 1993 to appropriate $1.4 billion in an effort to restore their liquidity.[33]

An effort was also made to integrate Hungary into the noncommunist world trading system. However, as long as Hungary remained a full-fledged member of the Council of Mutual Economic Assistance (CMEA) and subservient to the Soviet Union, its ability to compete internationally was limited.[34] In fact, since exports and imports within CMEA were determined by administrative fiat, not by competitive decisions based on price and quality, Hungarian enterprises had little incentive to engage in product innovation and quality control. Hungarian economists warned their countrymen that someday they would suffer as the quality of their goods fell further and further below the standards set in the West. But other than complain that members of CMEA should adopt a system using world dollar prices in their dealings with one another, Hungary could do relatively little to reform CMEA and reorient its trade from the East to the West. Nevertheless, the Hungarian authorities did try to inject some element of competitiveness into their system. The Hungarians were among the first in the communist world to allow their enterprises to form joint ventures with Western corporations. Moreover, Hungarian enterprises were allowed to buy and sell in international markets without having to go through the Ministry of Foreign Trade and its "impex," or foreign trade organizations. By 1984 over two hundred companies had such privileges.[35]

However, Hungary remained committed, though reluctantly, to CMEA and government control of foreign trade. CMEA was a political obligation, not an economic choice. Of necessity Hungary continued its eastward orientation.

V

This orientation did not change until Gorbachev began to introduce his own reforms in the Soviet Union. Since at least 1848 Russia as the conservative gendarme of Europe had actively interfered to oppose domestic reform in Hungary. The Soviets, as we saw, continued this tradition. The Hungarians were always aware that they dare not take what the Soviet Union might find too great a step away from communism or toward political alliances with Western countries. Imagine the confusion, therefore, when in 1988 Gorbachev's call for perestroika and then glasnost pushed the Soviet Union into the forefront of the reform process, thereby undercutting Hungarian hard-liners in their efforts to obstruct Hungarian reforms.

The May 1988 Conference of the Hungarian Socialist Workers Party provided a major opportunity to take advantage of the new liberalism coming out of the Soviet Union. At the time the Hungarian Communist Party still monopolized power, and until the party conference little thought was given to ending that monopoly. It was anticipated that the main result would be a more liberal, yet still monopolist, party. But with Gorbachev's call for democracy, secret competitive elections in his own country, and a visit to Czechoslovakia in April of 1987, during which he urged greater liberalization within Eastern Europe, East European reformers realized that they had an unprecedented opening.[36] By mid-1989 and the death of János Kádár, Hungary's leader for thirty years, the Hungarian communists were forced by public pressure to agree to a multiparty system, free elections, freedom of the press, and a guarantee of civil rights.[37]

VI

Whereas such fast-moving political change did not result immediately in far-reaching economic changes in Russia, it did in Hungary. In part, this was because Hungary had already broken with communist orthodoxy. Gorbachev turned out to be much warier of economic than of political liberalization. By contrast in 1989 the Hungarian government ended restrictions on the number of employees a private business could hire and the size of a firm's capital.[38] Taking advantage of the new liberalization and attempting to fill the vacuum created by the central planners who had put so much emphasis on shutting down small shops and creating monopolies, private entrepreneurs established an estimated sixty thousand new firms in 1991 alone. At the same time a major campaign was launched to privatize the state industrial sector. But like the privatization campaigns in other former communist countries, Hungary's has been erratic.[39] While Hungary has been slow to increase private landownership in agriculture, it has had great success in privatizing small shops.

Yet there has been considerable confusion over who has the right to own the urban land. In Budapest control over the land and housing was turned over to the local neighborhood districts, but control of the major utilities such as water, gas, and transportation was assigned to the municipal government.[40] These different jurisdictions led to differing regulations, taxation, and definitions as to who was entitled to reclaim and assign ownership.

Despite the uncertainty over landownership rights, Hungary has been more successful than any of its neighbors at encouraging foreign investment.[41] Unlike Russia, it did not hesitate to bring in foreign capital. As of 1991, foreigners had invested $1.5 billion, and joint ventures numbered 5,600. By 1993 the total invested had grown to about $5.5 billion.[42] Western firms such as General Electric, Audi-Volkswagen, and Suzuki have committed themselves to major investments.[43] General Electric, for example, has poured close to $550 million into what once was the state-owned Tungsram electric bulb factory.[44] The results have been mixed, at best. General Electric says it lost money for three consecutive years beginning in 1990. The overstaffed work force and inefficient work habits developed during the communist years have taken longer to change than expected. Although GE reduced its inherited work force of 18,000 to 10,000, as of 1994 it was still losing money. Nonetheless, Hungary's low labor cost of about $1.40 an hour, in contrast to the much higher wages of $22 an hour being paid in West Germany, have made Hungary, as well as Poland, the Czech Republic, and Slovakia, especially attractive to foreign investors. Thus, despite its present inability to earn a profit, Tungsram's labor costs were so low that GE decided to transfer the manufacture of all its lighting production in England and Western Europe to Hungary.[45] While the bureaucracy in these countries is still difficult to deal with, and the work habits still very much influenced by a communist bureaucratic culture, the low wages, access to West European borders, workable transportation and communications, and reasonably stable governments have served to attract many Western manufacturers. Consequently, because Hungary's wages are so low, General Motors has tentatively selected Hungary instead of Spain as the site for the construction of a major plant. As of 1992 the share of foreign ownership in Hungarian industry amounted to 4 percent.[46] The Hungarian government's goal was to increase this to 30 percent by 1995. By contrast, despite enormous interest from outside investors, actual foreign investment in the much larger Russia amounts to not much more than $1 billion. Russian wages are also low, but political conditions, as the December 1993 election shows, are unstable, and Russian authorities continue to argue over whether they want foreign investment or not.

Price reform in Hungary is also far advanced compared with that in Russia. Since January 1991 some 90 percent of the country's producer and consumer goods prices have been determined by the market.[47] Except for subsidies on transportation and some public housing, most other consumer price subsidies have been eliminated. A new accounting law has been partly effective.[48] Firms with debts that are ninety days overdue are now declared to be bankrupt.[49] This has led to a major increase in declarations of bankruptcy, which in turn has caused a sharp increase in overt unemployment. The unemployment rate rose from about 1 percent in January 1990 to about 14 percent in early 1993.[50] Russia has so far refrained from implementing such measures, for fear it could become a very serious political problem. For the same reasons the larger Hungarian state enterprises have not been forced into bankruptcy. The Hungarian commercial banks have been reluctant to push too hard, lest they will also become insolvent.

In 1991 Hungary finally no longer had to subordinate its trade to the requirements of the disintegrating CMEA bloc, something its economists had been recommending for years. As requested, the Soviets switched the bulk of the CMEA pricing and paying process from barter and transferrable rubles to dollars. But the sudden change proved to be disruptive in both Hungary and Russia. Russian exporters collected the dollars, but failed to pass on their earnings to importers throughout the Soviet Union. Consequently, by late 1991, Soviet imports from Eastern Europe had all but evaporated. Ironically, denied their old sales opportunities, many Hungarian exporters began to yearn for larger Russian contracts.[51] Out of necessity Hungary and the other East European countries began exporting their goods to the capitalist world, particularly Western Europe. Thus, whereas one-half of Hungary's exports in 1988 were directed to members of CMEA, in 1991 the share fell to 20 percent.[52] By 1992 Hungary was selling only 10 percent of its exports to the former Soviet Union. As before World War II, Germany became Hungary's major trading partner. This near-disappearance of the Soviet Union as a trading partner accelerated the process of structural economic change.[53] Hungarian industry could no longer find outlets for its heavy-industry products, so it began to switch to the production of consumer goods. By 1993 Hungary's economy, including its unemployment and its large foreign debt, bore a much stronger resemblance to the economies of Western Europe than to those of the former Soviet Union or Hungary in 1955.

While Hungary's economic problems are far from resolved and the reform process is by no means completed, the reform route Hungary has chosen has several attractive aspects. Despite a serious drop in 1992 in its GNP, its earlier growth has provided its people with a rather good standard of living, at least by East European standards.[54] It has become a favorite of foreign investors, who regard it as a low-cost, low-inflation, politically stable area. That assumes, of course, that the return to power of the Communist Party in the guise of the Hungarian Socialist Party will not bring with it a reversal of the reform process. Unlike Russia's shock therapy, Hungary's gradual reform has made it possible to avoid hyperinflation and, until recently, crippling national unemployment. That is why there is growing concern inside the country about the sudden 14 percent rate of unemployment. It was this unemployment as much as anything that precipitated the May 1994 vote to bring back the communists.

VII

An important lesson of the Hungarian reform process for Russia is that reform should begin by generating new and meaningful competition with state-owned industry. Without that, price liberalization will inevitably cause an inflationary jolt and ongoing price escalation, because there is no competition to help bring prices down. Such new businesses are also needed to produce more consumer goods and to absorb the slack in jobs created by the fall in output in the state industrial sector, including the military-industrial complex. Consequently, it is essential to stimulate the formation of new businesses and services at the wholesaling and manufacturing levels as well as in retailing. Simultaneous steps will have to be taken to re-create the financial, legal, and economic infrastructure provided by banks, commercial law codes, courts, financial markets, and liberalized prices without which a market cannot operate.

Privatization of existing state monopolies, while important, does not necessarily produce competition. If the enterprise was a monopoly when under state control, it is likely to remain a monopoly even when privatized. Some effort must be made not only to encourage the formation of brand-new business but to divide up state enterprises before or, if need be, after they are demonopolized. One way is to open up the country to foreign trade both because it provides goods and technology for modernization and because imports create price competition.

As the Hungarian reforms show, in order for new-business formation to succeed, prices must be made flexible.[55] When inflation is under control and competing enterprises are already in existence, price decontrol can be introduced gradually without fear of hyperinflation. At the same time businesses must know that they will be able to take advantage of profit opportunities resulting from the subsequent higher prices. If prices remain fixed, they will limit or even preclude the earning of entrepreneurial profits and thus discourage prospective entrepreneurs from expanding supplies to meet demand, which, of course, is the way to hold down inflation. Price flexibility is also needed to attract foreign investors who are seeking a profit. Therefore, in addition to new-business formation, simultaneous price liberalization, even if in stages, is as essential to the gradual process of reform as to shock therapy.

VIII

Despite occasional setbacks, Poland's transformation ranks as one of the most encouraging developments inside the former communist world. Given a 16 percent unemployment rate, an out-of-touch state industrial sector that continues to operate much as it always has, and an Italian-like turnover of governments, it may be a bit premature to congratulate the Poles on their miraculous transformation from centrally planned communism to market-determined democracy, but so far they have been more successful in their efforts than any but a few dreamers anticipated. Their economic growth rate, which became positive in late 1992, compares very favorably with Russia's, and their political freedom and democracy puts China to shame. There is much that Russia, as well as China, can learn from the Polish example.

As of now, Poland is the one former communist country that has successfully combined democracy and positive economic growth in its move to a market economy. Equally impressive, it has done this in a relatively short time. Not surprisingly, after fifty-five years of fratricidal economic and political chaos, Poland still has far to go. There is no guarantee that it will be able to absorb its unemployed and privatize and transform its state enterprises rapidly enough to prevent political and economic unrest. Yet it has come a long way from when the reforms began in 1988. At that time, of all the communist countries, Poland appeared the least likely to succeed. There seemed to be no way to bridge the gap between the military-dominated Communist Party, led by General Wojciech Jaruzelski, and the worker-dominated Solidarity movement, led by Lech Walesa. Poland had come close to war with the Soviet Union, which had seriously considered sending in troops to occupy Poland in December 1981. As if all that were not enough, Poland had defaulted on its foreign debt and was unable to repay $45 billion to lenders in the West.

Yet in 1989, after decades of battle and self-flagellation, the undoable was somehow done. The warring parties inside the country agreed to work out their differences over a "roundtable" and attack the chaos in their economy with what became known in Poland as the Balcerowicz Plan and in the outside world as shock therapy.

IX

Like Hungary, Poland had had communism impressed on it in 1945. As a result communism did not wear well, and so in 1956, 1968, 1970, and 1980 there were violent protests, almost always accompanied by bloodshed and the threat of even greater violence against this alien system. The Polish desire for a free, independent noncommunist state periodically crashed into the geopolitical reality of a Russia to the east that had historically been hostile and that was now the homeland of communism, and an East Germany to the west that had been equally hostile and was now a fanatical convert to communism. On the surface, however, Poland in some ways seemed to be a prototypical communist country. Like the Soviet Union, it was a modern communist industrial state. It had nationalized and merged private industrial enterprises into state monopolies and conglomerates, distinguished by the large size of the work force in each factory. As in the Soviet Union, this was designed to take advantage of economies of scale. There were two significant differences, however. First, Polish peasants had managed to resist several efforts at collectivization. Second, the government always seemed to tolerate a very small private service sector in retailing, construction, and even manufacturing. These institutional nuances, as we will see, facilitated the introduction of shock therapy; the absence of similar private farms and business enterprise was something Russia sorely missed.

Edward Gierek, who took over leadership of the party and government after an outbreak of unrest in 1970, sought to promote Poland's economic growth by massive purchases of Western machinery and equipment. By the end of the decade, he had committed Poland to a $25 billion debt. To his dismay, this Western technology, designed for a market system where resource use was determined by demand, not political consideration, did not mix well with Polish communism. The exports that were to be produced by these machines and that Gierek counted on to pay back the debt never fully materialized. On the contrary, the debt grew to $40 billion, and the need to service that debt exacerbated Poland's domestic economic difficulties. In August 1980 this sparked a new surge of labor unrest and subsequent government repression.

The events of 1980 gave birth to something unprecedented in the communist world, an independent labor union. Led by Lech Walesa, the shipyard workers in Gdansk organized themselves and workers elsewhere into what came to be called the Solidarity movement. After some initial violence, the communist-led government agreed to work with this new labor movement, and for a time it looked as if the alliance might work. It was ironic that what many called the first truly proletarian labor movement evolved out of a communist, not a capitalist, state. Some labor groups in surrounding communist countries wanted to learn more about, if not adopt, this new model. To prevent any such thing the Polish government came under increasing pressure to clamp down on Solidarity. Hard-liners in East Germany, Czechoslovakia, and the Soviet Union were particularly insistent. In response, on December 13, 1981, General Jaruzelski, who had become prime minister in February 1981, declared martial law. The brave experiment ended with the leaders of Solidarity either under arrest or in hiding.

Despite the crackdown that followed, even Jaruzelski after a year or so, came to see the need for some changes in the Polish economic system. In a move reminiscent of the events in Hungary after the revolution in 1956, the Polish government on January 1, 1982, tried to decentralize decision making in the economy. However, whereas in Hungary a coalition of former antagonists began to work with the government, members of Solidarity refused to work with Jaruzelski. That contributed to the failure of Jaruzelski's initial efforts. An attempt to decontrol prices in October 1987 also failed.[56] Unlike their Hungarian counterparts, Polish reformers were not yet ready to compromise. There seemed to be no way out of the ideological and personal impasse the Poles had created for themselves.

X

Because of the standoff between the government and the labor movement, the economy continued to deteriorate throughout most of the decade. Then, after another round of strikes in mid-1988, a turning point in history occurred, as two bitter enemies—the Jaruzelski government and the leadership of Solidarity—decided to work with each other to find a way out of their economic and political dead end. Both sides had come to recognize that failure to act was creating enormous devastation in the economy.[57] Similar efforts over the years had always failed. This time, though, Gorbachev was head of the party in Moscow, and he firmly believed that unless the Communist Party leadership in Eastern Europe showed the way to reform from above, the parties would sooner or later be overwhelmed from below.

Ideological deviation and a multiparty political system of the sort being contemplated in Poland would never have been tolerated by a Khrushchev or a Brezhnev, both of whom sent Russian troops into Eastern Europe for far less serious deviations. By contrast Gorbachev tolerated the Polish reforms and muzzled the Soviet defenders of the status quo. Another important difference between the success of the 1989 and the failure of the earlier reform efforts was that the consistently hard-line leaders in East Germany were no longer in a position to say, much less do, anything about ideological deviation in Poland. They had become too distracted by their own ideological upheavals.

Gorbachev encouraged Jaruzelski to work out his differences with Solidarity over what came to be called the Roundtable. Instead of responding to the 1988 worker strikes with the usual confrontation between workers and police, the government offered to consider legalizing Solidarity if its leaders agreed to end the strike and sit down and talk.[58] Such an agreement was finally reached in January 1989. There followed a series of additional discussions that culminated in April 1989 with the government's agreeing to hold free elections later in the summer. While Jaruzelski agreed that all the seats in the upper house could be contested, he insisted that in the important lower house, or Sejm, 65 percent of the seats would remain uncontested and be set aside for members of the ruling Polish United Workers Party (the Communist Party).[59] Much to everyone's surprise, Solidarity won all the contested seats in the Sejm and ninety-nine of the one hundred seats in the upper house.[60] Despite the defection of what he thought were deputies firmly committed to his candidacy, Jaruzelski nonetheless ended up with a one-vote margin, enough for him to be reelected president. His failure to attract more of a popular vote was so humiliating, however, that he decided not to form a government. Consequently, in August 1989 a noncommunist, Tadeusz Mazowiecki, became prime minister, the first time a noncommunist prime minister had governed Poland since immediately after World War II.[61]

As the first legitimately elected Polish government in forty years, the Mazowiecki regime took the election to be a clear mandate for action and change, and it therefore moved quickly to dismantle the centrally planned economic system. Such a popular mandate would have been of immeasurable help to both Gorbachev and Yeltsin—assuming, of course, that the Russian people could have agreed among themselves, as the Poles did, on a common goal. The Russians did approve a question on the April 1993 referendum indicating support for Yeltsin's economic reforms, but the referendum was so loosely worded and encumbered with so many political implications that nobody quite knew what approval meant.

To help him in his reform effort Mazowiecki appointed Leszek Balcerowicz minister of finance and deputy prime minister. A member of the Polish United Workers Party until 1981, Balcerowicz subsequently became a consultant to a Solidarity union group. Trained as an economist at the Warsaw School of Planning and Statistics as well as at St. John's University, in New York, he did most of his professional work at the Polish Economic Development Institute.

Balcerowicz wasted no time. In late September 1989 he presented a reform plan to the annual meeting of the finance ministers of the G-7 major industrial powers in Washington and a few days later to the Polish people.[62] Normally, such a plan is presented at home first, but since Balcerowicz sought substantial loan and debt forgiveness from Western governments, he took advantage of the gathering of the finance ministers to get their approval.

As would happen in the Soviet Union and Russia, announcing a reform plan in advance, especially if it involves price liberalization, risks further inflation as everyone seeks to buy before prices go up. Prices had already been increasing after the Jaruzelski government's failed effort at decentralization in 1987. Moreover, in 1989 the Jaruzelski government issued some decrees further increasing inflationary pressures. For example, to win political favor, in April 1989 it agreed to index wages to 80 percent of the increase in prices in August 1989.[63] It also freed food prices and cut virtually all farm subsidies.[64] (Some insist the August 1989 price liberalization decision was a last-ditch effort to saddle the incoming Solidarity government with an impossible burden, which would be sure to discredit it and ultimately bring about its downfall.)[65] By December 1989, prices on the black market were increasing at a rate of 27 percent a month. As a consequence state stores, with their fixed prices, ended up with empty shelves. In addition the budget deficit continued to grow while the GNP began to shrink. Furthermore, external conditions were unhelpful. Oil prices were going up because of the Persian Gulf war and blockade of Iraq (an important trading partner and supplier of oil for Poland), and Polish trade with CMEA was sharply cut back. The CMEA collapse was most acutely felt in 1991, but trade in 1990 also suffered. As the economic situation deteriorated, it was too late for gradual reforms like those in Hungary. Drastic measures were needed.

XI

What came to be called the Balcerowicz Plan was put into effect on January 1, 1990. Like successful reforms of the sort we have already described in West Germany and Japan and like those prescribed by the International Monetary Fund, the Polish reforms sought to carry out a number of steps simultaneously: cut demand, dampen inflationary expectations, open up markets inside and outside Poland, and create new market institutions and infrastructure.[66]

Balcerowicz moved boldly and comprehensively. He and his advisers had already worked out many of their ideas in the spring of 1989. As their first step, on January 1, 1990, the prices of 80 percent of all consumer goods were set free.[67] Though some controls were kept on energy, housing, and other miscellaneous products, deregulation eliminated the need for most price subsidies. This deregulation, plus cuts in the military budget, made possible substantial reductions in government expenditures, so the deficit was reduced from over 15 percent to 7.5 percent of the GNP. On the monetary side, interest rates were raised to as much as 36 percent a month, or 432 percent a year, and lending procedures were tightened.[68] To encourage exports, the zloty was on January 1990 devalued from 600 zlotys to the dollar to 9,500 zlotys. To prevent further devaluation, the Poles were able to obtain from the West a one-billion-dollar stabilization fund for the zloty. Because the devaluation was so successful, the Poles did not have to draw on this money. In an effort to lessen inflationary pressures, the wage indexation rate was lowered to 30 percent of the inflation rate, from the 80 percent rate established by the Jaruzelski government. By February 1990 indexation was reduced further, to 20 percent. In an effort to restrain wage increases, an excise wage tax was levied on enterprises that voluntarily raised wages beyond certain limits. Finally, in hopes of generating meaningful competition in the marketplace, the Mazowiecki government relaxed regulations restricting the creation of new businesses. At the same time it announced plans to begin the privatization of state enterprises and the demonopolization of key markets. Compared with the subsequent Gaidar reforms in Russia, this was a much more dynamic and relevant undertaking.

XII

The initial response to these radical reforms was not exactly what the planners had anticipated. They had expected an immediate jump in prices of about 40 percent per month, not the 73 to 78 percent that actually occurred.[69] Similarly, they had anticipated a minor fall in output; instead, industrial production dropped sharply. At this point the Polish statistics become even less trustworthy than normal, but official reports indicate that output in January dropped by more than 30 percent.[70] Conditions improved somewhat in the months that followed: inflation rose by only 20 percent a month in February and fell to a significantly lower 5 percent a month in March and 3 to 5 percent thereafter. This rate was still high, but lower than that of the prereform era. Industrial output also stabilized a bit, but one did not need statistics to appreciate that the industrial restructuring became ever more disruptive. Poland's dinosaur-like state industrial enterprises were no more amenable to revitalization than their counterparts in Russia and Hungary were.

Other sectors of the economy, however, began to respond in a more positive way. The long-standing budget deficits turned into budget surpluses, and the tightened credit conditions combined with cutbacks in government spending to force businessmen and ordinary citizens alike to dip into their dollar savings to finance their needs.[71] As a result the zloty began to stabilize. Within limits it even became convertible into German marks. This gave traders the opportunity to make the short drive to Berlin to buy Western commodities and return to sell them at home. The flow of Western products and an increase in output from the private peasant and trade sectors helped moderate the inflation. Gradually, the queues that had been a constant part of Polish life since the start of World War II began to shorten. At the same time the end of controls allowed Poles to seek higher profits for their goods in the West. Because of a 35 percent increase in hard-currency exports, Poland began to accumulate a foreign-trade surplus in 1990.[72] Usually, just the opposite happens when an economy is initially opened up this way. This was certainly true in Russia. Some time is needed for traders to adjust to the new conditions. But in Poland convertibility made the zloty so cheap that the changes occurred almost immediately. Even some state enterprises responded. The Gdansk shipyard, for instance, where Lech Walesa helped create the Solidarity movement, almost went bankrupt in the 1980s. Yet, because its wages were one to two dollars an hour, compared with as much as twenty-four dollars in the outside world, Poland had by 1990 become a major competitor in the world market for shipbuilding, even though the productivity of its labor was about 50 percent of that of Asia and Western Europe. This wage difference provided the Poles, like the Hungarians, with a competitive advantage.[73] The Russians for a time had the same cost advantage in terms of labor, but their political and economic chaos more than offset the lower wages.

Equally important for the success of their reforms, unlike the Russians, the Poles responded enthusiastically to the opportunity to open up new businesses. According to Jeffrey Sachs, who became a consultant to Balcerowicz and who had also helped mobilize support for shock therapy among Solidarity's political leaders at a crucial August 1989 strategy meeting, by mid-1993 some 1.7 million new private businesses had been created.[74] What makes this especially impressive is that the Polish work force numbered only seventeen million. Whereas in 1988 the share of the private sector in industrial output was only 10 percent, by mid-1991 it had doubled, and by 1993 it had more than doubled again.[75] In mid-1993 the private sector thus accounted for 56 percent of the total industrial employment and for over 50 percent of the total industrial output.[76] Almost all the country's retailing was also in the hands of private owners. Given the relatively short time in which all of this occurred, the formation of new businesses in Poland (green-fieldization), as distinct from privatization of existing state industry, compares favorably with what took place in China. The reverse happened in Russia, where, as we saw, the emphasis was on privatization, not on green-fieldization

While overall the reform process in Poland has been a success, Polish critics have noted that the privatization of state industry has not been as rapid as initially promised. Mazowiecki's government submitted a privatization plan in mid-1990; like similar plans in Russia and other former communist countries, it met fierce resistance from factory directors and the work force.[77] The government of Jan Bielecki, successor to Mazowiecki, tried to accelerate the process, but again without much success.[78]

The successful privatization of state industry, whether it involves auctions, issuance of vouchers, or simply a management-worker takeover, does not come easily. As we saw with Russia and will see with China, because privatization directly threatens long-standing bureaucratic interests, it is the most difficult element of the reform. Fortunately for Poland, green-fieldization was more important. Since Russia chose the route of privatization, this has hurt its reform effort.

Just as the peasants expected that the land reform would make them owners of the land, so managers and workers assumed that with privatization the factories where they had worked most of their lives would become theirs. That holds for Russia as well as for Poland. The general public, however, having sacrificed all these years to pay for the diversion of resources into industry and agriculture, tends to believe that it too should be allowed a share in the parcelization of the country's assets. Moreover, state bureaucrats seldom relinquish their authority and perquisites voluntarily.[79] Although a small number of Polish state enterprises, accounting for 14 percent of the assets and 10 percent of the employment, have been privatized, the bulk of the state sector has not yet resolved the ownership problem or come to terms with the new market conditions.[80]

Still, while state industry was stagnating, enough new private businesses were established that by late 1992 they made up for the decline in the state sector. As a result Poland's industrial production actually began to increase again. In 1993 the economic growth of about 4 percent a year in Poland was the highest in Europe. In that sense shock therapy was successful. This was after output in mid-1991 had fallen as much as 20 percent from the January 1990 level.[81] But the increase in private production was still not enough to absorb all the workers who were being laid off from the state sector. By mid-1993 the unemployment rate had climbed to 14 percent.[82] As in Russia, in Poland the state sector, even the portion that had become privatized, was having difficulty responding to market conditions and competition. Yet whereas the state subsidies were cut in Poland, they continued for a time to be issued in Russia, so while industrial output dropped, employment stayed relatively constant. Sometimes that required having Russians come to work and do nothing.

The fear that unemployment will spread even further in Poland has created considerable unrest. The workers in the state-owned coal mines and steel mills have been particularly militant. There has also been widespread opposition to shock therapy. In response the public in 1993 voted the Communist Party, with its call for a slower-paced and more humane reform, back into power in an agrarian-communist coalition government. So far, however, the newest version of communism has been relatively benign and has continued to support economic reform and markets, even if at a slow pace. Nonetheless, there is always the danger that Poland's leadership will not be able to maintain its unique combination of democracy and economic reform. As in Hungary, in Poland sustained economic growth would be the best way of strengthening the process.

XIII

Several notable features of the Balcerowicz reforms are relevant to Russia. The Polish vote for Solidarity in the 1989 election—and, by inference, the rejection of the Jaruzelski leadership—was crucial. This clear mandate for change provided an important cushion for the very difficult transition from central plan to market. Reflecting this willingness to proceed with change, Balcerowicz, the architect of this painful process, stayed on in the government even though Mazowiecki, the initial prime minister, was forced from office and replaced by Bielecki.[83] Although Balcerowicz's successors spoke for a time about reversing course, they have all held to the basic reform agenda, again reflecting a broad base of popular support for the reforms.

The political support for Yeltsin during and after the August 1991 coup and the referendum of 1993 also reflected the Russian public's acceptance of the need for change. But Yeltsin, Gaidar, and his advisers overlooked the fact that Russia lacked the nascent market infrastructure that existed in Poland. Some Poles in January 1990 also insisted that reform was premature because Poland's market was not developed enough. But whereas in Poland the preexisting private commercial sector amounted to 10 percent of the economy and 80 percent of the peasants had never moved off of their own private farms, in Russia at best only 2 to 3 percent of the farms and businesses were operated independently of the state. Nonetheless, even though about 40 percent of Poland's total employment, including 20 percent in construction and 10 to 15 percent in industry, was private, it would be an exaggeration to say that any of these businesses in Poland operated as freely as their counterparts in the West.[84] The Polish government continued to exercise many controls, direct and indirect. Still, in contrast to Russia, where at the start of the Yeltsin reform in 1992 barely a fraction worked in the private sector, in Poland the private constituency, after some hesitation, responded willingly to the reform's market stimuli of higher prices and relaxed controls. Moreover, because it was easiest for new and existing entrepreneurs to increase the production of food and consumer goods, the reforms brought an immediate improvement in the lives of the Polish people, at least of those who could afford the high prices. Because of the continuation of the collective farms in Russia and its other erratic policies, there was no such improvement there and thus even less support for the reform process than existed in Poland.

Reform in Poland was also facilitated by a widely held consensus that Poland's future lay in Western Europe, not in the East or in Russia. This meant not only embracing market and democratic institutions but also, in the extreme case, seeking membership in NATO and the Common Market. Of course, not everyone was eager or willing to break with the past, but those looking eastward and supporting authoritarian rule constituted a much smaller percentage of the population in Poland than did their counterparts in Russia, where there was a much greater dichotomy, as well as a historical struggle between Westernizers and Slavophiles. This made it possible for an able and committed leader like Tadeusz Mazowiecki and one of his successors, Hanna Suchocka, to undertake daring, even painful reforms that opened Poland to the world.

The bigger question in Poland is not whether there is broad

public support for Western-type reforms but whether the West Europeans will allow Poland to integrate itself into the West European economy and political alliances. As a new kid on the block, Poland is blamed for disrupting European markets by dumping metallurgical products into an already saturated economy. Many West European politicians also fret that Poland's democratic roots are not yet deeply grounded enough and that thus Poland is not a reliable political partner. To complicate matters even more, Yeltsin has warned that Russia would oppose any effort to make Poland a full member of NATO. Led by the United States, the members of NATO have agreed not to upset the Russians. Such a standoffish attitude by the West undermines the transforming and integrating process.

XIV

Poland's relative success so far has undoubtedly been helped by the presence of political consensus and the absence of ethnic factions. By contrast Russia's lack of consensus and its ethnic conflicts make it more difficult for the reformers to generate support for economic reforms. Poland was also lucky in that the reforms were attempted after only forty years or so of communism, not after a seventy-year siege, as in Russia. Poland did not escape the drive to amalgamate competitors into monopolies, but their roots were not dug as deeply or spread as broadly. Moreover, it has the benefit of a small but substantial private infrastructure in agriculture, services, and even industry. The unleashing of economic incentives thus awakened dormant but potentially responsive decision-making bodies, which reacted much as their peers in the noncommunist world might have.

Absent a similar nonstate economic sector in Russia, the unleashing of economic incentives is taking much longer to penetrate the incentive-resistant barriers erected during the seventy years of Russian communism. Shock therapy worked in Poland because institutions were in place that reacted to the sudden application of decontrolled prices and economic incentives. For societies without such institutions, a gradual approach is the preferred strategy. This means allowing only partial and gradual price decontrol until the new private agricultural and entrepreneurial sector can be nursed into being. Sooner or later the barriers in Russia will be penetrated, however, or they will simply wear away. It would be wrong to insist that Russia will never reform. But compared with that of Hungary and Poland and the even faster-responding China, which we will examine in the next chapter, the disruption and suffering of Russia is likely to last longer. It remains unknown whether the Russians will ever be able to form a consensus about the nature of the reform they want, whether the benefits of the reform will be realized soon enough to warrant the costs, and whether the Russian people will tolerate what may often appear to be a never-ending series of experiments and supposed remedies.

Some liken the successive Russian reforms to the remedies the local Russian Orthodox priest prescribed to a peasant who found that his chickens were dying.

"Feed them aspirin," the priest urged.

Seeing the peasant a few days later, the priest asked whether the medicine had worked. "Not really. Another fifty died."

"Well, my son, try penicillin."

After a week the priest again inquired about the chickens. "Any better luck?"

"No. This time one hundred died."

"Then try castor oil," urged the priest.

Another week passed, and the priest again sought out the peasant.

"What happened this time?"

"This time they all died!"

Stunned, the priest shook his head from side to side, "What a pity! What a pity! I have so many other remedies I wanted to try."

9.

China as a Model

Given the differences in culture, size of population, importance of industry, and ethnic makeup, many observers, including Yegor Gaidar, insist that the Chinese reform experience is not a good model for the Soviet or the Russian transition.[1] To some extent they are right. But by the same criteria all countries are different, and no model or pattern of development in one country can be applied strictly to another country. Thus, by comparison with Russia, all East European countries are too small or their populations too homogeneous. None was without markets or subjected to Communist Party dictates or an antimarket mentality for more than forty-five years. Moreover, 80 percent of the farms in Poland escaped collectivization, and for decades Hungary and Poland were considerably more tolerant of private commercial activity. As for the West Germans and the Japanese, they, unlike the Russians, had the good fortune to be occupied by U.S. troops during the hardest days of the economic reform. Despite the ensuing economic upheaval, the presence of U.S. occupation forces ensured political tranquillity without tainting the newly born democratic governments.[2]

I

The point is that no comparisons are perfect. For that matter, the Chinese and Russian leaderships even insist that they seek different goals. For example, the Russians no longer talk about socialism. In contrast Chinese officials assert that they are still building socialism, but with Chinese characteristics. However, with its dynamic and burgeoning private sector, stock markets, and expanding exports, China might more aptly be said to be building capitalism with Chinese characteristics.[3] Despite an unwillingness by both parties to be compared to each other, it turns out that Russian and Chinese reforms have considerably more in common than might at first appear.

To be sure, there are some striking differences between China and the Soviet Union. Before it disintegrated, the Soviet Union consisted of 293 million people; Russia has just a bit more than half of this total, or 147 million.[4] China's population in 1991 was estimated to be 1.15 billion, or almost four times larger than the Soviet Union's and seven times larger than Russia's.[5]

There was also a significant difference in the makeup of those populations. Whereas 80 percent of the Chinese population is rural, 34 percent of the population in the former Soviet Union and 26 percent in Russia are considered rural.[6] Consequently, a much larger percentage of the Soviet-Russian population is employed in industry, specifically state industry. On the basis of the size of the industrial sector, some observers conclude that reform in Russia will be more difficult to implement because state industry has almost everywhere, including China, been the most difficult to transform. As Anders Åslund has explained, "primitive economies dominated by agriculture such as the Chinese and Vietnamese economies" are easier to transform because "it is much easier to establish small-scale economic units based on the family with quasi property rights."[7]

Of course, that statement was made after the fact. Before 1978 few if any analysts showed such clarity of vision about China's transformation under Deng Xiaoping's leadership. No one had expected China, with its many poor peasants, to create a vibrant economy so quickly. Chiang Kai-shek and Mao Zedong had failed to do so. If anything, a good argument could have been made that Russia was more likely than China to make the transformation. After all, Russia had proportionally more urban residents and factory workers familiar with machinery, as well as a more literate population. Thus the Russians should have been more amenable to new ideas and change. In contrast peasants are noted for their conservatism and reluctance to reform. Moreover, given the overcrowding in the Chinese countryside and what some regarded as a Malthusian crisis, it would be easy to agree with those who held that retaining centralized and state control in Chinese agriculture was more important than ever.

It was not only that China had more peasants than Russia but that their agricultural practices were very dissimilar. For example, Chinese agriculture is highly labor intensive and Russian agriculture is not. Russian farms rely on big open fields and are considerably more mechanized than those in China and farther from their markets. Russia's climate is more severe than China's, and its rural population is older and includes a larger percentage of females.

The differences in their ethnic makeup are even harder to explain away. Over 90 percent of the Chinese people are Han Chinese. Admittedly, many of them speak very different dialects, and communication between regions can be difficult. Still, that situation differs from that of the former Soviet Union and Russia, where there are over one hundred different ethnic groups. Only about one-half of the people of the Soviet Union considered themselves Russians. Even within Russia itself about 20 percent of the population consists of non-Russians. This ethnic diversity was a major cause of tension in the Gorbachev era. After the breakup of the Soviet Union, Yeltsin no longer had to deal directly with many of those ethnic problems, but ethnic tensions did not disappear. There remain serious ethnic controversies among members of the Commonwealth of Independent

States, and they complicate economic reform for all of them. By contrast, China's tensions with Tibet and the Moslem areas in the northwest do not interfere with the economic reforms in the rest of China.

Many analysts insist that another underlying reason for the different ways in which China and Russia have responded to reform is that the Chinese are more attuned to market-type relations. The Chinese have traditionally operated small businesses and services independently of the state. Other analysts point to the large number of successful Chinese entrepreneurs outside of China. By contrast the Russians have historically had a more difficult time with markets and commerce. That helps explain why relatively few successful ethnic Russian businessmen are found overseas.

The Chinese reform process was also facilitated by the fact that China had to endure less than thirty years of the Leninist-Stalinist system, which lasted almost seventy years in Russia. Consequently, many Chinese still remembered how to deal with markets and market networks. In the Soviet Union very few were left who had experience with the prerevolutionary markets. Thus the preference for the state as the economic decision maker rather than the individual, family, or clan was much stronger in Russia than in China.

The Chinese reformers themselves also acknowledge that the Cultural Revolution made it easier to implement far-reaching reforms because it undermined the party bureaucracy and controls. When Deng Xiaoping regained power in late 1978, the party and government cadres were in disarray. Consequently, there was little resistance when the peasants began to take land out of the commune and work it themselves on long-term leases. Earlier attempts to do the same thing during the Great Leap Forward in China, in 1962, had been stopped by Mao Zedong. Unlike Mao, Deng not only allowed the peasant takeover but made it formal policy in 1982. By contrast in Russia the party bureaucracy remained strong enough to oppose such actions. Moreover, as we have seen, Gorbachev himself was opposed to the breakup of the collective farms. Yeltsin has been more supportive, but he had difficulty in persuading the pre–October 1993 parliament to support him. Even with a new post–October 1993 parliament, the local rural bureaucracy has continued to resist anything that might diminish its authority.

But while the Cultural Revolution opened the way for Chinese economic reform, it acted more as a stun gun than as a permanent immobilizer. Eventually, in the early 1980s, the Chinese Communist Party regained its sense of control, but by then economic reforms were already successfully under way, so the party elders concerned themselves primarily with restraining political liberalization. Occasionally, there was some economic retrenchment as well, but with Deng's unrelenting advocacy the economic reforms continued to move ahead. By contrast, although Gorbachev also started with economic reforms, when he encountered stony opposition from the party, he turned to political reform in order to undermine the opposition. If anything, Gorbachev takes pride in the "political reforms that we have undertaken . . . and the political pluralism and dissidence which is now permitted and free elections and the division of powers. . . . Our reforms mean above all, a revolution in the minds of men. That is why they are so different."[8]

However, Gorbachev insists that until he had introduced the country to this new, pervasive form of democracy, he could not break up the collective farms and mandate a return to private property. To my suggestion that he might have been a more successful economic reformer if he had copied the Chinese strategy of allowing the peasants to take over the land and others to set up private businesses, he replied,

> Professor Marshall Goldman . . . believes that we ought to have begun not by trying to change people, change the mindset of the people, but by immediately attacking the problem of property . . . but I can imagine what would have happened if I, General Secretary of the Communist Party, Mikhail Gorbachev, followed his advice and said from the start, "What I

> think we must have is private property. The party should be removed to the background, etc., etc.;" I would have been removed within three days.[9]

In other words, he felt he had to shake up the party hierarchy first and to do that he had to put in place a democratic system. However, it is hard to imagine that Gorbachev, even if the reaction of his colleagues on the Politburo or the Central Committee had been positive, would at the time have attempted such a course of action. As late as 1992 he himself was still opposed to the idea of private ownership of land.

II

There are, then, major dissimilarities between Russia and China. However, on closer look, what are sometimes regarded as large differences turn out not to be so large after all. In any event, some of these "contrasts" offer important lessons for Russia as it seeks to learn from China's movement away from a centralized command economy. Take the image of the hardworking Chinese entrepreneurial peasant and sweatshop laborer. This stereotype stands in sharp contrast to that of the slothful Russian peasant asleep on his stove and the drunken, lazy Russian worker. Yet in the prereform communist era, with its absence of meaningful material incentives, Chinese workers and peasants also developed the same slothful ways. Visitors to China's state-run factories (not the private factories) were then, and are now, struck by the large number of Chinese workers on their unauthorized *xiuxi*, or nap. Conditions in the countryside were little different. This was vividly pointed out to me during my first visit to China, in 1979. The post–Cultural Revolution economic reforms had not been fully implemented, and China was still trying to recover from years of economic mismanagement. The Sinologist economists I was traveling with had just come back from a visit to a still-existing agricultural commune. The trip had made an immense impression on them. One of them said, "After three decades of communism, I now agree that Mao has done the impossible—he has created lazy Chinese." It was as if Mao had lobotomized the Chinese workers and removed their work incentives. Remember that millions of Chinese died of starvation during the Great Leap Forward of the late 1950s when material incentives were suppressed, but when material incentives were reintroduced, in 1978, agricultural and industrial productivity increased at a rate of 9 percent a year. This indicates the potential that was lost under Mao (1949–76).

Russian workers undoubtedly have similar suppressed potential. Many of the new independent Russian farmers report productivity increases of 100 percent or more once they have broken off from the collective farms and formed their own farms.[10] Similarly, a fascinating story in the *New York Times* told of a Polish contractor's preference for Russian and Ukrainian migrant workers, who work much harder and professionally than local Polish workers.[11] The reason was simple; he offered wages higher than those they received in Russia and in Ukraine.

After the claim that the work culture differs, the argument used most by those who dismiss the Chinese analogy is that industry plays a much more important role in the Russian economy. Since Russia's industry was purposely developed for central planning, not for competitive markets, and much of it is obsolete or oriented for military production, that argument cannot be discounted. As we saw, one of Yeltsin's biggest problems is that the members of the pre–October 1993 Congress of People's Deputies as well as the military-industrial bureaucracy insisted on continuing this investment in obsolete state enterprises, thus diverting support for new and presumably more competitive enterprises.

However, while the percentage of GNP and population engaged in the state industrial sector is considerably smaller in China than in Russia, because of the larger Chinese population the absolute number of Chinese workers in industry is actually larger. Thus while there were 35 million industrial workers in the Soviet Union and 23 million workers in present-day Russia, there were 47 million industrial workers in China in 1980 and 107 million in 1992.[12] Therefore, the reforming of state industry has also been a problem in China. Indeed, some state Chinese enterprises are only now slowly being privatized after a decade of trying. Similarly, it is estimated that two-thirds of China's state factories lose money.[13] Nevertheless, the difficulty of dealing with state industry did not postpone China's overall reform. The Chinese simply concentrated on other opportunities, especially the creation of nonstate farms, services, and manufacturing. State industry has had an increasingly smaller share in China's overall GNP. Deng Furong, one of China's leading economists and a member of the Standing Committee of the National People's Congress, has estimated that at present its share is less than 50 percent.[14]

When some state enterprises in China find themselves no longer economically competitive, they attempt to transform themselves. For example, by 1991 the Number One Beijing Textile and Dyeing Plant was close to bankruptcy. It had ceased to be competitive. Township and private factories in the Chinese countryside had learned how to produce better-quality and lower-cost cloth. (It came as a shock to this Western economist to discover that what he had always regarded as the cheapest labor in the world, Beijing labor, was in turn being outproduced by even cheaper labor in the Chinese countryside.) After two years of losses, the factory manager decided that rather than go bankrupt, it would be better to lay off a portion of the factory's three thousand employees and tear down one-third of its buildings. Located in downtown Beijing, the factory buildings were replaced with a commercial center consisting of a multistory office building, a hotel, and a shopping mall. State-owned textile plants in Shanghai, Guangzhou, and Shenzhen are giving way to similar structures for similar reasons. In contrast most of the effort in Russia has focused on first privatizing and then sustaining state industries. This is a much more difficult approach than encouraging the creation of brand-new businesses, which are less likely to be trapped in the ways of centrally planned behavior.

Even in agriculture China and Russia show some similarities. Agricultural specialists tend to agree that it will be difficult to reform Russian agriculture as long as there is inadequate crop storage space and an underdeveloped highway system. The total length of the Soviet highway system used for general transport purposes was actually less in 1990 than in 1980, when one-quarter of the state farms in the Russian Republic had no road linking them with the rest of the nation.[15] Chinese agriculture suffered from the same deficiencies. Yet the Chinese increased their output and shipments to urban areas with only a modest increase in highway construction. It was not more highways that made the difference; it was the fact that Chinese peasants were allowed to operate on their own. When they were the ones who stood to suffer, if there was any crop loss, they no longer left their crops outdoors, as they had before, but began to store them in their houses—at least until they could put enough aside to build additional storage facilities. In the same way, the transportation problem was solved when the peasants sold their crops to new private businesses that operated trucking services. Alternatively, many peasants simply placed their crops on their bicycles and drove into town. Granted, the Russians are not into bicycles; the point is that when there is an incentive, there is more likely to be a way.

It is also true that the crop profiles of the two countries are very different. However, until the Chinese began their reforms, they, like their Moscow mentors, were forced to plant grains, either rice or wheat. Once the Chinese peasants were allowed to make their own decisions and satisfy their own needs, though, they turned to producing vegetables and fruits for themselves as well as for market. Having been deprived and closely controlled for so long, Chinese peasants had developed a high elasticity of demand. The Chinese leadership ultimately had to understand and accept that there would be a significant increase in output only when the peasants were allowed to satisfy their own needs first. Once they had satisfied their own needs, the peasants did turn their efforts to selling outside their villages. There is every reason to believe that the Russian peasants will respond in the same way.

Given the scale of Russian agriculture, critics of the Chinese analogy argue that the breakup of the vast Russian communal fields will result in a sharp drop in output because the existing machinery stock with its large tractors, combines, and harvesters cannot be used effectively on smaller fields. Yet the highest productivity in Russian agriculture comes not from the large farms and their theoretical economies of scale but from the small garden plots, which are limited in size to .5 hectares, or 1.2 acres.[16] In 1981 the Russian peasants were also authorized to lease another one and a half acres in order to grow fodder crops.[17] These subsidiary household plots accounted for about 4 percent of the arable land but yielded between 25 to 30 percent of the country's agriculture output.[18] Under Yeltsin the number of subsidiary plots has grown to 48 million; according to some reports, they account for 8 percent of the arable land.[19] The private farms that are being spun off collective farms in Russia average about 41 hectares, or 100 acres, per holder.[20] The working of such a farm requires more machinery than the smaller garden plots. Admittedly, many of these new private farms are having a hard time. They suffer from lack of credit, simple machinery, seed, pesticides, and fertilizer, from delays in payment for crop sales, and from a distorted price system. Directors of the state farms have also made a concerted effort to sabotage private farming. This explains why substantial numbers of private farms have already been forced to close.[21] In 1992, for example, as many as five thousand farms were abandoned; in 1993, fourteen thousand. As we noted earlier when citing these data, Russian agricultural reform will not be easy. At the same time those private Russian farmers who have persevered have been able to double and in some cases triple their profits.

Despite the differences, the Chinese experience suggests that even a moderate increase in agricultural production would have a positive impact, both material and psychological, on the overall reform process. Thus the increase in Chinese agricultural output and income, beginning in the late 1970s and continuing into the early 1980s, not only raised peasant incomes but also increased the flow of food to the urban areas. Gradually, this eliminated the shortages that had before been a hallmark of all socialist economies, China included. These early successes created a mood very different from that found in most of Eastern Europe and the former Soviet Union. The Chinese public generally felt that the economic reforms had worked and made their lives better. In contrast Russia's reforms have not yet improved the livelihood of most Russians—just the opposite—and the vote for extremists in December 1993 reflects the continuing disillusionment with the Russian reform process.

If the Russians had begun their transformation effort by turning over the land to the peasants, the outcome might well have been different. Certainly, it would have been worth a try. It is instructive that, throughout Asia, the countries that have undergone the most successful economic transformations all began their reform effort with an agricultural land reform. That was the case in Japan, South Korea, Taiwan, and now China. Agricultural reform, in turn, led the way to reform of the industrial sector. Granted that agricultural conditions in Russia are different from those in Asia; however, even a modest improvement would have helped the reform process.

Despite his earlier explicit rejection of that notion, Gorbachev has belatedly come to acknowledge that perhaps he should have begun with agricultural reform after all: "I consider it my biggest miscalculation that we did not take agriculture as the starting point of the reform process and that we stopped half way."[22]

In defending his reluctance to carry out more far-reaching reforms, Gorbachev, as we saw, insisted that he lacked the political power to move as boldly as Deng Xiaoping had. There was indeed nothing like the Cultural Revolution in the Soviet Union's recent history. Nevertheless, Gorbachev seemed to have all the power he needed to purge the Politburo. No other general secretary of the Central Committee had ever moved so rapidly to dismiss the officials he disliked as Gorbachev did in 1985–86. Unfortunately, some of the new appointees turned out to be as conservative as those who were purged. The failure to push for more sweeping reforms had as much to do with Gorbachev's own reservations about the breakup of the collective farms and private farming as with his supposed lack of power.

Similarly, Yeltsin also had a chance to implement agricultural reforms but hesitated. As we noted earlier, in the aftermath of his resistance to the August 1991 coup attempt, he could have done almost anything he wanted to. Instead, he allowed the enthusiasm of the moment to dissipate, and he disappeared from Moscow soon thereafter for several weeks. In retrospect it appears he also lost the chance to promulgate a constitution that in August 1991 could have provided him with the power he needed to carry out the reforms. As he was to do in December 1993, he could also have insisted that an earlier constitution address the issue of private farming and landownership. Though the impact of the collapse of the August putsch was not as far-reaching as the Cultural Revolution's, it did serve to discredit those in the party and government leadership who opposed the reforms. However, taking advantage of Yeltsin's inaction, the Russian bureaucracy rallied and, under the crafty leadership of Ruslan Khasbulatov, began to thwart most of Yeltsin's subsequent reform efforts. The April 1993 referendum provided Yeltsin with a second chance, as did his closing of the Parliament in September 1993 and the vote for the new constitution in December 1993. But whereas in August 1991 Yeltsin was the undisputed hero, after September and the bloody shelling of the White House in October 1993 he had the power but not the same moral authority he had enjoyed in the earlier, much less controversial period. It is likely that he will never regain the power to act that he had at his disposal but failed to use in August 1991.

III

Probably the biggest difference between Russian and Chinese reforms came in agriculture. By 1982 the bulk of China's peasants were farming for themselves, in what was first called the contract or family responsibility system. There were other, equally important differences.

While some Chinese peasants were escaping the communes, others began to set out on their own as traders and artisans. Nudged in part by local Communist Party officials eager to increase tax revenues from nonagricultural economic activities, a growing number of peasants began to expand their handicraft household efforts into small manufacturing shops.[23] Before long, manufacturing became more important in some villages than agriculture. Some Chinese villages I have visited prided themselves on how high labor productivity had become in agriculture, something that most economists would not have expected to see in a land with over 1.1 billion people. In this way they could free up more labor for work in manufacturing. Nothing comparable happened under Yeltsin.

A similar movement away from total dependence on employment within the state sector occurred in China's cities. Almost overnight urban residents began to hawk food and other consumer goods and services on street corners, in stalls, and eventually in little shops. The pace was breathtaking. During my initial visit to China, from December 1979 to January 1980, I could see that the first private traders had already begun to appear timidly on the streets, primarily in regions outside of Beijing. The number of vendors on the corner, particularly peasants selling their crops, had increased significantly by the time I next visited, two and a half years later. By then some cadre members had regrouped and begun to express their resentment over what they saw as their loss of privilege and status. For the first time ordinary people, especially those with money, were able to buy goods previously available only to those with government *guangxi*, or connections.

In 1984 my wife and I encountered our first private store in the streets of Beijing. So impressed were we by what we saw that we wrote an article for the *New York Times* about how private business had come to Goldfish Lane in Beijing. Upon our return to Beijing two years later, we immediately went back to Goldfish Lane to see what had changed. The street was now filled with half a dozen or so shops, and our old friends were doing even better than before. They explained that someone had described their new venture in the *New York Times* and that in the wake of that article a flood of American visitors had come and bought up whatever they could find. When we returned in 1988, our shop had disappeared. After a good deal of searching, we discovered that it had been relocated on a neighboring street, while the narrow alley that had been Goldfish Lane had also disappeared. In its place was a spacious avenue flanked on either side by two luxury thirty-story hotel and office buildings.

As to private enterprise, the big difference between Gorbachev's and Deng Xiaoping's moves to the market was that Deng Xiaoping did not limit entry. Equally important, he seemed to have a better understanding of what the purpose of economic reform should be. By saying publicly that it is good to enrich yourself and that cat color is not important but catching mice is, Deng acknowledged that the goal of economic reform was to make people's daily lives better. What was the point of an ideology that talked about equality but ignored the consumer? Poorer but purer was no longer a desirable goal.

IV

Once the Chinese reform process was set in motion, economic conditions improved rapidly. Given the chance to enjoy the results of their work, the Chinese peasants quickly found ways to increase their output. They also learned that they could usually eliminate occasional cadre obstruction by co-opting party officials. When necessary the cadres were assigned the better plots of land or equipment like trucks or small tractors. It also helped that the unleashing of the peasants coincided with the widespread creation of new private services. Like mosquitoes after a wet spring, the private entrepreneurs swarmed all over the countryside, eager to transport and sell newly produced goods. The explosion in the number of independent farmers and private traders and artisans made it difficult for a mafia-like operation to exert widespread control. Remnants of some of the old triads or gangs did survive and new ones emerged, but overwhelmed by the numbers of sellers and quantities of foods produced, they were unable to achieve an inhibition of general retailing activities or production in any way comparable to the Russian mafia's.

The rapidity of this new growth was very important for other reasons as well. Deng had the good sense in the early days of the reform to divert extra consumer goods to the countryside. This was done to reassure the peasants that they had something to gain for all their new hard work. That policy reinforced the peasants' willingness to support the new reforms.

This rapid growth in agricultural output and the private sector more than compensated for the inevitable slowdown that occurred in China's state military and civilian industrial sector. China's leaders recognized that they had to show immediate results in order to sustain support for the reforms. This recognition evidently eluded the Russian leaders. To Gaidar and most of his Russian and foreign advisers, a successful reform meant curbing the money supply and credit, restructuring state industry, and closing down much of the heavy and munitions industries. Consequently, when Russian industrial production fell by 20 percent in early 1992, Gaidar was convinced that the drop in production (which also included a decline in consumer goods production) was, if anything, a sign that the reforms were taking hold.[24] He explained, "So far, there has not been a single post communist country that has undergone stabilization of the economy and the launching of market mechanisms without a recession of at least twenty percent."[25] Earlier Ed Hewett, an

American economist, made the same point: "We will have to disregard longheld notions of what constitutes 'good' or 'bad' news for the Soviet economy. Typically we have regarded slow growth . . . as signs of trouble. They can mean that, but over the next few years they may also be a sign of success. . . . A successful economic reform will involve considerable pain now."[26] But this was a misunderstanding of what should have taken place. While such cutbacks in production were undoubtedly necessary, particularly in the munitions industry, Gaidar and his team failed to see that they had to be more than offset by a higher output of consumer goods. Increased production of consumer goods in China not only helped provide jobs but also demonstrated to consumers that reform could improve the quality of their lives. As we just noted, by 1993 more than 50 percent of China's industrial output was being produced by the nonstate sector.[27] This is particularly impressive because industrial production in the nonstate sector was as little as 15 percent in the early 1980s.[28] In some ways it was less costly economically and certainly politically to keep the workers in state enterprises on the job, even if they did nothing, than to throw them out into the street.

Some would argue that because the state dominates a much larger proportion of the economy in Russia than it did in China, it is unrealistic to expect such compensating growth in Russia. Its growth would probably take a form different from China's. Nevertheless, the Russians could have followed China's example in encouraging the opening of brand-new or green-field businesses and farms in both the cities and the villages. In 1992, for example, 1.25 million new firms opened in China, an increase of 26 percent over the rate in 1991.[29] The opening of new businesses and enterprises is where most of China's growth has come from. Hardly any growth has so far come from the privatization of the state sector.

V

After some initial ambivalence the Chinese began to accept foreign investment. Beginning in 1987, when Gorbachev authorized the creation of joint ventures and also began to contemplate the formation of special economic zones, the Soviets appeared ready to react the same way. But whereas the Chinese moved ahead and actively sought out foreign investment in the first year of their reform, the Soviets, and particularly the Russians, had mixed reactions to the idea of foreign investment in their domestic economy. In the earlier Mao era, the Chinese attitude toward foreign interaction and investment was also hostile, a legacy of long-standing Chinese xenophobia, which continued under Mao. Until the mid-1970s foreign businessmen, for example, were seldom allowed beyond the Canton trade fair. Even then not everyone was allowed into Canton. Under Deng, however, the atmosphere changed, though joint ventures were at first closely monitored. The emphasis was to be on exports, not on sales by joint ventures in the domestic market. Because of such controls and restrictions, there were for several years only a few joint ventures, and not many of these made money. Between 1979 and 1982 only 83 joint ventures were registered, and 107 were established in 1983.[30] The big increase began in 1984, when 741 were formed. It was about then that the joint ventures run by overseas Chinese, particularly those from Hong Kong, started to make money on a regular basis. Soon thereafter many non-Chinese joint ventures also began to prosper. The special economic zones that were set up in several coastal areas became especially attractive for foreign investors, and increasing numbers of foreign investors began to establish wholly owned subsidiaries as well. Thanks to the profits that were being made, the number of new joint ventures opened in 1985 doubled and continued to grow until the June 4, 1989, crackdown in Tiananmen Square.[31] However, interest increased again in 1991, when 8,395 joint ventures were registered, and the numbers kept on rising in 1992 and 1993.[32]

It would be misleading to suggest that everyone in China welcomed foreign investors. Like Russia's, some of China's senior leaders were reluctant to open their country to foreign involvement. Visits to the special economic zones reduced some of them to tears of bitterness—to them it seemed that China was again permitting the kind of hated foreign coastal concessions that had so disgraced and humiliated prerevolutionary China. As in Russia, there was opposition that took the form of bureaucratic arbitrariness and harassment. There were also managerial and labor problems. On occasion U.S. businesses, such as the AMC jeep project in Beijing, even had to call in not only the U.S. ambassador for help in dealing with unyielding Chinese officials but the U.S. secretary of state as well.[33] Nonetheless, with Deng Xiaoping's affirmation of support for foreign investment, the investment process has continued and become regularized with less interference from senior officials. Before long, manufacturers in Hong Kong and thereafter Taiwan and even South Korea began to transfer their operations to China to take advantage of the cheap labor and welcoming environment. In 1992, foreigners committed themselves to investing $68.5 billion in China, a more than fivefold increase over 1991. It was anticipated the figure would rise again in 1993, to $80 billion.[34] Given its cheap raw materials and labor, Russia could be equally attractive to West European manufacturers. But more than cheap labor is needed. There also has to be an assurance of state order and an operating economic infrastructure. That will be some time in coming.

Without doubt foreign, especially overseas, Chinese financial, technological, and managerial transfer has been very important for China. The impact has contributed to the high rate of industrial growth as well as to the stunning increase of Chinese exports. The value of China's exports rose from $40 billion in 1987 to over $80 billion in 1992. China's bilateral trade surplus with the United States, which was about $20 billion in 1993, is now second in size only to Japan's.[35] Yet the role of foreign investment must be kept in perspective. According to Deng Furong, foreign investment constitutes only 2 percent of the country's total investment. This should be remembered by those who lament the absence of a loyal group of overseas Russians willing to invest in Russia.

The investment climate in the Soviet Union and Russia was very different. When Russian joint ventures were authorized in 1987, the initial response was also modest. Gradually, more and more foreigners came in search of investment, but as the foreign partners found themselves confronted with more and more obstacles, their enthusiasm soon waned. Some Soviet bureaucrats seemed to fear that some of the joint ventures would actually make money.[36] They were worried they would be accused of selling out their country. In other instances there were openly expressed fears that Western competitors would drive locally owned enterprises out of business. That was the rationale for the November 1993 decision to ban Western bankers from taking deposits from Russians. Western bankers were disturbed by the decision, because it contradicted an earlier treaty commitment made by the Russian government that allowed Western banks to serve Russian customers. Moreover, several banks, including Citibank and Chase Manhattan, had obtained official authorization to open such accounts only weeks before the Yeltsin government announced it had changed its mind. However, Russian bankers had demanded that they be given more time to learn how to compete. They were afraid that if foreign banks were allowed in, the Russian banks would lose their best customers. Eager to win the support of the Russian bankers in the December 12, 1993, election for parliament, the leaders of the government, especially Yegor Gaidar, who had organized his own political party, reversed the government's earlier decision. Such a sign of protectionism, even though later it was partially reversed, inevitably discourages Western investors.

The best way to attract investment would have been to encourage some visible, profitable demonstration projects, much as the Chinese did. Creating a successful model would have attracted other investors to Russia and encouraged other joint ventures in their struggles with a bureaucracy bred in the belief that joint ventures were to be hampered, not helped. The ultimate success of the Beijing Jeep–American Motors joint venture served this purpose in China. "Desperate to attract foreign investment, China could not afford a 'model' failure."[37] While top leaders such as Gorbachev and Yeltsin were often helpful intermediaries, local Russian bureaucrats seemed to vie with one another to erect trade barriers, raise taxes, complicate banking and foreign-exchange relationships, frustrate the search for offices, apartments, phones, and office equipment, hamper access to factory site locations, and demand bribes. The Soviets and the Russians also promised to establish special economic zones. One or two have been agreed to, at least on paper, but Russia, unlike China, has few that are operating.

The initial investors in China and in Russia were attracted by the idea of gaining access to giant untapped markets. In contrast both the Chinese and the Russians wanted investors who were going to manufacture for export. Ultimately, that suited foreign investors in China, especially when they came to appreciate that not only was Chinese labor cheap, but after a few years of exposure to noncommunist ways and material incentives, Chinese workers could regain their productive work habits. In contrast the Russian work force, while cheap, is not suited to the type of labor-intensive work done in China. The Russians have come to think of themselves as more suited for a capital-intensive work style that stresses heavy industry and machinery, not hand labor. Foreign investors in Russia eventually became interested in exports—but of raw material, not labor-intensive products. But exports of raw materials raised the fears among Russians, particularly the nationalists, that they would be exploited by foreigners. Reflecting that paranoia, Russian authorities in June 1993 refused to allow any joint venture to ship petroleum through Russian pipelines to the outside world. This decision, though soon rescinded, was costly not only to the joint ventures but to the reformist faction of the Russian government seeking to attract more investment. Frustrated by recurrent battles of this sort, a growing number of potential investors, particularly in the energy field, have begun to redirect their investments away from Russia to its neighbors, above all Kazakhstan, which has tried to be accommodating, not off-putting, to investors.

VI

What lessons does the Chinese case hold for Yeltsin and his team of reformers? The Chinese experience demonstrates that shock therapy is not the only way to proceed. To the shock therapists who warn that step-by-step, gradual economic reform is like crossing an abyss in two leaps, the Chinese gradualists respond that economic reform should be like crossing a river by feeling for one rock at a time.[38]

This battle of analogies can be misleading. As we will discuss in the concluding chapter, there clearly are some reform measures that because of their intractability must be addressed together and immediately. At the same time other measures, particularly those involving the creation of new institutions, can and should evolve gradually and, indeed, must be carried out simultaneously with a variety of fiscal and monetary measures.

It would have been much better for Russia if such measures had been adopted in the early years of the Gorbachev era, but some can still be undertaken. Thus although Yeltsin's October 1993 decree allowing the peasants to form their own private farms deserves praise, the odds are that implementation of this reform will take years. Committees will have to be set up to judge who will get the richest land, and their arguments are likely to drag on for many months if not years. The Russian leaders would be better advised to set private farming in motion at once by also announcing that, as an interim measure, every peasant may double the size of his garden plot. There would be less room for bureaucratic obstruction this way, because the peasants have been allowed to have their own gardens for decades, and those garden plots have been expanded and reduced before. Even Stalin ordered them expanded during World War II. Given this precedent, the leaders should wait six months and then announce that the peasants may double the size of their gardens again. The result could be a very quick payoff of more fruit, vegetables, and meat in the markets. Yeltsin should also suspend the requirement that new businesses seek licenses from government regulators. As in China, those who open businesses should be required to do no more than get a license and pay a small registration fee at a local government office.[39] Special encouragement for new-business development should also be provided even if, despite Prime Minister Chernomyrdin's protestations, Russia becomes one vast bazaar. As an economist at the Institute of Economics at the Chinese Academy of Social Science put it, "If Deng Xiaoping had reacted like Chernomyrdin, China would not have grown either." By all means continue privatization of state industry, but the most promising growth will eventually come from green-field or new start-ups.

Designing a new policy for foreign investment will probably prove more difficult, primarily because the Russians are split over whether their country should remain inward looking or have closer economic relations with the West. It may still be possible to depend solely on domestic resources, but it becomes harder and harder to do that in an age of rapidly moving technology. Even the Japanese found they could not do without foreign help. While they restricted the amount of foreign investment, they nonetheless relied heavily on foreign patent licenses. Because Russia's capital and technology needs are so enormous, it is unrealistic to expect Russia to reenter the world economic community solely on the basis of grants, loans, and patents. As China's experience clearly indicates, meaningful growth in the early stages needs foreign investment and technology as well as domestic saving and investment, not capital flight.

In China as the annual economic growth rate began to reach the double-digit range, bureaucratic obstructionism became less and less of a problem. It has not disappeared completely, and probably never will, but government interference is much easier to deal with when opportunities in the nonstate sector become attractive and ubiquitous. There are numerous instances in both China and Russia of former agents of the security forces and the KGB who have established themselves in their own businesses. Typically, they operate as representatives of what at one time were state enterprises that dealt with foreign entities.[40] At that point it often appears that everyone can make money, and thus relatively few choose to be left behind and defend what have since become discredited values and restraints.[41] My son discovered in 1988 that his elite students in the Beijing Foreign Service Institute, the future foreign-service officers of China, had become so attracted by the opportunities that had been opened for international business that the majority switched from diplomatic service and went into business.

As China's new entrepreneurs continue to grow in numbers and become increasingly independent of the state for their jobs and well-being, this middle class has the potential for forming a core that is essential for the building of any viable democratic society. If that happens, the economic reforms will have set in motion political reforms much as they have done elsewhere in East Asia. It would obviously be better if economic and political reform occurred simultaneously. The developments in Poland suggest that this is not impossible. In Russia, by contrast, the Gorbachev-initiated effort at political reform preceded meaningful economic reforms. As a consequence Russia still lacks the base of an economically independent middle class that a viable and durable democracy must ultimately have.

10.

Economic Aid: Great Expectations–Massive Disappointments

The Grand Bargain (see Chapter 4) was just the first of many efforts by the West to help the countries of the former Soviet Union in their struggle to democratize and switch to a market system. In almost each case, Western leaders have been quick to pay lip service to the idea of providing sizable quantities of financial help, but slow to appropriate the actual funds. And when finally pressured into coming up with the funds, they are unsure about how such aid should be used and for what purpose. The resulting flow of financial and technical support has been considerably more meager than the Russians were led to believe it would be. Inevitably, this has caused mutual recrimination not only between Western and Russian government officials but within the ranks of Western advisers. Similar quarrels have divided Russian economists, some of whom feel Russia is not ready to absorb large quantities of aid.[1]

Central to any effort to provide Russia with meaningful economic aid is the enormity of the region's aid requirements. Russia is a large country, and its infrastructure and capital stock are outdated and inappropriately conceived. A substantial portion of the industrial sector of the former Soviet Union is inadvertently engaged in value subtracting, not value adding. Wastefulness permeates the whole system. Many factories would be better off simply reshipping the raw material components they expect to use rather than trying to process them. Nor is it easy to remedy this problem. Because it is a systemic defect, a legacy of the central-planning system, it cannot be solved merely by importing a modern piece of equipment. Take the simple case of Russian wrapping paper, which is coarse and dull. Even if new papermaking machinery is imported, the procedures used in packing and shipping the paper remain crude. Rolls of paper tend to arrive crushed. Thus much more than equipment is needed to manufacture the paper. New inks and dyes also require new machinery and shipping procedures. Other societies have managed to make such "whole system" transformations, but it cannot be done easily or quickly. Although until 1989 East Germany was the most industrially advanced East European country, West Germany has had to spend over $100 billion a year in private investment and state aid to rehabilitate the region's industry and try to bring it up to international standards. So far there is still relatively little to show for West Germany's massive aid.

If $100 billion a year seems inadequate for the former East Germany, a country of 17 million, imagine how much more will be needed for Russia and its 147 million people. One thing seems clear: government-to-government aid alone or even government aid as the predominant form of support will not do the job. Private investment, both domestic and foreign, is also needed. The Marshall Plan was significant not only because it provided American government financial support but also because it enabled the Europeans themselves to put their economic houses in order and establish priorities. This in turn attracted foreign and domestic investment. Private investment also made the difference in Germany and Japan after World War II and, to a degree, in Poland, Hungary, and China. Since private investment is usually more closely monitored, it can provide more of an economic stimulus than government-to-government lending can.

I

Private investors can be very demanding. They want a good return on their money, and they want to be sure that their assets are protected and usually redeemable. Having worked with several corporations seeking to invest in the former communist world, I can attest that the decision of whether or not to invest is made in much the same way, regardless of the nature of the corporation. The decisions are very much influenced by macro conditions—a stable government, legal procedures (both civil and commercial), controlled inflation, a customer base, and adequate disposable incomes. At the same time, however, a corporation's investments (very much a micro matter) are determined by individual executives. They ask whether there is a large cheap and adept work force, as well as raw materials, industrial components, adequate highway network, communications infrastructure, and accessible and easy border crossings. Some investors will accept something less than all these conditions, but almost always they want to be sure that, at the very least, the trend is toward meeting these criteria, not backing away from them.

There are two quite different reasons for investing in the former communist world: for their cheap labor in order to manufacture and for their new markets in order to sell. Those interested in Eastern Europe and China are looking first of all for cheap labor. As we have seen, low-wage countries like Hungary, Poland, the Czech Republic, and Slovakia, with their wage rates of two to three dollars or so an hour for skilled machinists, have become extraordinarily attractive when compared to Germany, with its rate of twenty-two dollars or more an hour. The interest is particularly keen when major suppliers are under enormous pressure from customers like General Motors to lower their costs.[2] In fact, one reason why East Germany is lagging behind Poland and Hungary in its recovery is that East German labor costs are approximately fifteen dollars an hour.[3] At those rates East Germany holds relatively little attraction for Western manufacturers. Japan is drawn to China for much the same reason.

Japan Air Lines, for example, has found that plane maintenance in China costs one-tenth as much as similar operations in Japan. Transferring aircraft maintenance to China is an attractive way to reduce costs for an airline that is losing five hundred million dollars a year.[4] Even though Russian wage rates are also very low, few Western manufacturers of machinery are interested in Russia because of its low wage costs. High-tech firms have hired Russian scientists and engineers, but usually for software research, more than hardware manufacturing. The strong support expressed for the neo-fascist Vladimir Zhirinovsky in the December 1993 election suggests that Russia lacks the stability foreign investors seek. Conditions are just too chaotic for foreigners to manufacture and transport complicated products.

Offsetting Eastern Europe's lower labor costs is its lower labor productivity, a communist legacy. Nevertheless, the lower labor costs still make the former Soviet bloc countries attractive. To lure investors it is thus essential to keep the wage rate low. Yet these low-wage rates are fodder for nationalists as well as communists who decry what they see as Western capitalist exploitation of the local labor force. A solution in Poland, Hungary, the former Czechoslovakia, and Russia is to increase labor productivity faster than wages.

While manufacturers of industrial components focus on finding cheap labor, manufacturers of consumer goods also look for larger bases of customers with disposable income. In addition to offering a cheap adept work force, China has become increasingly attractive because of its market potential. The prospect of millions of new customers has also attracted consumer goods companies such as cigarette manufacturers, soap producers, and food suppliers to Russia.

II

This background makes it clear that to the goal of helping these countries stabilize their political structures and economies and build their infrastructures must be added the goal of facilitating the opening of new private businesses and farms. Under George Bush the United States established half a dozen Enterprise Funds in Poland, Hungary, Bulgaria, the Czech Republic, and Slovakia to assist in financing new local businesses.[5] The British established a counterpart, called a "Know How" fund. The operating approach of these funds is to be responsive and nonbureaucratic. In Poland, for example, the U.S.-Polish Enterprise Fund provided over a thousand small-business loans in a two-year period. President Bill Clinton has established a similar Russian-American Enterprise Fund, under the chairmanship of Gerald Corrigan, the former president of the New York Federal Reserve Bank, and requested $300 million to finance new ventures and businessmen unable to obtain sufficient internal funding. This fund is charged with facilitating the creation of new businesses and is not intended for the privatization of already existing enterprises. Toward the same end, the United States should also establish a Farm Fund and a Marketing Fund to foster the formation of a private core of essential economic institutions.

While the overall effort has been very effective, some abuses have led to criticism of the Hungarian-American Enterprise Fund. Critics have pointed to the Hungarian fund's willingness to pay excessively high salaries. Some of these salaries went to American executives with political connections to high-ranking Republicans, including former President Ronald Reagan. This creates the impression that such funds are a form of patronage for American politicians.[6] These abuses vindicate those who advocate more regulation. More regulation might reduce the abuses, but it would also eliminate the ability of such funds to move quickly and responsively to the needs of the prospective businessmen and businesswomen in Eastern Europe.

An effort has also been made to combine U.S. government funding with private management and incentives to stimulate not only new private businesses in Russia and Eastern Europe but American private investment as well. On September 2, 1993, the U.S. government announced an unusual type of private-public venture capital investment.[7] This $100 million Russian Country Fund is to be managed by Paine Webber Incorporated, with $25 million to be supplied by the Russian government and $50 million of that amount to be guaranteed by the Overseas Private Investment Corporation (OPIC), a federal agency.[8] Paine Webber seeks to invest this fund in Russian enterprises, particularly in the high-tech and energy areas, more or less in the way venture capital funds are invested in the United States. Morgan Stanley, Solomon Brothers, and CS First Boston have similar initiatives. At the same time OPIC has agreed to provide an additional $28 million of loan guarantees for Texaco for a project to develop Russian oil fields. The OPIC guarantee is meant to protect Texaco in case a new Russian government decides to nationalize foreign investment. OPIC has also agreed to underwrite a somewhat similar effort by Du Pont and its subsidiary Conoco to develop Russia's energy resources. By providing such guarantees against political interference, OPIC hopes to encourage other American investors as well.

During the last years of the Gorbachev era, the Batterymarch Financial Management, under the leadership of Dean LeBaron, also tried to seek out potential investment. LeBaron sought to utilize some of the research talent employed in military enterprises in Leningrad and to direct this know-how into commercial ventures. His initial goal was to raise one billion dollars to underwrite such efforts. He eventually obtained commitments of several hundred million dollars, but his Leningrad counterparts were unable to establish enterprises that could show profits. He therefore abandoned his effort, although some of the projects he had been considering did eventually develop commercially viable products.[9] George Yurchyshyn, a former vice president for the Bank of Boston, organized a similar venture, the Ukraine Fund, to invest in small- and medium-size private businesses in Ukraine. Such efforts have the potential of producing significant profits, but in the short run they entail enormous risks. That is why OPIC underwriting (paid for by the U.S. taxpayer) can be very helpful.

The U.S. government has also taken the lead in seeking to assist the privatization of state industries. Prior to the July 1993 Group of Seven meeting, in Tokyo, the United States sought to put together a four-billion-dollar fund for that purpose. But the Japanese in particular protested against such a large sum. Indeed, given an exchange rate of one thousand rubles to the dollar, it would have been hard to find viable projects that could profitably absorb such large sums of money. In the end the G-7 agreed to contribute three billion dollars, but even that seems excessive. There were more than enough state enterprises willing to accept the money; the problem was that many of them were inherently unprofitable. And there is the danger that many enterprises will be privatized by their former managers but will continue to operate much as they did when the same managers were state employees.[10] American aid should not be used to prop up the old apparatchiks and the old system.

In addition to helping start new businesses, Western funding to Russia should be used to help build the infrastructure that attracted foreign investors to Eastern Europe. It should encourage the World Bank to assist in the building of communications and the training of banking, managerial, and business personnel. Because of its political importance, the Russian military should be supported in its efforts to demobilize. That entails funding the construction of civilian apartments and job training. Toward the same end the advanced industrial nations could also help the Russians establish a version of the GI Bill of Rights program, with its support for mortgages, college education, and veterans' benefits.

None of this will be easy, because it means finding Russian entrepreneurs willing to take on completely new and difficult challenges. Moreover, it risks interfering unduly in Russian internal affairs. Many apparatchiks see such initiatives as a threat to their own status and power.

There is also the prospect that a significant share of the funding might not reach Russia. The Agency for International Development (AID), our main aid-dispensing agency, has adopted the traditional approach to these new government initiatives. The administrator of AID, J. Brian Atwood, in testimony before the U.S. Senate, even boasts that to reduce the risk of a misuse of funds, "no dollar and virtually no commodities are provided directly to Russian entities." That is why AID relies so heavily on consultants or what are called the Beltway bandits. These private research institutes and consultants earn their way by preparing studies of what should be or has been done. As the U.S. government undertakes to spend hundreds of millions of dollars on Russia, the Beltway bandits have begun to vie for this new flow of funds. Although many of these firms specialize in domestic American concerns or arms control, the vast majority have virtually no experience with Eastern Europe, the Soviet Union, or communism. But they are good at preparing and submitting proposals and rounding up relevant consultants.

An example of their procedures can be seen in AID's effort to deal with Russia's very serious environmental problems. In the traditional pattern AID sent out "requests for proposals." Attracted by the tens of millions of dollars being offered by AID, at least four different groups have called the Russian Research Center at Harvard looking for experts on the Russian environment. A substantial portion (sometimes the bulk) of such funding will therefore go to underwriting reports on the environment rather than to allocating those funds for equipment and procedures that would deal directly with Russia's environmental crisis. Andrei Nechayev, the minister of the economy, complained during a spring 1992 visit to Harvard, "The Russians are paying for these stacks of worthless pages," which do nothing to solve his country's problems. The U.S. government would not need to turn to these Beltway bidders if the Russians themselves had worked out a careful plan for the use of the aid, as the West Europeans did during the Marshall Plan era. Knowing how they wanted to spend the money, the West Europeans spared the U.S. government the need to come up with ways to do so.

In the early months of the Gaidar administration, many Western economic advisers lobbied earnestly for what came to be called the "ruble stabilization fund." Patterned after the "zloty stabilization fund" in Poland, the proposed $6 billion ruble fund was intended to support the ruble exchange rate with hard currency. The fact that $1 billion from the world financial community was available in Poland to prop up the zloty helped prevent fluctuations in the zloty exchange rate and facilitated exports and imports. It provided a sense that the zloty was worth buying and holding. But a zloty or a ruble stabilization fund can work to discourage speculation only when there is an infrastructure that can put the currency to use. The zloty fund in Poland succeeded because the Poles had a private sector, however modest, ready and able to respond to internal as well as export opportunities. The Russians had no such sector. Russia's industrial monopolies were not adequately equipped to respond to domestic markets, let alone sell to foreign markets. A ruble stabilization fund will work only if the country has a dormant hard-currency-earning capacity ready to generate a more systematic flow of *valuta*. Russia did not have such a capacity in early 1992, when some of its most outspoken Western advocates were pressuring the IMF to provide such support.[11]

While foreign economic support of Russia is essential if the reforms are to succeed, those who favor foreign aid should also understand that, to the extent that foreign aid is used successfully, it may ultimately cost American jobs in specific economic sectors. If the American aid, for example, leads Russian farmers to increase their grain harvest, it might mean smaller exports of wheat to Russia. A similar result might occur if the Russians increased their exports of raw materials and machinery. Russians and East Europeans have already encountered fierce protectionism in Western Europe. Trade barriers have been erected, in particular, against East European and Russian sales of aluminum, steel, and agricultural products. Although overall the West Europeans in 1993 enjoyed a substantial trade surplus with Russia, the Common Market authorities sought to force Russia to shrink its exports of aluminum to less than 20 percent of 1992 levels.[12]

III

Not all the resistance to increased trade between Russia and the West comes from the West. Some Russians are equally, if not more, critical of various aspects of foreign trade. Much of the opposition reflects historical xenophobia made worse by the fact that many Russians are deeply hurt by Russia's unexpected and sudden decline as a superpower. The post-1991 surge of imported foreign consumer goods has no doubt adversely affected Russian producers. That explains the promises of higher tariffs and reduced grain imports made before the December 1993 elections for parliament.[13] The tariffs were introduced in March 1994, although their implementation was delayed to July 1994. Some of the more outspoken critics of the reform process like Vladimir Zhirinovsky feel that Gorbachev and Yeltsin are merely stooges of the West. Why else would they have allowed the collapse of the Soviet Union and Russian military and economic might? Such critics have seen the reforms as a devious plot to grab control of Russia's raw material wealth, and their views account in part for the appearance of "Yankee get out of Russia" graffiti which began to appear in 1994. These sentiments are not just the ravings of xenophobic fanatics. In early 1992 Georgi Matyukhin, the chairman of the Central Bank, criticized the move to ruble convertibility and opening the Russian economy to foreigners. He feared that the falling value of the ruble would eventually "allow our whole republic to be bought for a dollar."[14]

Yeltsin has at times resisted IMF conditions for support. In April 1992 when the IMF spelled out some particularly onerous requirements for foreign financial support, Yeltsin responded, "We do not intend to work under the direct orders of the IMF. We do not agree completely with the organization's viewpoint and we will stick to our point of view."[15] Many others have raised equally, if not more, strong protests.[16]

As potential recipients of aid in other countries have discovered, IMF terms can be harsh and demanding. There doubtless is some justification for Yeltsin's complaints. At the same time it would be a mistake to be too lax. Given the importance of seeing the Russian reforms succeed, G-7 leaders have put enormous political pressure on the world's lending organizations to relax their credit standards in order to accommodate the Russians and start the flow of funding. Giving in, the IMF has created what it calls a "systemic transformation facility" (STF).[17] Under these terms, it has put aside $3 billion for the Russians, $1.5 billion of which has already been delivered. Countries formerly a part of the Soviet Union can qualify for this money merely by "demonstrating a credible reform strategy." This means establishing strict limits on central-bank credit creation, letting interest rates rise, reducing subsidies, and establishing a budget that will hold down inflation.

At least three problems arise from such a special arrangement. The wrong message is transmitted when the Russians come to perceive that credit terms can be stretched. Given that they already tend to treat credit obligations lightly, there is a danger that they will not learn how important such obligations are and that capital flight will continue. There is also a strong likelihood that, once such concessions have been made, some Western advisers will seek to obtain even more concessions—after all, since an exception was made once, why can't it be made again? A problem here is that some Western advisers have come to act more as advocates than as analysts. Finally, other debtor nations of the world will come to wonder why they are not entitled to similar concessions. This could put the whole international lending effort at risk. For that reason some new organizations should be created just for the purpose of providing Russia aid with fewer or no strings attached. To use the IMF for this purpose undercuts the IMF's credibility in its work elsewhere in the world.

IV

With or without international or foreign government credits and guarantees, those making investments in Russia should be aware that there is an erratic quality to doing business in Russia. Whereas in the Soviet period contracts were difficult to negotiate but, once agreed to, rigidly enforced, in the postcommunist era they are often broken. Taxes are raised and lowered. Commitments are agreed to, but the bills are not paid. In one case a private Swiss firm ended up with an overdue Russian debt of $250 million. Philip Morris claims it is owed $78 million by the Russian government. Government debts are treated no better. The Russians defaulted on more than $1 billion of American loans extended for grain sales. Japan and Germany have had to deal with similar defaults. The Russians asked the Koreans whether they could repay their $1.5 billion debt with a shipment of military weapons.[18] Overall, Russia in 1993 was in arrears $70 billion of foreign debt.

Yet, because it is potentially such a rich market and source of raw materials, foreign firms keep seeking a niche for themselves. Some are able to sell consumer goods in hard-currency shops; others try to open their own outlets or buy their own buildings. Yet even here there is uncertainty. Ostensible owners or lessees of a piece of land or building have repeatedly been evicted, usually by municipal authorities. Those affected included foreigners and Russians. This often happens when there is a change of mayors and the new mayor accuses the old one of corruption and proceeds to invalidate many existing agreements. In June 1994 Mayor Luzhkov of Moscow decreed that all property belonged to the city and that the Ministry of State Property had no right to sell it. Even the Ministry of State Property canceled one of its contracts and sought to regain control of one of its buildings. This is the same organization entrusted with creating the new sense of ownership and appreciation for private property.[19]

The Russians have not yet created user-friendly conditions for foreign firms. Western joint venture partners often face all the disadvantages of having to operate like a Russian entity while paying the higher tax and fees a wholly owned Western firm must pay. Moreover, the managing Russian partners of a joint venture frequently demand a Mercedes, a fancy apartment, and special privileges for friends. The Russian manager of the joint venture Alphagraphics provided printing services at no charge for his personal friends. The American junior partner protested, but to no avail. The accumulated costs of such abuses led Combustion Engineering in the late 1980s to walk away from one of its joint ventures, the first established by an American partner. Petro-Canada of Calgary closed its Moscow office in December 1993 when it encountered similar difficulties.

Some Russian firms do not abide by their agreements with foreign investors. A Japanese partner in a joint venture agreed that the Russian firm would sell within Russia and the Japanese firm would earn its money through exports. The Russian partners, however, could not resist the temptation to export and thereby earn *valuta,* so they violated the agreement and ended up competing with their Japanese partners. The Japanese walked out of the agreement. Similarly, a West Coast American venture capital firm signed what it thought was an "exclusive agreement" to manufacture a new Russian drug for sale in the West. Before long, however, the Russian partners had signed several such "exclusive agreements."

Foreign firms that decide to try their hand at investing in Russia are under enormous pressure to seek as quick a payback on their investment as possible. Given the unstable political and economic conditions and the periodic confrontations between reformers and those opposed to reform, it is not surprising that investors will try to take their money out of the country as fast as possible. This results in a predominance of get-rich-quick schemes, which the Russians tend to view as exploitive. Their preference, understandably enough, is for long-term investors. When they find themselves with the short-term investors, they tend to be suspicious of any involvement with foreign institutions.

By the same token, foreign investors often find themselves disillusioned by what they encounter. It is particularly disarming when someone who appears outwardly the same as his counterpart in Western Europe behaves in a manner that is often very different. Still very much influenced by the behavior encouraged in the days of central planning, most Russians continue to do no more than they are told to do and seldom take the initiative. I never cease to be astounded when the phone rings on an unoccupied desk in an office in Moscow. Even if three or four office workers are sitting at adjacent or even back-to-back desks, they almost never bother to pick up their colleague's phone and take a message. There are usually no answering machines, but if it is not their phone, it is not their business, even if they work for the same enterprise.

As if uninspired work habits, broken contracts, and archaic banking practices were not enough, a particularly troublesome development is the mafia's growing encroachment on the foreign community. Initially, the mafia restricted itself to muscling in on domestically owned businesses. Harassing the foreign community would have meant running up against the KGB. Gradually, however, as central power became weak and ineffectual, the mafia extended its reach to foreign businesses. A Scandinavian supplier of paper equipment, for example, reports that because the mafia controls all trucking in the country (a Russian version of how the Teamsters used to operate in the United States), it could not ship paper-machinery equipment to a Siberian factory without making a payoff. The firm refused to do so and lost the sale. Because containers are broken into, shippers avoid sending containers through the St. Petersburg port. They advise the trucking in of containers from Helsinki and riding shotgun until the final destination has been reached. That sometimes sounds simpler than it actually is. Having decided to open up a market for its cigarettes in Kazakhstan, an American manufacturer arranged for a protective unit of former Russian military personnel to accompany its train full of cigarettes from the port in Lithuania to Almy Ata. Armed guards were stationed on each boxcar. The train ultimately reached its destination but not before the mafia made three attempts with machine guns to raid the train. In another instance French businessmen in Moscow reported that a mafia representative demanded a 20 percent share of the expected gross revenue (not profit) of a new hotel that was about to open. The *Wall Street Journal* reported that an American supplier of communications services in Moscow agreed to turn over 10 percent of the gross revenue from his business, which he believed was the only way to protect his $2 million investment.[20] Those who refuse to pay bribes or accept unwanted partners risk a violent response. The Coca-Cola factory in Moscow, for example, was attacked by a rocket-propelled grenade; the attacker remains unknown.[21] In the fall of 1993 several foreigners were attacked by and some died at the hands of the mafia. With the mafia now controlling 70 to 80 percent of all Russian private business and banking, bribes, protection rackets, and violence have become part of the daily business life in much of Russia, and their targets are increasingly foreigners. One major American company now assigns personnel bodyguards to all its expatriate employees, and at least one major Western company was reported to have relocated its headquarters from Moscow to Vienna, for the safety of its employees' families.

V

Governmental aid and private investment from the West can accomplish only so much. The highest priority should be to reinvigorate once healthy economic endeavors and institutions. It thus makes sense to support oil development work and to revive abandoned oil fields. By utilizing already existing, if deteriorated, pipelines and refining infrastructures, the country could relatively quickly avail itself of a needed source of export earnings. In the same way foreign aid should be used to foster the formation of an institutional network of small shops and distributional facilities. The danger is that a climate of near-anarchy and lawlessness offers no assurance that the resources will be used as intended or, for that matter, even remain inside the country. It complicates the situation even more that many economic advisers insist that reform will begin only when the country's macroeconomic conditions have stabilized. In their view the emphasis should be on providing economic aid to support the ruble and facilitating privatization and the conversion of munitions industries to civilian production. The problem is that there is not enough money or investment interest to address all or even a small portion of those needs. This leads to bitter attacks on and rebuttals by the aid-giving institutions, neither of which do much to advance the reform effort.[22] Even Al Gore, the U.S. vice president, has criticized the IMF. At best, then, economic support from the outside world is likely to be meager and of marginal help to the reform process. The odds are that, even if the West were somehow able to increase its support, it would not have the impact intended until the Russians themselves came around to putting their political, social, and economic house in order. Of course, foreign economic help, even at the margin, is intended to facilitate that process. But too much chaos leaves a real danger that outside aid will not only be ineffective but worsen the situation. The capital flight and the willingness of some Western firms to bribe and corrupt their way into the domestic economy illustrate how good intentions can become counterproductive.

11. The Clash between Economics and History

Russia and, earlier, the Soviet Union have been preoccupied with the travails of far-reaching reform for almost a decade. If it was not clear in 1985 when Gorbachev became general secretary, it is clear today that economic reform has not and will not come easily to Russia. The confluence of history, culture, and communism has created a present-day Russia whose economy differs from that of other countries of the world, even those that were also communist. Reform is not impossible in Russia—in fact, it is already under way—and there has been some progress, but the process is likely to continue to be much slower, more agonizing, and more difficult than elsewhere in the former communist world.

While a review of reform efforts in other countries provides a helpful perspective, future proposals for reform must also take into account Russia's specific history, culture, and institutions. We will now try to combine these two approaches.

I

Specialists have been interested for some time in the best way to help countries extract themselves from economic sloth or chaos and develop their economies. These efforts predate the collapse of the communist movement. Economic revitalization in the Third World was an especially serious concern in the post–World War II era.[1]

A new generation began to concern itself with economic development in the late 1980s. Familiar with the challenges, although not the historical specifics and culture, many of these specialists included Eastern Europe and the countries of the former communist world in their analyses.[2] Most of their remedies for the former communist world differed little, if at all, from their prescriptions for the Third World.

It is probably misleading to divide these analysts into differing schools of thought; good economists usually recognize that there are few if any absolutes in economics. Sooner or later, most economists would agree on a uniform package of reforms. They differ in regard to the pace and sequence. Some, as we have seen, advocate shock therapy; others, such as Ronald McKinnon, Peter Murrell, and János Kornai, advocate gradual reform.[3]

Much as we have, Murrell warns against overreliance on price reform, particularly when there is no free entry. Without competition, price reform, rather than helping, creates "large immediate costs . . . and few immediate benefits." He argues that price reform should come only after new organizations and businesses have been created. Consequently, it is more important to promote reforms that facilitate the formation of new institutions than to begin with price reform. For this reason foreign investment should be directed to fostering such new economic activity. This neo-Schumpeterian approach argues against comprehensive reform and in favor of a "search for sectors in which the process of free entry is least likely to damage established interests." For many of the reasons we have pointed to, Murrell is particularly skeptical about the likelihood of radically revitalizing large industrial enterprises.[4]

McKinnon places more emphasis on macro concerns, especially on the need to reduce the budget deficit of a country undergoing transition. Consequently, he urges cutting expenditures and instituting new tax laws. After addressing the fiscal imbalance, he stresses the need to bring inflation under control. He would do this by introducing positive real interest rates—that is, rates that are higher than the rate of inflation. Only when fiscal restraint is instituted is financial liberalization advisable. McKinnon also argues that newly privatized enterprises should not initially be allowed to borrow from state banks. This policy would reduce the risk of default and the continuing resort to the soft-budget mentality. Instead, he wants new enterprises to rely on self-finance. This he holds is not as difficult as it sounds. Economies newly converted from central planning offer enormous profit opportunities that one can seize by opening small trading and processing ventures. As in China, they require very little capital and are easy to expand. Finally, McKinnon also recommends decontrol of foreign trade. The first step in that process is to adopt a unified exchange rate. Prior to 1990 Russia had several hundred different exchange rates for different kinds of products. Only after exchange rates have been unified can the monopoly of the Ministry of Foreign Trade and the use of quotas be abolished and the right to export and import subject to the payment of tariffs be available to anyone. Because in 1991 Yeltsin's government reversed the order of the reform process by ending the state monopoly before establishing a unified exchange rate, it created chaos in the foreign-trade sector. This reversal by stimulating the export and import of the wrong kind of goods complicated the domestic reform process. To McKinnon the sequence of reforms is crucial: fiscal control before domestic financial reform, and exchange uniformity before deregulation of foreign trade. Decontrolling domestic prices should accompany a freeing of foreign trade—but only after a tightening of fiscal and monetary controls. McKinnon explains that such a sequence is the best way to curb inflation and that a similar scenario underlay the success of the 1948 West German reform.[5]

While clearly preferring a greater role for the private sector, Kornai has accepted the reality that the state cannot be made to disappear with the wave of a magic wand. Because the state has dominated economic matters so thoroughly and for so long, it is not easy to reduce its influence. Rather than sequencing them as

McKinnon recommends, Kornai believes that budget and price reforms, along with currency convertibility, should be carried out first and simultaneously. In addition, because the government is so deeply entrenched, a "huge injection of market forces" is also necessary. Balancing supply and demand, however, will take time. Because it is an "iterative process," new owners and new enterprises feed on each other and cannot be created overnight.[6]

The advocates of shock therapy agree with much of the economic reasoning of the gradualists, but they believe that results will come faster if fiscal, monetary, and price reforms are implemented all at once. Without simultaneous reforms there cannot be meaningful prices. Without meaningful prices resource use will be distorted, and speculators, not producers, will emerge as the chief beneficiaries. Fiscal and monetary reforms will be more effective if the reform is comprehensive, addressing every sector of the economy at the same time.[7] Proponents of shock therapy recognize the upheaval an across-the-board reform produces, but they argue sequential reform is not painless either; it just prolongs the process. It is a choice, therefore, between removing a large bandage with one quick jerk or lifting it bit by bit. One may hurt less than the other, but neither is free of pain.[8]

Those in favor of shock therapy note that in Poland and Russia, the two countries that adopted a variant of it, there was not much choice. Both countries were caught up in a runaway inflation. At the same time, the use of price controls in many state stores all but guaranteed the illegal sale of their goods out the back door. The result was that the shelves of state stores were nearly empty. To prevent political upheaval and disruption and a possible return to authoritarian government, a quick, comprehensive response was necessary.

Still, as we have seen, critical to the success of shock therapy is the existence of a dormant, even undeveloped market infrastructure that can be jolted into action. Without it inflation is likely to grow even faster, and shock therapy may create as many problems as it solves.

II

Designing an economic reform strategy for Russia that produces better results is not easy. Without actually carrying out another strategy, it is unfair to second-guess the prevailing approach in Russia. Nevertheless, Table 11-1 attempts to compare the different reforms we have considered, along with some elements of the gradualist and shock therapy approaches, in an effort to see which measures have worked and which have failed.

Finding and implementing the most effective model of reform was just one of Russia's problems. The country's leaders also had three other important tasks: (1) building a democratic political system and the accompanying infrastructure, (2) shrinking the country's massive military-industrial complex and converting it to civilian production, and (3) containing the ethnic tensions unleashed by the dissolution of the Soviet Union. Taking advantage of the growing chaos in the economy and society, one ethnic group after another began to insist on more autonomy. With the breakup of the Soviet Union, ethnic conflicts intensified even in Russia itself. Thus the Chechens and Tatars in Russia demanded more economic control over their resources and sought independence from Russia, just as in 1991 many of the republics sought independence from the Soviet Union. Any one of these three issues would by itself be enough to debilitate most normal governments. When combined with the effort to implement economic reform, they posed a challenge that was overwhelming.

For Yeltsin and his successors the effort at reform has become more complex because so many of the already attempted reforms have yielded such meager results. Despite six years of reform under Gorbachev and two under Yeltsin, most Russians had by 1994 come to feel that the economy was in a poorer condition than it had been during the communist era. In addition, the Russians can no longer pride themselves on being a world superpower.

The December 1993 protest vote shows that many regarded the move to democratic government and a market economy as

Table 11-1 Conditions prior to Reform

		West Germany	Japan	Hungary	Poland	China	Soviet Union	Russia
Ownership of Business	State			x	x	x	x	x
	Cooperative			x	x			x
	Private	x	x	x	x			x
Ownership of Agriculture	State			x	x	x	x	x
	Cooperative			x	x			
	Large Landlords		x					
	Private	x	x	x	x			
Functioning markets		x	x	x	x			
Political System	Foreign Military Presence	x	x	x	x			
	Authoritarian-Totalitarian					x	x	
	Partial Democracy			x				
	Near Full Democracy	x	x		x			x
Major Ethnic Problems								x

Nature of Reform

		West Germany	Japan	Hungary	Poland	China	Soviet Union	Russia
APPROACH	Shock Therapy	x	x		x			x
	Gradual			x		x	x	
OWNERSHIP OF BUSINESS (after reform)	State			x	x	x	x	x
	Cooperative			x	x	x	x	x
	Private	x	x	x	x	x	x	x
PRIVATIZATION OF STATE ENTERPRISES				x	x	x		x
OPENNESS TO FOREIGN TRADE (after reform)	State			x	•	•	x	x
	Cooperative			x			•	•
	Private	x	x	x	x	x	•	•
FUNCTIONING MARKETS	Extensive	x	x	x	x	x		
	Limited							x
MACRO POLICY	Currency Reform or Devaluation	x			x		•	
	Sharp Budget Cuts	x	x		x			x
WAGE CONTROL					x			
OPENNESS TO FOREIGN TRADE	Restricted						x	
	Partial	x	x	x	x	x		x
CONVERTIBILITY OF CURRENCY	Restricted						x	
	Partial	x	x	x		x		x
	Near Full (noncapital flows)				x			

•Small Amount

wrongheaded. Except for a small number of entrepreneurs who have benefited, we in the West do not fully appreciate that a large number of Russians are very unhappy with the economic reforms. Many wish to reintroduce elements of the old system.[9] Thus while Russian economic reformers and their Western advisers regarded the July 1993 currency reform, which invalidated all pre-1993 money, as a know-nothing act on the part of Viktor Gerashchenko, the head of the Central Bank, and Oleg Lobov and Oleg Soskovets, two conservative deputy prime ministers, Gerashchenko, Lobov, and Soskovets regarded it as an effort on their part to bring sanity to the economy. They saw it as an attempt, as it were, to reach back for elements, if not large portions, of central planning. It certainly was not a random act, never to be repeated again. In their eyes they were patriots trying to restore the grandeur of the former central-planning system. To them it is the reformists who are the deconstructionists, beguiled by an approach that goes against the best interests of their country.

This resistance to change is a part of a centuries old struggle between Westerners and Slavophiles that is likely to continue into the future even if the economic situation should improve. The Slavophiles oppose any policy that ties Russia more closely to the West or leads to a dilution of Russian traditions in favor of Western mores and practices. Their concerns go beyond economic reform, extending to what they see as the clash between the Western way of life and Russian culture, traditions, and spirit. In the mid-nineteenth century Ivan Turgenev described this struggle in his novel *Fathers and Sons.* Present-day Slavophiles, epitomized by Aleksandr Solzhenitsyn, believe in the superiority of the Russian soul and regard Western values as corrupt. They prefer the way of life represented by Russian peasants and the Russian Orthodox church. In contrast Westernizers, like the late Andrei Sakharov, believe that unless Russia shakes off the influence of this Slavophile mentality and desire for isolation from the West, it will be perpetually condemned to technological and industrial backwardness and authoritarian governments. In their eyes Russia's salvation lies in its becoming integrated into the West, economically competitive, and more democratic. The reformers who swept into the government during the Gaidar era embraced the vision and attitudes of the Westernizers.

Given the enormity of the change required in order for the reforms to succeed, it would be easy to accept the argument that Russia is trapped by its history and will never be able to implement the reforms that would mark a break with its past. That would be an incorrect conclusion, but it would also be wrong to assume that the reforms will be completed anytime soon. Because a large portion of the population has lived under authoritarian regimes for so much of its history, resistance to Westernization is deeply imbedded. Thus it is not surprising that Russians feel relatively comfortable with more centralized control, rather than with a freer market economy. This could change, but the very different makeup of the population's political profile brings with it a braking influence on any far-reaching reform.

In terms of its receptivity to change, Russia in some ways resembles Iran. To many of us in the West, the shah's reforms made good sense. We had difficulty understanding why the Iranian public would welcome a return to the traditions of fundamentalists and an Ayatollah Khomeini. In the same way Russia's population responds differently to economic stimuli than do Poles, Hungarians, or Chinese. Given their willingness to tolerate several centuries of czarist rule and decades of totalitarian communist regimes, the vote in December 1993 certainly seems to confirm the impression that a disproportionate number of Russians not only accept but feel comfortable with a more authoritarian form of government than their counterparts in the West would tolerate.

III

The earlier communist destruction of Russia's market economic infrastructure and the difference in attitudes made it inevitable that the reform process would be more prolonged and painful in Russia than elsewhere. Nonetheless, it is possible that a different approach might have been more effective and less painful. At the time Gorbachev began his reforms, in 1985, the Soviet Union was not suffering from hyperinflation and destabilizing budget deficits. Moreover, though the shelves of consumer goods shops were not overloaded, they were not as empty as they were to become by the time Gorbachev left office, in December 1991. At that early date there was at least a possibility that Gorbachev could have followed the Chinese and the Hungarian examples and embarked on a course of gradual reform. Instead of beginning with the intensification and acceleration of machine tool production, he should have launched an effort to build new institutions, especially those that serve consumers, such as new businesses in agriculture, trade, services, and manufacturing. This process should have been as comprehensive as possible. The larger the number of those involved, the more difficult it would have been for a racketeer or mafia group to assert control. The reconstitution of the small-sized manufacturing, agriculture, and service infrastructure destroyed by Stalin should also have been a major priority, particularly if market signals were ever to play a meaningful role.

By all means, Gorbachev or his successors should also have encouraged the privatization of state industries, but not as the main focus of the reform. To privatize Russia's huge structure will take a long time. State-owned industrial dinosaurs such as GAZ and Magnitogorsk were designed for the central-planning era and are ill suited for a market environment. Even after privatization, the bulk of them will continue to be unprofitable. Some may be responsive to the more productive ways of private ownership, some may become joint ventures with the West, but the vast majority are saddled with overstaffing and obsolete equipment. It is hard to see how they can be anything but a drag on the economy even if run as private businesses.

Gorbachev should have paid more attention to fiscal and monetary control. It was during his tenure that a negligible budget deficit reached levels of 10 percent or more of the GNP. He should also have pursued a gradual liberalization of prices. As the experiences of both Hungary and China demonstrate, this is not an easy process to control. In these countries there were retreats and restarts until the process achieved a certain balance between price flexibility and tolerable inflation. It is hard to see how gradual reform, problematic as it might have been, would have produced any more chaos or upheaval than now exists.

IV

After almost six years of Gorbachev's economic mismanagement, it was probably too late, and conditions were too serious for Yeltsin to attempt gradual reform. As we saw, the GNP was down, prices were up, state stores were empty, and the budget deficit was at least 20 percent of the GNP. Almost as much money was printed to finance the budget in 1991 as between 1947 and the end of 1990. In addition the private sector opened up by Gorbachev had come under the control of the mafia.

To their credit, Gaidar and Yeltsin moved quickly to meet this economic crisis. But they and their advisers assumed that they were working in an environment of economic crisis more or less similar to those that sometimes occur in the West. This was a serious error. Certainly, some of the measures just recommended for use by Gorbachev also could have been adopted by Yeltsin, especially the abolition of restraints on the opening of new businesses and farms. Yeltsin should have eliminated virtually any regulation that inhibited the formation of new businesses and farms, including the need for permits and licenses. Anyone wanting to set up his or her own private operation should have been allowed to do so by merely sending in a notice by postcard and paying a minimum registration fee. This would have helped to limit the extortion and graft that eventually proved to be so corrosive. As was noted earlier, several prospective entrepreneurs told me that because of new regulations, taxes, restraints, corruption, and mafia interference, it had by 1993 actually become more difficult to open new businesses than it had been in 1992.[10] Admittedly, the lack of control also led to abuses, unaesthetic scenes, and even public health nuisances, but such matters could have been addressed in time. The main priority in the beginning should have been to stimulate new-business formation as rapidly as possible.

Yeltsin could also have allowed private ownership of land. An increase in agricultural output is impossible without a sense of security. Although private ownership was not introduced in China, long-term leases served much the same purpose. If ideological nostalgia prevented ownership or even leasing, another solution would have been simply to increase the size of each peasant's garden plot. If it was good enough for Stalin in World War II, Yeltsin could have done the same thing. Permitting the buying and selling or leasing of land would have eliminated much of the ambiguity that currently exists. This is true not only for agriculture but also for industry and commerce.

Another missed opportunity of the Yeltsin-Gaidar team was its failure to deal immediately with the money overhang created during the Gorbachev era. They could have shrunk the money supply by instituting something like the 1947 swap of ten old rubles for one new ruble. Former Prime Minister Valentin Pavlov's ill-conceived currency reform of January 1991 and Viktor Gerashchenko's repeat effort in July 1993 have discredited anything associated with currency reform. Pavlov's reforms sought to invalidate only fifty- and one-hundred-ruble notes, and Gerashchenko attempted to eliminate only rubles printed before 1993. Focusing just on special ruble notes angered the people who happened to be holding those notes. In contrast, by calling in all notes regardless of their date of issue, Stalin was in 1947 able to shrink the size of the overall money supply. Those affected the most were holders of large money hoards and deposits. Inevitably, many innocent people also suffered in such a broad effort, but those most deeply affected were wartime speculators and others who had probably earned their money in what at the time was regarded as a dishonest way. The Erhard reform in postwar Germany had much the same positive effect.

If Yeltsin had taken the lead to introduce such across-the-board currency reforms in January 1992 and if he had moved at the same time to balance the budget and curb the printing of new money, he would have had more leeway in addressing some of his other problems. Of course, these are big ifs, but a currency reform would certainly have made the fiscal and monetary tightening easier to implement and helped with several aspects of Yeltsin's overall program. If Yeltsin, for example, had eliminated a substantial portion of the money overhang, his reforms would have had a less negative impact on those with fixed incomes and on retirees. With less money in circulation, prices might not have risen so quickly after they were decontrolled.

A currency reform with less price volatility would have also allowed the authorities to extend price decontrol to more energy products, especially oil. Because energy prices were never fully decontrolled, the domestic price of Russian oil in 1993 rose to only about 30 percent of the world price. Under these circumstances an enormous profit was to be made by smuggling oil out of Russia. Those in charge of issuing the export permits found it hard to resist the temptation to accept a cut for being so helpful.[11] But a currency reform would have resulted in less money in circulation and a lower inflationary potential, and allowing oil prices to rise to world levels would therefore have been less risky. If exorbitant profits could no longer have been made by selling cheap oil at higher world prices, the export permits would automatically have lost most of their value. Thus much of the corruption involved in the issuance of export permits would have been eliminated.

A currency reform might also have led to a more rapid move toward ruble convertibility. While hard-currency auctions brought limited convertibility, fewer rubles in circulation and accompanying efforts to balance the budget would have helped to slow the printing of new rubles, restrained domestic inflation, and halted the fall in the value of the ruble relative to foreign currencies.

The authorities should also have eliminated the currency declaration forms required of all arriving and departing visitors and residents. For reasons that have long since lost their relevance, it continues to be a violation of the law to bring in or take rubles out of the country. But given the fall in the value of the ruble, visitors should have been encouraged to take rubles out of the country. The fewer rubles inside Russia, the better. Similarly, requiring exporters to convert their hard-currency export earnings (especially as much as 50 percent of their gross revenue) into rubles with the Russian state bank was counterproductive. It is the most effective method for discouraging legal exports. Moreover, the export taxes introduced by Gaidar to collect a share of the profits from the export value of raw materials were other disincentives to a legal export trade. In mid-1993 the theoretical tax rate of the combined total of the different taxes levied on exporters exceeded 120 percent of profits. Many economists argue that lightly taxed exports are more likely to generate greater revenue for the state than heavily taxed exports. Using police to track down export earnings illegally deposited in foreign banks, as the Russian authorities did for a time, has proven to be equally unsuccessful. The state would benefit more by the use of import tariffs and the introduction of what might be called an exploitation tax on all mining and drilling activity. The latter tax would be the opposite of a depletion allowance, which is traditionally used to stimulate oil drilling and mineral exploration. Instead of the depletion credit, producers would pay a royalty-like fee to the state for everything they took out of the ground. This would apply to products for use in Russia as well as for export.

While a good currency reform would have gone a long way toward dampening inflationary pressures, the effort could also have been reinforced by the introduction of an excess-wage tax similar to the one used in Poland to restrain wages increases. As was noted in Chapter 8, in January 1990, the first month of their reform, Polish managers were allowed to increase wages a maximum of 30 percent. If wages were raised more than that, they had to pay a substantial excise tax out of their profits. In February and March 1990 the nontaxable limit on wage increases was lowered to 20 percent. Admittedly, such a tax adds to the red tape, but, like the Poles, the Russians who toyed unsuccessfully with a similar concept could gradually have diminished the impact in tandem with the drop in inflationary pressure.

As we already saw, the Gaidar team did not have much time to draw up and implement its reforms. But in addition to the appropriate steps they did take, they should have accelerated the reintroduction of commercial codes. Instead of searching for foreign business codes that might be suitable for Russian needs, they might also have benefited by exhuming prerevolutionary Russian codes. Undoubtedly codes and practices of seventy years ago would have had to be modified to reflect modern practices, but transplanting foreign codes without allowance for the unique Russian context was a formula for continuing confusion.

One of the biggest obstacles to the regeneration of manufacturing in Russia has been the four to eight weeks or more that it takes a manufacturer to collect his payment after the goods are shipped and the buyer instructs her banks to pay her bills. With an inflation rate hovering around 20 percent a month, that is a major disincentive. The banks become major beneficiaries of this long delay, since they almost always end up paying the shipper 20 to 40 percent less in real terms than the shipper was entitled to. In retrospect it is clear that special care should have been taken to facilitate the transfer of money between banks, especially those in different cities.

V

To assist future reform efforts, it might be useful to summarize the steps that should have been introduced in January 1992 when the Russian price reforms were put into effect. Table 11-2 does this and also allows us to compare our model with what the Gaidar team actually did. Notice that our model borrows the wage restraints and the currency convertibility steps from Poland, the currency reforms from West Germany, and land reform and freedom of entry for new enterprises from China.

Of course, it is much easier and usually less damaging to second-guess than to have to draw up and execute actual reforms. But with an economy on the verge of hyperinflation, and under crisis-like time pressures, Gaidar and his reform team, with little actual administrative experience, were bound to encounter diffi-

Table 11-2 Reforms Gorbachev Should Have Introduced

1. Facilitate the formation of new private businesses in manufacturing, agriculture, and services
2. Privatize existing state enterprises, beginning with agriculture and services and then proceeding to manufacturing
3. Gradual decontrol of prices
4. Control fiscal policy

Reforms Yeltsin and Gaidar Should Have Introduced

1. Facilitate the formation of new private businesses in manufacturing, agriculture, and services
2. Privatize ownership of land and/or allow leasing
3. Currency reform
*4. Decontrol prices
5. Excess wage tax
*6. Control fiscal policy
7. Ruble convertibility
*8. Privatize existing state enterprises
9. Reintroduce commercial business codes
10. Facilitate money transfers between banks

* Steps taken by Yeltsin and Gaidar in the first stages of the reform

culties. Economic reform in Russia in late 1991, however, was more than a classroom exercise. It deeply affected people's lives and, as much as anything, gave rise to the reactionary backlash mirrored in the gains of the neofascist Liberal Democratic Party in December 1993. More attention should have been devoted not only to the successes and failures of reforms elsewhere in the communist and noncommunist world but also to Russia's unique cultural and economic infrastructure. Even then measures that work elsewhere in the world may not be suitable for Russia. Given the magnitude of the task, it is unlikely, even with these considerations, that a more comprehensive economic reform would have succeeded quickly. The economic reformers often seemed to neglect the fact that Russia had taken on many of the trappings of a democratic society. This meant that when the reform process began to pinch, the reformers had to pull back if they wanted to stay in office. A meaningful drop in the GNP and a significant growth in unemployment were almost certain to spark a political backlash. For that reason whenever widespread layoffs were likely, considerable resistance to economic restructuring was also likely. That explains why there was so little concern about the growth of unpaid interenterprise debt and why there has been such a strong lobby for industrial subsidies; both techniques helped sustain otherwise unprofitable industrial operations.

By early 1994, however, the continued emphasis on dampening inflation eventually began to have an impact even on the industrial monopolies. There was a limit to how long the enterprises could avoid paying their suppliers' bills and workers' salaries. Beginning in 1994 when the unpaid debt reached 25 trillion rubles, more and more enterprises began to insist on payment before delivery. In addition, despite holding second and third jobs, many workers began to find that without their basic salaries they could no longer buy what they needed. As a result inventories began to accumulate, even of oil, and it became very difficult to increase prices. Some of the oil companies, for example, announced that they would freeze prices—something they had not done for almost a decade. While such an inventory buildup meant lower rates of inflation, it also meant layoffs of workers, plant closings, and growing political stress. Admittedly, no matter what type of reform had been introduced, sooner or later Russian leaders would have had to face up to these problems—that is what restructuring is all about. However, rather than shock therapy, a more gradual approach to reform, especially if accompanied by the formation of a new marketing infrastructure and newly created private businesses, might have slowed somewhat the drop in the GNP and lessened the accompanying social upheaval.

VI

The integration of old world communism with new market institutions has not been easy. There are many pitfalls on the road to success. It might be instructive, therefore, to conclude this study by examining two attempts to apply market procedures in helping Russia develop its economic potential, with results that have been mixed at best. These examples are meant to provide insight for future reformers as well as investors.

There is general agreement that raw material development is one of the most logical activities for Russians to pursue. Their country has rich deposits of valuable minerals, and before the onset of perestroika the Soviets were the world's leading producers of such products as oil and gas. Thus it should not be too difficult to revive those operations. Enhancement of oil output with Western help would seem to be a particularly attractive example of how Western market experience and technical expertise can facilitate Russian economic revival. However, natural as this partnership might seem to be, it has in several instances suffered because the market, state control, and Russian nationalism clashed. The fate of the joint venture White Nights shows what can happen when the Russians suddenly discover that foreign investors are about to profit from the development of Russia's raw materials.

White Nights was in many ways a Russian initiative. Crude oil output in the West Varyegan and Tagrinskoye fields at Raduzhny, in the Tuimen region of West Siberia, was declining at a rate of about 20 percent a year.[12] Production, which was 550,000 barrels per day (bpd) in 1988, dropped to 250,000 bpd in 1990 and to 180,000 bpd in 1992.[13] This decline was due in part to the tendency of Russian operators to inject large quantities of water in order to increase pressure in the well. In the short run this increases oil extraction, but in the long run output drops more rapidly than otherwise because the oil drillers after a time spend as much time pumping out the water as they do pumping out the oil. Oil production was also adversely affected by the outbreak of war between Armenia and Azerbaijan. Because Azerbaijan had become the only source for most of the Soviet Union's oil equipment, the war disrupted its normal industrial operations and interfered with its supply of oil equipment.

In an effort to increase output, Anatoly Sivac, the general director of the Varyegan Oil and Gas Production Association (Vareganneftegas) (VNG), decided to seek foreign assistance. He approached Giles Labbe, a Texas oilman, and his partner Gordon Andrus, a New York lawyer who had formed a company called Anglo-Suisse, which specialized in increasing yields from worked-over oil fields.[14] After some success in Morocco, Pakistan, and Indonesia, they were eager to try their hand in Siberia, notorious for its poor drilling practices. The two sides reached an agreement in November 1990 to form a joint venture, with the equity allocated fifty-fifty. Because Anglo-Suisse was short of funds, however, it sold 45 percent of the joint venture to Phibro Energy Products, a subsidiary of Solomon Brothers. This left Anglo-Suisse with 5 percent.[15] The initial charter called for each side to put up $40 million. But after operations began, in July 1991, Phibro had to put up another $76 million in early 1992 in what it euphemistically called "a voluntary loan."

Recognizing Russian sensitivities about extracting oil from untapped oil fields, the White Nights venture was designed to increase output from already exploited oil fields, which had seen their best days. The existing Russian company, VNG, agreed to maintain operation of the oil field, on the assumption that output would decline about 25 percent a year, producing about 20,000 bpd in 1992–93. That oil could be sold on the domestic market. Anything that the joint venture could produce above that level with the application of Western technology was to be divided fifty-fifty and could be exported. In 1991 and 1992 that extra output amounted to about 7,000 bpd to 8,000 bpd.

In a search for tax revenue, however, the newly installed Russian government imposed an oil export tax of approximately five to six dollars a barrel in early 1992. The tax was reduced by a third in September 1992, but was increased again on January 1, 1993, to almost its original level.[16] Most of the initiative for this tax came from the International Monetary Fund, which was looking for as many sources of taxation as possible to help balance the Russian national budget.[17]

The problem was that for White Nights this retroactively imposed tax amounted to about 25 percent of the joint venture's total gross revenue (the world price then was about twenty dollars a barrel) and made no allowance for costs. Had they known there would have been such a confiscatory tax, the American partners would probably have negotiated different terms or not signed the contract at all.[18] After considerable effort White Nights convinced the Russian government that such a tax was indeed unfair. Thus on July 27, 1992, Acting Prime Minister Yegor Gaidar agreed to exempt joint ventures with a foreign equity that exceeded 30 percent and if they were formed before January 1992, when the tax was levied. The exempt joint venture also had to be in the business of obtaining its revenue from the sale of increased output above what Russian efforts alone would have yielded. White Nights qualified on all three counts. Nevertheless, a commission established to certify the exemptions refused to issue an exemption. After an appeal White Nights was still forced to put millions of dollars in an escrow account in case the exemption was ultimately not granted. Even without a tax of five dollars a barrel, however, their operation was unprofitable. Consequently, their Western oil drilling and servicing facility was abandoned, and all but a few of the 105 foreign workers who came in 1991 returned home.

By 1993 the White Nights operation was effectively bankrupt, but the American partners refused to pull out until they could retrieve some of their $110 million investment. In rapid succession the four different taxes in effect when White Nights signed its contract were increased to eleven.[19] The export tax, income tax, excise tax, subsurface royalty tax, mineral use tax, mineral rehabilitation tax, geological tax, port fees, value-added tax, and mandatory conversion of 50 percent of all hard-currency exports into rubles in fact exceeded total revenue.[20]

In addition to the taxes, White Nights had to contend with some in the Russian bureaucracy who challenged the joint venture's very existence.[21] It had been registered in 1990 as a Soviet company, but since there was no longer a Soviet Union, technically White Nights no longer existed. Next White Nights discovered in November 1991 that Vneshekonombank had frozen $2.8 million of its operating funds.[22] As we saw earlier, this was a consequence of the run on Vneshekonombank. The freezing of all *valuta* deposits was not directed specifically against White Nights, but that was little consolation.

White Nights also encountered a ruble shortage. Its partner VNG, which was responsible for covering the ruble costs of the Russian work force of 1,400, ran out of rubles. Again, this problem was not peculiar to White Nights. It was due in part to inflation and in part to the fact that customers stopped paying their suppliers. As we saw, beginning in 1992, Russian enterprises throughout the country began to have the same difficulty. When White Nights sought to cover its payroll by flying in a planeload of rubles, "the bank stole it and used it to pay other people's payrolls."[23]

Even when White Nights was authorized to export its oil, it

was not easy. Breaking a year-old contract, Transneft, the monopoly controlling the oil pipelines, doubled the fees White Nights had to pay and divided the pipeline and created two separate companies and, as a consequence, two different negotiating entities.[24] In addition, even though only joint ventures had to pay hard currency to ship their oil through the pipeline, White Nights and other joint ventures still had to compete for slots in the pipeline with the domestic oil production associations, which usually had priority. Moreover, White Nights had to reroute its oil from the Black Sea, where it had been assigned originally, to the Baltic Sea, where the port fee and theft were higher. Finally, in June 1993, oil shipments from all the joint ventures were suspended for most of the month.[25]

While taxes and the Russian bureaucracy were the main causes of its difficulties, White Nights had other problems as well. The natural drop in production was steeper than had been anticipated. The fields assigned to White Nights were "the dogs," the least promising of all.[26] Not that White Nights expected special treatment, but because it was one of the first to risk its own money in such an effort, it had assumed that the Russians would take extra steps to ensure its success. If this "demonstration project" made money, others would surely follow. White Nights had also regarded this first project as just a beginning and was eager to bid on other projects in the area.

What explains the Russians' apparent lack of cooperation? They complained that the Americans were paying the expatriate staff about $8,000 a month, while they themselves were receiving approximately $500 a month.[27] Moreover, the Americans had built themselves Western living accommodations, while the Russians continued to live in their shabby, substandard concrete apartment houses. Most important, the Russians resented losing control over their raw materials.[28] By October 1993 there were signs that the Russian partner was becoming more cooperative, yet, as one Russian energy official put it, Russians will "never let foreign devils have the life-blood of Russia."[29]

VII

Despite repeated White Nights type of experiences, there have also been some promising pockets of development, both foreign and domestic. For example, after starting poorly and finding that its assembly plant in Estonia was now in another country and thus unsuited for the production of products within Russia, Polaroid suddenly discovered it had unknowingly tapped a major market for its cameras and film. With pleasure as well as an acknowledged degree of awe, Polaroid found that Russia had become its fourth- or fifth-largest market for cameras and film, with sales approaching $100 million a year. It turns out that instant photography, in which the film is automatically developed in the camera, was just what Russian photographers needed. Because of the historical neglect of consumer needs, Gosplan had never provided enough resources for film-developing laboratories and camera stores. Picture takers were therefore forced to develop their film in their bathroom sinks at home. Even though the film is expensive by Russian standards, Polaroid cameras eliminated all that trouble.

A few other Western firms have also established profitable businesses. While the majority have been overwhelmed with punitive and ever-expanding taxes (Western firms are viewed as the best source of tax revenue not only for the national but also for the local treasuries), the mafia (some Western firms are forced to pay one or another mafia group as a form of tax, and others decide to hire their own security force, but the cost is much the same), and unpaid debts (successful businesses now insist on cash and refuse credit), there is enormous potential for those able to take advantage of the lack of competition and the Russian hunger for consumer goods. Coca-Cola and Pepsi, along with several Western cigarette, candy, soap, and food manufacturers, have enjoyed such strong sales that they have decided to commit themselves to building manufacturing facilities that will be staffed by Russian workers and supplied by a broadening base of locally produced supplies and raw materials.

Some domestic success stories have also appeared. The reform effort in Sakhalin, an island on the Pacific Rim just north of Japan, demonstrates that the Russians can carry out genuine reforms with a motivated population and an effective leader. Sensing that the island's economy was lagging behind that of its neighbors, the local authorities sought outside help. Like the residents in a Wild West movie who advertise for a sheriff, the residents of Sakhalin looked about for a reformer with an economic program. An unlikely candidate, Valentine Fedorov, an outsider from Moscow and at the time the prorector of Moscow's Plekhanov Economic Institute, decided to seek the post. To everyone's amazement, he ran in a local election for governor of the island in 1990 and won.

Unlike most economists who concentrated on the privatization of state industry, his main emphasis was on creation of brand-new private enterprises in retailing, services, farming, and manufacturing. Yuzhnii Sakhalinsk, the capital of the island, already had numerous stores that had been privatized and brand-new ones, as did other Russian cities. Fedorov understood, however, that to sustain a market environment and facilitate the coming together of buyers and sellers, he also had to change attitudes and the general economic climate. Toward that end he encouraged the establishment of a permanent fairground—cum flea market—about a mile outside the city, where budding merchants could comfortably and safely offer their goods (including handicrafts and small manufactured items). Business hours were from 9:00 A.M. to 4:00 P.M. each Saturday and Sunday. The proprietors of this for-profit fairground charged exhibitors and visitors a modest fee, and called their operation "Fedorovka," after their benefactor.

More important, at a time when most private farmers elsewhere in Russia could only lease their land, Fedorov encouraged local peasants to break away from the collective and set up there own private farms. He arranged for them to gain title and become owners, not renters. Between January and June 1992 over one thousand private farms were established. In addition,

Fedorov promoted the formation of new private food-processing, fishing, and manufacturing activities. When I visited the island in July 1992, a number of individually owned fish-processing plants with refrigerated storage space were already up and operating. Atypically for Russia, they had been built in less than two years. As of mid-1992 there were five thousand such ventures in Sakhalin either already operating or in the construction stage, all launched since Fedorov arrived on the scene.

Until my visit I had met many clever buyers and sellers and providers of valuable services, but never a manufacturer. Given their absence for sixty years or more in Russia, the establishment of retailing and service enterprises filled a critical need, but real economic reform also requires the development of new private manufacturing. However, private Russian manufacturing enterprises as of 1992 were still rare.

In Sakhalin I finally met Russian manufacturers. Some of the most successful new-business owners were actually operating before Fedorov's arrival, but were doing it illegally. Not surprisingly, some had served time in jail for activities for which Fedorov honored them in 1992. One of the most successful businessmen had been operating an illegal fur-processing business in the basement (literally an underground business) of the State Railroad Administration building. He shaped the furs into hats, dolls, and mink and sable coats and sold them. While he bought most of the furs from trappers, like a character out of the mystery novel *Gorki Park*, he also bred his own sables. When Fedorov arrived and made these activities open and legitimate, the fur dealer expanded into new endeavors. He opened up a fishing venture, which soon boasted twelve employees. In a year or so, he expected to complete the construction of an old-fashioned Russian bathhouse next to his fishing grounds for tourists.

Yet even where reform seemed relatively successful, the reformers often encountered considerable resistance. In April 1993, amid accusations of corruption and the abuse of state and social interests, Fedorov was forced out of office as governor of Sakhalin and replaced by a more traditional administrator. At about the same time several other reformist governors in other cities of the Russian far east were also removed. Each was replaced by an administrator more in tune with the traditional practices of state control represented by holdovers from the pre-Gorbachev era.

The fate of the reforms set in motion by regional leaders like Fedorov once they are removed from office is uncertain. Although many, if not all, of the newly created ventures are allowed to continue their operations, the underlying climate, with its ongoing emphasis on bureaucratic or mafia control, is less welcoming to new-business development than it was in the early months of the Yeltsin era. This is especially true of manufacturing, which requires a longer period to recoup its initial investment.

As the example of Sakhalin suggests, even when the reforms seem to be going well, their opponents may still have the power to reverse the process. That the reformers in Sakhalin had to retreat illustrates how difficult and erratic the reform effort in a country like Russia, with its deeply embedded antimarket traditions, may be.

VIII

Because the potential is so enormous, the reform of the Russian economy has proven to be very frustrating. The wealth of natural resources and human talent make it hard to understand why the results thus far have been so disappointing. Because other countries have done much better with much less, it is not surprising that many Russians attribute the collapse of their country's economy to foreign intrigue. Not only during the December 1993 elections but traditionally, that has been a common explanation for Russia's problems. Masonic-Zionist conspiracies are especially popular scapegoats. Many Russians also believe that the United States has been secretly undermining their efforts.

Russia's delayed and sometimes negative responses to reform have little to do with conspiracies, however, and much to do with its legacies, particularly its lack of experience with the market. It is also a consequence of the fact that many of the reforms were ill conceived, not least for their assumption that Russia was just like any Western country. But without responsive institutions such as private farms, shops, and factories as well as a distribution and marketing infrastructure, the chances of the successful application of shock therapy were small. Even with the necessary infrastructure there is no guarantee that shock therapy will succeed. Nor should it be ignored that the application of shock therapy when the institutions necessary for its implementation are not in place is more likely to complicate than to simplify attempts to reform Russia's economy and raise its standard of living.

Some Western analysts have argued that the political process and the absence of a working constitution and a stable political tradition where members of the government not only enact laws but implement them has also hurt the reform effort. The resulting political infighting and lack of a clear relationship between the executive branch and the parliament have produced gridlock. This has allowed the communist apparatchiks who were never removed from power to obstruct reform. This is all true, but such explanations overlook the fact that in January 1992, when Gaidar took over the reform process, Yeltsin had put in place Russia's most reform-minded government since the revolution. But its concentration on fiscal and monetary control, to the neglect of the formation of competitive enterprises and the establishment of market institutions, led to increasing inflation and declining living standards. These leaders all seem to have forgotten that, as a minimum, a successful reform must make the life of the average consumer better. That was not the top priority of either Gorbachev or Yeltsin. Gaidar seemed more concerned about such matters than Gorbachev, but even he worried more about inflation than about increasing the flow of consumer goods to households. If he had succeeded in his fight against inflation, he might have helped his cause, but his chances of success were crippled by the very absence of a market infrastructure. In any case, he did not do very well. He predicted that there would be some inflation and that prices would double. Instead, they rose twenty-four-fold in 1992 and tenfold in 1993. He also predicted that there would be a short-lived drop in the GNP, but it lasted for more than two years. Admittedly the rate of inflation did begin to taper off in 1994, but only because industrial production, at least in the state sector, began to fall at an accelerating pace. By May 1994, it was dropping at an annual rate of 29 percent. Most important of all, the output of consumer goods did not go up but actually fell—so much for bettering the lives of the consumer. The resulting public outcry provoked a political reaction and a determination by a growing segment of both the pre- and post-October 1993 parliaments to oppose radical economic reformers and Gaidar himself. Inappropriate economic reforms or programs are likely to strengthen the hands of the antimarket reformers and unleash fierce political infighting.

Nonetheless, those who seek to blame the failure of Russia's reforms on this or that Russian or Western reformer, as well as on the IMF, the G-7, or United States, are misinformed. In answer to people like Richard Nixon, both we and the Russians must understand that neither the reformers nor the West lost Russia. It was not ours to lose. Russian culture, the seventy years of communism, and its creation of new mind-sets and gigantomanian institutions made rapid economic reform impossible.

Reform will come to Russia, but slowly and sometimes gradually and sometimes in fits and starts. After all, societies much less well endowed have been able to reform themselves. Eventually, Russia will work its way out of what occasionally appears as a hopeless morass. Centuries of czarism and seventy years of communism have created a combination of obstacles that makes Russia a special case and its reform effort unusually difficult. They have also created a citizenry conditioned to wait for action initiated at the center, not at the periphery by individuals. An appropriate economic program therefore needs not only good leadership but a motivated public. Russia is not a prisoner of its history; reform is possible, but Americans as well as the Russians must come to realize that meaningful reform that makes life better for the man in the street will require extra time, insight, and patience.

All of this is not to argue that since reform is so difficult reformers can do as they please; on the contrary, Russia's reformers sometimes appear to have forgotten that, unlike those of the past, the Russians of today can express themselves politically when they feel abused by the economic system. Moreover, given their tradition, Russians have a greater tendency than many other peoples to fall back on extremist solutions. Consequently, overeager or misguided reformers risk bringing to power fascists and communists, as happened in December 1993, and making reform actually more difficult. Ill-designed reforms are not costless. It is not just that a poor reform sets the cause back to square one. As Zhirinovsky's election shows, a misconceived reform sets the process back to square minus one.

Fortunately, the Russians are a people famed for their patience. When I wondered aloud why it was that Russians seemed to tolerate so many shortages, a raging inflation, and a three-month delay in getting paid, one of my friends put it simply. "We Russians pride ourselves on our ability to suffer." However, as the revolutions of 1905 and 1917 show, even Russians have their limits. The government's challenge is to produce positive results before that limit is reached.

Notes

Abbreviations

FBIS	*Foreign Broadcast Information Service Daily Report: Soviet Union* (*Soviet Union* became *Central Eurasia* in Jan. 1992)
FBIS, China	*Foreign Broadcast Information Service Daily Report: China*
FT	*Financial Times*
Nar. khoz.	Tsentral'noe Statisticheskoe Upravlenie, *Narodnoe khoziaistvo SSSR* (cited with the statistical year)
NYT	*New York Times*
RFE/RL	Radio Free Europe/Radio Liberty
WSJ	*Wall Street Journal*

Preface

1. Boris Yeltsin, *Against the Grain: An Autobiography* (New York: Summit Books, 1990); Boris Yeltsin, *The Struggle for Russia* (New York: Random House, 1994); John Morrison, *Boris Yeltsin: From Bolshevik to Democrat* (New York: Dutton Books, 1991); Vladimir Solovyov and Elena Klepikova, *Boris Yeltsin: A Political Biography* (New York: G. P. Putnam's Sons, 1992); Angus Roxburgh, *The Second Russian Revolution: The Struggle for Power in the Kremlin* (London: BBC Books, 1991).

Chapter 1: The Reform That Never Was

1. *Boston Globe*, Oct. 11, 1992, p. 2.
2. Boris Yeltsin, *The Struggle for Russia* (New York: Random House, 1994).

3. Conversation with Ambassador Matlock.
4. *Newsweek*, Aug. 31, 1992, p. 40.
5. Ibid.
6. For a fuller analysis, see Marshall I. Goldman, *What Went Wrong with Perestroika* (New York: W. W. Norton, 1991).
7. Personal conversation with Gorbachev.
8. *FBIS*, March 2, 1992, p. 32.
9. Philip Hanson, "The Dimension of the Monopoly Problem," *RFE/RL Reports*, April 12, 1991, p. 12.
10. *Promyshlennost SSSR* (Moscow: Finansy i statistika, 1988), p. 14; *FT*, May 13, 1992, IV.
11. *Pravda*, Nov. 20, 1962, p. 5; Tatiana Zaslavskaia, "The Novosibirsk Report," *Survey* 28, no. 1 (Spring 1984): 88.
12. *Moscow News*, no. 43 (1992): 11.
13. Ed Hewett, in *NYT Book Review*, July 10, 1983, p. 28; Jan Vanous, in *NYT*, Nov. 19, 1992, p. A34.
14. *FBIS*, May 31, 1990, p. 35.
15. *NYT*, Oct. 9, 1992, p. A3.

Chapter 2: The Rise of Boris Yeltsin

1. Boris Yeltsin, *Against the Grain* (New York: Summit Books, 1990), pp. 88–90.
2. Ibid., pp. 88, 91–92, 99, 101.
3. Ibid., p. 115.
4. Ibid., p. 107.
5. John Morrison, *Boris Yeltsin* (New York: Dutton Books, 1991), p. 46.
6. Yeltsin, *Against the Grain*, p. 112.
7. Morrison, *Boris Yeltsin*, p. 52; *FBIS*, July 30, 1986, p. R27.
8. *Pravda*, March 17, 1987, p. 2.
9. Morrison, *Boris Yeltsin*, p. 54; RFE/RL, RL 206/88, May 20, 1988, p. 3.
10. Yeltsin, *Against the Grain*, p. 115.
11. *FBIS*, July 30, 1986, p. R27.
12. *Moskovskaia pravda*, April 14, 1987, p. 2.
13. *FBIS*, July 30, 1986, p. R27.
14. *Moskovskaia pravda*, March 15, 1987, p. 2.
15. *Pravda*, Nov. 13, 1987, p. 3; *FBIS*, Nov. 13, 1987, p. 66.
16. Yeltsin, *Against the Grain*, pp. 159, 166.
17. Ibid., p. 126.
18. Ibid., p. 183.
19. Ibid., pp. 126, 128, 188; Morrison, *Boris Yeltsin*, p. 59.

20. Morrison, *Boris Yeltsin*, p. 69.
21. Ibid., p. 70.
22. Yeltsin, *Against the Grain*, p. 36; Vladimir Solovyov and Elena Klepikova, *Boris Yeltsin* (New York: G. P. Putnam's Sons, 1992), p. 36.
23. Morrison, *Boris Yeltsin*, pp. 73, 94.
24. Yeltsin, *Against the Grain*, pp. 174, 219.
25. Ibid., p. 207; Morrison, *Boris Yeltsin*, p. 33; Marshall I. Goldman, *What Went Wrong with Perestroika* (New York: W. W. Norton, 1991), p. 70.
26. Yeltsin, *Against the Grain*, pp. 31, 36.
27. Morrison, *Boris Yeltsin*, p. 35.
28. Yeltsin, *Against the Grain*, p. 71.
29. Ibid., pp. 70–72.
30. Solovyov and Klepikova, *Boris Yeltsin*, p. 93.
31. Ibid., pp. 92, 94; Yeltsin, *Against the Grain*, p. 223.
32. Yeltsin, *Against the Grain*, p. 224; Solovyov and Klepikova, *Boris Yeltsin*, p. 98.
33. Solovyov and Klepikova, *Boris Yeltsin*, p. 92.
34. Ibid., p. 98; Yeltsin, *Against the Grain*, pp. 206, 208, 209.
35. Yeltsin, *Against the Grain*, p. 174.
36. Stephen White, *Gorbachev and After* (Cambridge: Cambridge University Press, 1992), p. 49.
37. Solovyov and Klepikova, *Boris Yeltsin*, p. 102.
38. Ibid., pp. 103, 159–62; White, *Gorbachev and After*, p. 55.
39. Morrison, *Boris Yeltsin*, p. 145.
40. Solovyov and Klepikova, *Boris Yeltsin*, p. 266.
41. *FBIS*, June 1, 1989, p. 25.
42. Morrison, *Boris Yeltsin*, pp. 98, 150; *FBIS*, March 17, 1989, p. 71.
43. Solovyov and Klepikova, *Boris Yeltsin*, p. 198.
44. Angus Roxburgh, *The Second Russian Revolution* (London: BBC Books, 1991), p. 180.
45. Ibid., p. 181.
46. Ibid.
47. Ibid.
48. Solovyov and Klepikova, *Boris Yeltsin*, p. 234.
49. Ibid., p. 235.
50. Ibid., p. 223.

Chapter 3: The Breakup of the Soviet Union

1. Vladimir Solovyov and Elena Klepikova, *Boris Yeltsin* (New York: G. P. Putnam's Sons, 1992), p. 225.

2. Ibid., p. 235.
3. John Morrison, *Boris Yeltsin* (New York: Dutton Books, 1991), p. 272.
4. Ibid.
5. *NYT*, Dec. 21, 1991, p. 5.
6. *Time*, May 11, 1992, p. 44.
7. Quoted in Solovyov and Klepikova, *Boris Yeltsin*, p. 221.
8. RFE/RL, vol. 1, no. 34, July 28, 1992, p. 15.
9. *Moscow News*, no. 36 (1991): 5; *FBIS*, Dec. 9, 1991, p. 51.
10. RFE/RL, vol. 7, no. 27, April 20, 1990, p. 1.
11. *FT*, Feb. 8, 1992, p. 37; Sovset, May 28, 1992, p. 3.
12. *FT*, March 31, 1992, p. 2.
13. RFE/RL, vol. 1, no. 38, Sept. 25, 1992, p. 26.
14. *FT*, July 9, 1993, p. 2.

Chapter 4: Economic Advice

1. Michael Alexeev, Clifford Gaddy, and Jim Leitzel, "Economics in the Former Soviet Union," *Journal of Economic Perspectives* 6, no. 2 (Spring 1992): 137.
2. David Joravsky, *The Lysenko Affair* (Cambridge: Harvard University Press, 1970), p. 50.
3. Angus Roxburgh, *The Second Russian Revolution* (London: BBC Books, 1991), p. 15.
4. Marshall I. Goldman, *Gorbachev's Challenge* (New York: W. W. Norton, 1987), p. 58.
5. Roxburgh, *Second Russian Revolution*, p. 14.
6. Ibid., p. 33. Anders Åslund, *Gorbachev's Struggle for Economic Reform: The Soviet Reform Process, 1985–88* (Ithaca: Cornell University Press, 1989), p. 4. Åslund writes that Aganbegyan and Gorbachev first met in 1979, but Zaslavskaia says that the meeting took place at an economic discussion in 1983. Anders Åslund, "Who Are Gorbachev's Economic Advisors?" (paper presented at the Kennan Institute, Wilson Center, Washington, D.C., Sept. 10, 1987), p. 12 (photocopy).
7. Personal correspondence.
8. Roxburgh, *Second Russian Revolution*, p. 34.
9. Åslund, *Gorbachev's Struggle*, p. 5.
10. *Pravda*, June 30, 1988, pp. 3–4.
11. Roxburgh, *Second Russian Revolution*, p. 147.
12. Ibid., p. 146.
13. *Ekonomicheskaia gazeta*, no. 27 (July 1989): 1.
14. Roxburgh, *Second Russian Revolution*, p. 147.
15. Åslund, *Gorbachev's Struggle*, p. 133.

16. Discussion with the vice chairman of the reform commision, June 1990.
17. Ed A. Hewett, *Reforming the Soviet Economy: Equality versus Efficiency* (Washington, D.C.: Brookings Institution, 1988), p. 300.
18. Nikolai Shmelev, "Avansy idolgi," *Novy mir*, June 1987, p. 142.
19. Åslund, *Gorbachev's Struggle*, pp. 74, 134.
20. Personal conversation.
21. Stephen White, *Gorbachev and After* (Cambridge: Cambridge University Press, 1992), p. 134.
22. *NYT*, May 25, 1990, p. A8; *FT*, May 31, 1990, p. 2.
23. Åslund, "Gorbachev, *Perestroyka*, and Economic Crisis," *Problems of Communism*, Jan.–April 1991, p. 33.
24. Ibid., p. 39.
25. John Morrison, *Boris Yeltsin* (New York: Dutton Books, 1991), p. 164.
26. Ibid., pp. 165–66.
27. Åslund, "Economic Crisis," p. 34.
28. Morrison, *Boris Yeltsin*, p. 166.
29. Ibid., pp. 167–68.
30. Quoted in *WSJ*, Oct. 26, 1990, p. A12.
31. Morrison, *Boris Yeltsin*, p. 169.
32. Ibid., p. 172.
33. *Pravda*, Oct. 18, 1990, p. 1.
34. Åslund, "Economic Crisis," p. 34.
35. Marshall I. Goldman, *The USSR in Crisis: The Failure of an Economic System* (New York: W. W. Norton, 1982).
36. Graham Allison and Robert Blackwill, "America's Stake in the Soviet Future," *Foreign Affairs* 70, no. 3 (Summer 1991): 77.
37. International Monetary Fund et al., *The Economy of the USSR: Summary and Recommendations* (Washington, D.C.: World Bank, Dec. 1990).
38. *FT*, April 4, 1991, p. 2.
39. Graham Allison and Gregory Yavlinsky, "Window of Opportunity" (J. F. Kennedy School of Government, Harvard University, and Center for Economic and Political Research, Leningrad, June 29, 1991).
40. Glenn Kaye, "A Conversation with the Revolutionary Jeffrey Sachs," *Harvard Magazine*, Nov.–Dec. 1992, p. 50; personal conversations.
41. *Washington Times*, June 25, 1991, p. 89.
42. "Of Building World Partnership: The Economic Declaration" (London Economic Summit, July 17, 1991).
43. "A Conversation with Graham Allison," *Harvard Gazette*, Oct. 4, 1991, p. 6.
44. *FT*, July 23, 1991, p. 2.

45. Michael Ellman, "Shock Therapy in Russia: Failure or Partial Success," *RFE/RL Research Report*, vol. 1, no. 34, Aug. 28, 1992, p. 49.
46. Peter Pringle, "Gaidar and Company," *Moscow Magazine*, June–July 1992, p. 31.
47. Ibid., p. 32.
48. Y. Gaidar, V. Koshkin, and F. Kovalev, *Rossiyskiie vestii*, Aug. 18, 1992, p. 1; *FBIS*, Aug. 19, 1992, p. 41.
49. *FBIS*, Aug. 19, 1992, p. 41.
50. Steven Erlanger, "Reform School," *NYT Magazine*, Nov. 29, 1992, p. 74.
51. Ibid.
52. Interview with Sergei Vasilyev.
53. Ibid.
54. Erlanger, "Reform School," p. 74.
55. *Business Week*, Feb. 24, 1992, p. 67.
56. Pringle, "Gaidar and Company," p. 33.
57. Interview with Sergei Vasilyev.
58. Pringle, "Gaidar and Company," p. 31.
59. Ibid.
60. Ibid.; *FT*, Oct. 30, 1991, p. 2; Nov. 11, 1991, p. 1.
61. Erlanger, "Reform School," p. 78.
62. *Business Week*, Feb. 24, 1992, p. 68; *FT*, April 16, 1992, p. 2.
63. *Izvestiia*, June 3, 1992, p. 2; *FT*, June 6, 1992, p. 4.
64. *WSJ*, June 15, 1992, p. A10; *NYT*, June 16, 1992, p. A13; *FT*, June 16, 1992, p. 1.
65. *Moscow Times*, Dec. 21, 1992, p. 8.
66. *NYT*, Dec. 15, 1992, p. A15.
67. *Commersant*, Dec. 22, 1992, p. 5.
68. *Izvestiia*, Dec. 2, 1991, p. 2; *NYT*, June 2, 1992, p. A8.

Chapter 5: Shock Therapy

1. Conversations with participants in the 1990 discussions of the 500-day plan.
2. Richard Layard, "Russia in Transition," *LSE Magazine*, Spring 1993, p. 4.
3. John Morrison, *Boris Yeltsin* (New York: Dutton Books, 1991), p. 155.
4. *FBIS*, Jan. 8, 1992, p. 45.
5. *NYT*, Dec. 5, 1993, p. 10F.
6. *FT*, Jan. 16, 1992, p. 22 (European ed.).
7. *Nezavisimaia gazeta*, Feb. 27, 1992, p. 5.

8. *FBIS*, Jan. 8, 1992, p. 45.
9. *WSJ*, Oct. 7, 1992, p. A13; *FT*, July 17, 1992, p. 3.
10. *Ukrainian Weekly*, Feb. 14, 1993, p. 3; March 21, 1993, p. 4.
11. *Ekonomika i zhizn*, no. 10 (March 1992): 9; *WSJ* , Dec. 24, 1991, p. B3.
12. *Ekonomika i zhizn*, no. 46 (Nov. 1992): 1.
13. Vladimir V. Popov, comments at seminar, Russian Research Center, Harvard University, Nov. 5, 1992; *Commersant*, Dec. 15, 1992, pp. 4, 22; *FBIS*, Jan. 7, 1992, p. 45; *RFE/RL Sovset*, July 27, 1992, p. 7; Layard, " Russia in Transition," p. 4.
14. *FBIS*, Aug. 10, 1992, p. 39; Dec. 14, 1992, pp. 11–12; RFE/RL, March 14, 1994, p. 1.
15. *FBIS*, Nov. 16, 1992, p. 24.
16. *WSJ*, June 16, 1992, p. A12.
17. *WSJ*, Nov. 15, 1991, p. A6.
18. *Pravda*, Nov. 19, 1992, p. 3; *NYT*, Feb. 1, 1993, p. A1; *WSJ*, April 6, 1993, p. A10.
19. *FBIS*, April 19, 1993, p. 62.
20. *FBIS*, Dec. 31, 1992, p. 47; Debevoise and Plimpton, "Letter to Clients," Feb. 6, 1992, Debevoise and Plimpton, 875 Third Avenue, New York.
21. *WSJ*, Sept. 13, 1992, p. A6.
22. Ibid.
23. *Commersant*, March 2, 1992, p. 15.
24. *FBIS*, June 4, 1992, p. 41.
25. *NYT*, March 28, 1993, p. 6.
26. Ibid.
27. *RFE/RL Research Report*, suppl., vol. 2, no. 7, 1993, p. 7; *WSJ*, Sept. 3, 1992, p. A6.
28. *NYT*, April 4, 1993, p. 8.
29. *FT*, April 5, 1993, p. 1; *WSJ*, April 6, 1993, p. C14.
30. *Interfax Financial Report*, March 12–19, 1993, p. 6.
31. *FBIS*, Dec. 5, 1991, p. 45.
32. Ibid.
33. *Ekonomicheskaia gazeta*, no. 10 (March 1992): 9.
34. *FT*, May 27, 1993, p. viii.
35. *Ekonomika i zhizn*, no. 6 (Feb. 1993): 3.
36. Ibid., no. 4 (Jan. 1993): 14.

Chapter 6: Privatization

1. Stephen K. Wegren, "Private Farming and Agrarian Reform in Russia," *Problems of Communism*, May–June 1992, p. 107.

2. Ibid., p. 108.
3. Ibid.
4. *Vremiia*, April 6, 1989; *FBIS*, April 19, 1989, p. 70.
5. *FBIS*, Dec. 2, 1992, p. 31.
6. *Ekonomika i zhizn*, no. 6 (Feb. 1994): 8.
7. *FT*, Oct. 29, 1993, p. 3.
8. *Moscow News*, no. 33 (1988): 8; no. 7 (1989): 13; no. 11 (1989): 3.
9. *Pravda*, Dec. 1, 1990, p. 4.
10. *NYT* Dec. 29, 1991, p. 10.
11. *Moskovskie novosti*, Aug. 23, 1992, p. 11; *FBIS*, Aug. 24, 1992, p. 30.
12. *NYT*, March 16, 1989, p. A14; Marshall I. Goldman, *What Went Wrong with Perestroika* (New York: W. W. Norton, 1991), p. 112.
13. *FBIS*, Aug. 24, 1992, p. 31.
14. *FBIS*, Dec. 7, 1992, p. 7; *RFE/RL Research Report*, vol. 2, no. 7, Feb. 12, 1993, p. 37.
15. *FBIS*, Jan. 2, 1992, p. 61; April 6, 1992, p. 27; *Rossiiskaia gazeta*, Dec. 31, 1991, p. 3; March 31, 1992, p. 2; *Ekonomika i zhizn*, no. 9 (Feb. 1991): 18; Wegren, "Private Farming," p. 111.
16. *FBIS*, March 22, 1993, p. 74.
17. *RFE/RL Research Report*, vol. 2, no. 7, Feb. 12, 1993, p. 36.
18. Wegren, "Private Farming," p. 109.
19. *FBIS*, Dec. 7, 1992, p. 7.
20. Wegren, "Private Farming."
21. *FBIS*, Dec. 7, 1992, p. 7.
22. *WSJ*, Feb. 26, 1993, p. B5; *RFE/RL Research Bulletin*, vol. 10, no. 5, March 2, 1993, p. 5.
23. *FT*, June 3, 1993, p. 30; *Ekonomika i zhizn*, no. 6 (Feb. 1994): 8.
24. *RFE/RL Research Bulletin*, vol. 10, no. 5, March 2, 1993, p. 5.
25. Marshall I. Goldman, *Gorbachev's Challenge* (New York: W. W. Norton, 1987), p. 238.
26. *FBIS*, Dec. 23, 1993, p. 63.
27. *FT*, Jan. 18, 1993, p. 2.
28. *Rossiiskaia gazeta*, Feb. 1, 1992, p. 2; Feb. 4, 1992, p. 1; *Washington Post*, March 27, 1992, p. A26.
29. *FBIS*, Aug. 20, 1992, p. 18.
30. *Nezavisimaia gazeta*, Dec. 16, 1992, p. 2.
31. *Moscow News*, no. 31 (1992): 2.
32. *NYT*, May 13, 1993, p. A4.
33. Interview with vendors on the Arbat in 1992.
34. *Washington Post*, March 27, 1992, p. A26.
35. *FBIS*, Jan. 27, 1993, p. 33.

36. Ibid. ; Feb. 5, 1993, p. 21.
37. Lecture by and interview with Anatoly Chubais, Moscow and St. Petersburg, June 23 and 27, 1993; *NYT*, Nov. 10, 1993, p. D1.
38. *FT*, Dec. 6, 1993, p. 2.
39. *FT*, Jan. 15, 1993, p. 2.
40. *FT*, Oct. 31, 1992, p. 16; *The World Bank in Transition* 4, no. 2 (March 1993): 2; *NYT*, March 17, 1994, p. A16.
41. *FT*, Feb. 13, 1993, p. 3.
42. *Business Week*, July 27, 1992, p. 52; *FT*, Oct. 2, 1992, p. 16; "Russia's Privatization Program," *International Economic Review*, Sept. 1992, p. 15; *Economist*, July 18, 1992, p. 70; *Ekonomicheskaia gazeta*, no. 9 (Feb. 1992): 17.
43. *RFE/RL Research Report*, vol. 2, no. 7, Feb. 12, 1992, pp. 32–33; *The World Bank in Transition* 4, no. 2 (March 1993): 1; *Ekonomika i zhizn*, no. 2 (Jan. 1994): 14.
44. "Russia's Privatization Program," p. 19.
45. Ibid.
46. *FBIS*, April 19, 1993, p. 56.
47. *Ekonomika i zhizn*, no. 12 (March 1993): 3.
48. Konstantin Borovoi, comments at seminar, Russian Research Center, Harvard University, April 7, 1993; Konstantin Borovoi, *People, Events and Feelings: The Price of Freedom* (Moscow: Novosti, 1993); Lev Makarevich, "Commodities Are the Key," *Business in the USSR*, July–Aug. 1991, p. 16.
49. *FBIS*, Feb. 9, 1993, p. 23; *RFE/RL Sovset*, Dec. 4, 1992; *NYT*, Nov. 13, 1993, p. 3.
50. Andrei Shleifer, comments at seminar, Russian Research Center, Harvard University, Nov. 3, 1993.

Chapter 7: Lessons of History: Postwar West Germany and Japan

1. John G. Gurley, "Excess Liquidity and European Monetary Reforms, 1944–1952," *American Economic Review* 43 (1953): 80.
2. F. A. Lutz, "The German Currency Reform and the Revival of the German Economy," *Economica*, n.s., 16 (May 1949): 132.
3. Horst Mendershausen, "Prices, Money and the Distribution of Goods in Postwar Germany," *American Economic Review* 39 (1949): 649.
4. Fred H. Klopstock, "Monetary Reform in Western Germany," *Journal of Political Economy* 39 (1949): 278.
5. Mendershausen, "Prices," p. 655.
6. Gustav Stolper, Karl Häuser, and Knut Borchardt, *The German Econ-*

omy, 1870 to the Present (New York: Harcourt, Brace and World, 1967), p. 228.

7. Klopstock, "Monetary Reform," p. 284.
8. Lutz, "German Currency Reform," p. 131.
9. Ibid., p. 133.
10. Ibid.; Stolper et al., *German Economy*, p. 231.
11. Rudiger Dornbusch and Holger Wolf, "Monetary Overhang and Reform in the 1940s" (Cambridge: MIT, 1990, photocopy), p. 28.
12. Stolper et al., *German Economy*, p. 229; Karl Hardach, *The Political Economy of Germany in the Twentieth Century* (Berkeley: University of California Press, 1980), p. 182.
13. Stolper et al., *German Economy*, p. 238.
14. Dornbusch and Wolf, "Monetary Overhang," p. 27A, fig. 1.
15. Takatoshi Ito, *The Japanese Economy* (Cambridge: MIT Press, 1992), p. 54; Shigeto Tsuru, *Japanese Capitalism: Creative Defeat and Beyond* (Cambridge: Cambridge University Press, 1993), p. 18.
16. Ito, *Japanese Economy*, p. 54; Tsuru, *Japanese Capitalism*, p. 22.
17. Ito, *Japanese Economy*, p. 55.
18. Ibid., p. 52; Raymond W. Goldsmith, *The Financial Development of Japan, 1968–1977* (New Haven: Yale University Press, 1983), p. 133.
19. Goldsmith, *Financial Development*, p. 132.
20. Frances McCall Rosenbluth, *Financial Politics in Contemporary Japan* (Ithaca: Cornell University Press, 1989), p. 115; Tsuru, *Japanese Capitalism*, p. 46.
21. T. Nakamura, "Japanese Economic History" (1989), quoted in Katsuhiro Miyamoto, "Possible Lessons for the Russian Economic Reform with the Reference to the Postwar Japanese Economy" (Osaka Prefectural University, Oct. 1992), pp. 9, 25.
22. Rosenbluth, *Financial Politics*, p. 115.
23. Goldsmith, *Financial Development*, p. 141.
24. Ibid.
25. Ito, *Japanese Economy*, p. 53.
26. Miyamoto, "Possible Lessons," pp. 7–9; Tsuru, *Japanese Capitalism*, p. 55.
27. Tsuru, *Japanese Capitalism*, p. 58.
28. János Kornai, *The Road to a Free Economy* (New York: W. W. Norton, 1990), p. 49.
29. "A Conversation with Dwight Perkins," *Harvard Gazette*, July 26, 1991, p. 15.

30. Josselyn Hennessy, "The End of the German Miracle," *Journal of Economic Literature* 31 (June 1993): 882, quoted in Dornbusch and Wolf, "Monetary Overhang."

Chapter 8: Gradualism or Shock Therapy: Hungary versus Poland

1. Ivan T. Berend, *Hungarian Economic Reforms, 1953–1988* (New York: Cambridge University Press, 1990), p. 31.
2. Ibid., pp. 21, 24; Paul Marer, "Economic Reform in Hungary: From Central Planning to Regulated Market," in Joint Economic Committee, *East European Economies* (Washington, D.C.: Government Printing Office, 1986), p. 237; János Kornai, "The Hungarian Reform Process: Visions, Hopes, and Reality," *Journal of Economic Literature* 24 (1986): 1687; Jan Adam, book review, *Journal of Comparative Economics* 16 (Dec. 1992): 774–75.
3. Berend, *Reforms*, p. 94.
4. Kornai, "Reform Process," p. 1701.
5. Ibid., p. 1702; Marer, "Economic Reform," p. 57.
6. Thomas A. Vankai, "Hungarian Agricultural Performance and Prospects during the 1980's," in Joint Economic Committee, *East European Economies*, p. 341.
7. Ibid., pp. 356–57.
8. Michael Marrese, "Hungary's Economic Transformation: 25 Years of Reform Finally Yield Fragile Fruit" (Dec. 1991) (photocopy), p. 3.
9. Berend, *Reforms*, pp. 85–86, 90.
10. Marrese, "Transformation," p. 3.
11. Ibid. ; Berend, *Reforms*, pp. 126, 137.
12. Berend, *Reforms*, p. 129.
13. Ibid., pp. 169–70.
14. Marrese, "Transformation," p. 3.
15. Tamás Bauer, "Hungary: On the Way towards a Market Economy," in *The Central and East European Economies in the 1990s: Prospects and Constraints* (Brussels: NATO, 1990), p. 78.
16. Marer, "Economic Reform," p. 239.
17. Kornai, "Reform Process," p. 1973; Marrese, "Transformation," pp. 3–4.
18. Kornai, "Reform Process," pp. 1699–1700.
19. Berend, *Reforms*, p. 232.
20. Ibid.
21. Ibid., p. 201.

22. Ibid.
23. János Kornai, *Contradictions and Dilemmas* (Cambridge: MIT Press, 1986), p. 33.
24. Berend, *Reforms*, p. 243; Marrese, "Transformation," p. 4.
25. Marrese, "Transformation," p. 4.
26. Berend, *Reforms*, pp. 260, 267; Marer, "Economic Reform," p. 249; Mary C. DeFilippo, "Financial Sector Reform in Hungary, Poland and Russia: A Comparative Analysis" (Department of Economics, Wellesley College, April 29, 1993, photocopy), p. 27.
27. Berend, *Reforms*, p. 272.
28. Adam, review, p. 776.
29. Berend, *Reforms*, p. 264.
30. Saul Estrin, Paul Hare, and Marta Surányi, "Banking in Transition: Development and Current Problems in Hungary," *Soviet Studies* 44 (1992): 786.
31. DeFilippo, "Financial Sector Reform," p. 30.
32. Estrin, Hare, and Surányi, "Banking," p. 789.
33. *FT*, Dec. 14, 1993, p. 17.
34. Bauer, "Hungary," p. 79.
35. Berend, *Reforms*, pp. 270–71.
36. *NYT*, Feb. 5, 1989, p. 15.
37. Bauer, "Hungary" p. 80.
38. Valerie J. Chang and Catherine L. Mann, "Industry Restructuring and Export Performance: Evidence on the Transition in Hungary" (Board of Governors of the Federal Reserve System, International Finance Discussion Papers, no. 445, Washington, D.C., May 1993, photocopy), p. 8.
39. Central Intelligence Agency, *Eastern Europe: Struggling to Stay on the Reform Path* (Washington, D.C.: CIA, July 1992), p. 17; George Gluck, "Privatisation: The Hungarian Example," *International Company and Commercial Law Review*, Aug. 1993, p. 289.
40. CIA, *Eastern Europe*, p. 18.
41. Ibid., p. 20.
42. Robert Blackwill, "Eastern Europe: Reforms about to Pay Off" (Testimony to the Joint Economic Committee of Congress, June 11, 1993), p. 2; *FT*, Nov. 1, 1993, p. 13.
43. *FT*, July 19, 1993, p. vi.
44. *FT*, March 10, 1993, p. 17; *Business Week*, April 26, 1993, p. 103.
45. *NYT*, May 11, 1993, p. 2; *FT*, Jan. 26, 1994, p. 16.
46. CIA, *Eastern Europe*, p. 17.
47. Ibid., p. 18.
48. János Kornai, "The Postsocialist Transition and the State: Reflections

in the Light of Hungarian Fiscal Problems," *American Economic Review—Papers and Proceedings* 82 (1992): 8–9.

49. CIA, *Eastern Europe*, pp. 17–18.
50. Ibid., p. 19; János Kornai, "Transformation Recession" (Harvard Institute of Economic Research, Harvard University, July 1993, Discussion Paper No. 1648), p. 5.
51. Blackwill, "Eastern Europe," p. 10.
52. CIA, *Eastern Europe*, p. 20.
53. Estrin, Hare, and Surányi, "Banking," p. 801.
54. Kornai, "Transformation Recession," p. 2.
55. Chang and Mann, "Industry Restructuring," p. 8.
56. Branko Milanovic, "Poland's Quest for Economic Stabilisation, 1988–1991: Interaction of Political Economy and Economics," *Soviet Studies* 44 (1992): 512.
57. Marek Grela, "Polish Economic Reforms: Current Developments, Constraints and Prospects," in *Central and East European Economies in the 1990s*, p. 89.
58. Paul Marer, "Economic Transformation in Central and Eastern Europe," in *Making Markets: Economic Transformation in Eastern Europe and the Post-Soviet States*, ed. Shafiqul Islam and Michael Mandelbaum (New York: Council on Foreign Relations Press, 1992), p. 71.
59. Krzysztof Jasiewicz, "Polish Elections of 1990: Beyond the 'Pospolite Ruszenie,' " in *Polish Road from Socialism: The Economics, Sociology, and Politics of Transition*, ed. Walter D. Connor and Piotr Ploszajski (Armonk, N.Y.: M. E. Sharpe, 1992), p. 186.
60. Marer, "Economic Transformation," p. 71.
61. Jasiewicz, "Polish Elections," p. 186.
62. *FT*, Sept. 28, 1989, p. 4.
63. Stanislaw Wellisz, "Poland under 'Solidarity' Rule," *Journal of Economic Perspectives* 5, no. 4 (Fall 1991): 212.
64. Milanovic, "Poland's Quest," p. 519.
65. Ibid., p. 520.
66. Jan Winiecki, "The Polish Transition Progamme: Underpinnings, Results, Interpretations," *Soviet Studies* 44 (1992): 811.
67. Grela, "Polish Economic Reforms," p. 91.
68. Winiecki, "Polish Transition Programme," p. 815.
69. Ibid., p. 814; Wojciech Bienkowski, comments at seminar, Russian Research Center, Harvard University, April 18, 1990.
70. Winiecki, "Polish Transition Programme," p. 814.
71. Ibid., p. 816.

72. Ibid., p. 815; Milanovic, "Poland's Quest," p. 526.
73. *FT*, April 28, 1992, p. ix.
74. Jeffrey Sachs, comments at seminar, Russian Research Center, Harvard University, July 29, 1993.
75. Winiecki, "Polish Transition Programme," p. 831.
76. *NYT*, June 20, 1993, p. F7.
77. Kazimierz Z. Poznanski, "Privatisation of the Polish Economy: Problems of Transition," *Soviet Studies* 44 (1992): 644.
78. Ibid., pp. 645–46.
79. Ibid., p. 658.
80. CIA, *Eastern Europe*, p. 32.
81. Ibid., p. 14.
82. Blackwill, "Eastern Europe," p. 16.
83. Milanovic, "Poland's Quest," pp. 526–27.
84. Michael Ellman, "Shock Therapy in Russia: Failure or Partial Success," *RFE/RL Research Report*, vol. 1, no. 34, Aug. 28, 1992, p. 53; Winiecki, "Polish Transition Programme," p. 831.

Chapter 9: China as a Model

1. Anders Åslund, "Soviet and Chinese Reforms: Why They Must Be Different," *The World Today*, Nov. 1989, p. 188; Yegor Gaidar, *FBIS*, Oct. 7, 1992, p. 24.
2. *FBIS*, *China*, July 21, 1993, p. 37.
3. Ibid.
4. *Nar. khoz.*, 1990, p. 67; CIA, *Handbook of International Economic Statistics, 1993* (Washington, D.C.: Directorate of Intelligence, 1992), p. 38.
5. Ibid., p. 39.
6. *Nar. khoz.*, 1990, p. 68.
7. Anders Åslund, *Post-Communist Economic Revolutions: How Big a Bang?* (Washington, D.C.: Center for Strategic and International Studies, 1992), p. 89; Åslund, "Soviet and Chinese Reforms," p. 189.
8. *Institute of Politics Proceedings, 1990–91, 1991–92* (Cambridge: John F. Kennedy School of Government, Harvard University, 1992), p. 46.
9. Ibid.
10. *Christian Science Monitor*, Nov. 12, 1992, p. 11.
11. "Lured by Zlotys, Ivan as a Model Migrant Worker," *NYT*, Oct. 6, 1991, p. 14.
12. *Promyshlennost SSSR, 1987* (Moscow: Finansy i statistika, 1988), pp. 100, 113; *Statistical Yearbook of China, 1981* (Beijing: State Statistical

Bureau, 1982); *NYT*, April 2, 1993, p. A7. I am grateful to Nancy Hearst, the librarian at the John Fairbank Center for Asian Studies, Harvard University, for help with this and other Chinese statistical information.

13. *NYT*, May 2, 1993, p. E7; *WSJ*, Jan. 14, 1993, p. A12; *China Daily*, May 28, 1993, p. 4. The economist Deng Furong confirmed these figures in an interview in Beijing, July 1993.
14. *FBIS, China*, July 2, 1993, p. 37; Furlong interview.
15. *Nar. khoz.*, 1990, pp. 619, 622–23; *Izvestiia*, Feb. 4, 1982, p. 21.
16. Zhores Medvedev, *Soviet Agriculture* (New York: W. W. Norton, 1987), p. 374.
17. Ibid., p. 375.
18. Ibid., pp. 364–70; *Nar. khoz.*, 1985, p. 202; 1982, p. 193; Douglas Diamond, "Soviet Agricultural Plans for 1981–85," in *Russia at the Crossroads: The 26th Congress of the CPSU*, ed. Seweryn Bialer and Thane Gustafson (London: Allen and Unwin, 1982), p. 117.
19. *Izvestiia*, May 28, 1983, p. 2; *FBIS*, Feb. 1, 1983, p. 28.
20. *FBIS*, Aug. 25, 1992, p. 7.
21. *FT*, Jan. 28, 1993, p. 28; June 3, 1993, p. 30; *WSJ*, Feb. 4, 1993, p. A14; *Ekonomika i zhizn*, no. 6 (Feb. 1994): 8.
22. *Izvestiia*, Jan. 28, 1993, p. 2; *FBIS*, Feb. 1, 1993, p. 28.
23. Jean C. Oi, "Fiscal Reform and the Economic Foundations of Local State Corporations in China," *World Politics*, Oct. 1992, p. 115.
24. *Ekonomika i zhizn*, no. 23 (June 1993): 1.
25. *FBIS*, March 2, 1992, p. 29.
26. *NYT*, Jan. 1, 1988, p. 31.
27. *NYT*, May 2, 1993, p. E7.
28. *WSJ*, March 30, 1992, p. 12B.
29. *China Daily*, July 13, 1993, p. 4.
30. *FBIS, China*, Oct. 10, 1985, p. K4.
31. Ibid.; *China Statistical Yearbook, 1987* (Hong Kong: Longman, 1988).
32. *FT*, June 14, 1993, p. 2; *Christian Science Monitor*, Dec. 1, 1922, p. 8.
33. Jim Mann, *Beijing Jeep: The Short Unhappy Romance of American Business in China* (New York: Simon and Schuster, 1989); *FT*, June 16, 1993, p. 5.
34. *FT*, June 14, 1993, p. 1. Not all estimates of foreign investment are that high. *FT*, Jan. 14, 1994, p. 13.
35. *FT*, June 16, 1993, p. ii; Central Intelligence Agency, *China's Economy in 1992 and 1993: Grappling with the Risks of Rapid Growth* (Washington, D.C.: CIA, Aug. 1993), p. 10; *NYT*, Nov. 18, 1993, p. A12.
36. *Moscow News*, no. 16 (1987): 6.

37. *FT,* June 16, 1993, p. 5.
38. Wang Xiao-Qiang, " 'Groping for Stones to Cross the River': Chinese Price Reform against 'Big Bang' " (Department of Applied Economics, University of Cambridge, Discussion Papers on Economic Transition, no. DPET 9305, March 1993), p. 1; *FBIS, China,* July 2, 1993, p. 37.
39. *China Daily,* July 13, 1993, p. 4.
40. *Boston Globe,* Aug. 11, 1993, p. 9.
41. *NYT,* July 4, 1993, p. 3; *WSJ,* Jan. 26, 1994, p. A10.

Chapter 10: Economic Aid: Great Expectations—Massive Disappointments

1. Gregory Yavlinsky, "Western Aid Is No Help," *NYT,* July 28, 1993, p. A19.
2. *NYT,* May 11, 1993, p. D2.
3. Ibid.
4. *FT,* Sept. 3, 1993, p. D2.
5. *WSJ,* April 26, 1993, p. A8.
6. *FT,* Aug. 11, 1993, p. 2; *WSJ,* April 26, 1993, p. 8; *European WSJ,* June 21, 1993, p. 4.
7. *NYT,* Sept. 3, 1993, p. D1; *WSJ,* Sept. 3, 1993, p. A2.
8. *NYT,* Sept. 4, 1993, p. 37.
9. *WSJ,* Dec. 23, 1993, p. A4.
10. *Rossiyskiie vesti,* May 27, 1993; Oct. 13, 1993, p. 1.
11. *FT,* Dec. 14, 1992, p. 4; Jeffrey Sachs, "Home Alone: How to Save Yeltsin's Reforms," *New Republic,* Dec. 21, 1992, p. 25.
12. *FT,* Aug. 16, 1993, p. 13.
13. *FT,* Nov. 17, 1993, p. 2; Nov. 24, 1993, p. 16.
14. *Washington Post,* Jan. 14, 1992, p. A14.
15. *Boston Globe,* April 29, 1992, p. 2.
16. *Izvestiia,* April 4, 1992, p. 2; *NYT,* May 7, 1992, p. A27.
17. *FT,* May 27, 1993, p. iii; Sept. 24, 1993, p. 2.
18. *Boston Globe,* Aug. 24, 1993, p. 7; *WSJ,* March 1, 1994, p. A16.
19. *FT,* Aug. 23, 1993, p. 2.
20. *WSJ,* Sept. 10, 1993, p. A16.
21. *Atlantic Journal/Atlantic Constitution,* Nov. 13, 1993, p. A11.
22. *FT,* Nov. 11, 1993, p. 3; Nov. 17, 1993, p. 14; Nov. 22, 1993, p. 12.

Chapter 11: The Clash between Economics and History

1. W. W. Rostow, *The Stages of Economic Growth* (Cambridge: MIT Press, 1960); Alexander Gerschenkron, *Economic Backwardness in His-*

torical Perspective (Cambridge: Harvard University Press, 1962); Ragnar Nurske, *Problems of Capital Formation in Underdeveloped Countries* (New York: Oxford University Press, 1961).

2. Olivier Blanchard et al., *Reform in Eastern Europe* (Cambridge: MIT Press, 1991); Stanley Fischer, "Stabilization and Economic Reform in Russia," *Brookings Papers on Economic Activity*, 1992, no. 1; János Kornai, *The Road to a Free Economy: Shifting from a Socialist System: The Example of Hungary* (New York: W. W. Norton, 1990); János Kornai, Merton J. Peck, and Thomas J. Richardson, eds., *What Is to Be Done?* (New Haven: Yale University Press, 1991); Michael Keren and Gur Ofer, *Trials of Transition: Economic Reform in the Former Communist Bloc* (Denver: Westview Press, 1993); Ronald I. McKinnon, *The Order of Economic Liberalization: Financial Control in the Transition to a Market Economy* (Baltimore: Johns Hopkins University Press, 1991); Peter Murrell, *The Nature of Socialist Economies: Lessons from Eastern European Foreign Trade* (Princeton: Princeton University Press, 1990); Horst Siebert, ed., *The Transformation of Socialist Economies: Symposium 1991* (Tübingen: J. C. B. Mohr, 1992); Shafiqul Islam and Michael Mandelbaum, eds., *Making Markets* (New York: Council on Foreign Relations Press, 1993).
3. Murrell, *Socialist Economies*, p. 224. For a good summary see Mary C. DeFilippo, "Financial Sector Reform in Hungary, Poland and Russia: A Comparative Analysis" (Department of Economics, Wellesley College, April 29, 1993, photocopy), p. 14.
4. Murrell, *Socialist Economies*, pp. 225–26.
5. McKinnon, *Economic Liberalization*, pp. 4–8, 160–61.
6. Kornai, *Road;* Robert Kuttner, "The Dustbin of Economics," *New Republic*, Feb. 25, 1991, p. 26.
7. Stanley Fischer and Jacob Frenkel, "Macroeconomic Issues of Soviet Reform," *American Economic Review—Papers and Proceedings* 82 (1992): 37; David Lipton and Jeffrey D. Sachs, "Prospects for Russia's Economic Reforms, *Brookings Papers on Economic Activity*, 1992, no. 2, p. 213; Jeffrey D. Sachs and David Lipton, "Poland's Economic Reform," *Foreign Affairs* 69, no. 3 (summer 1990): 47.
8. Gur Ofer, "Stabilizing and Restructuring the Former Soviet Economy: Big Bang or Gradual Sequence," in Keren and Ofer, *Trials*, p. 83.
9. *Nezavisimaia gazeta*, Aug. 6, 1993, p. 1; *FBIS*, Aug. 6, 1993, pp. 16–18; Aug. 9, 1993, p. 22; *NYT*, Aug. 7, 1993, p. 4.
10. *Rossiyskaia gazeta*, Aug. 3, 1993, p. 3.
11. *FT*, Aug. 19, 1993, p. 2.
12. *Petroleum Economist*, special supplement, June 1992, p. 8.

13. Ann Inse, "American Know-how and Russian Oil," *NYT Magazine*, March 7, 1993, p. 57.
14. *WSJ*, Jan. 29, 1992, p. A8.
15. *East/West Executive Guide*, Feb. 1993, p. 3.
16. Ibid., p. 30.
17. Imse, "American Know-how," p. 30.
18. Ronald Benson, president of Phibro, comments at Russian Research Center-Harriman Institute Seminar, Arden House, New York, April 12, 1992.
19. *East/West Executive Guide*, p. 32.
20. Imse, "American Know-how," p. 29.
21. *Pravda*, Feb. 12, 1992, p. 2.
22. Imse, "American Know-how," p. 57.
23. Ibid.
24. Benson, comments, April 12, 1992.
25. *Nezavisimaia gazeta*, June 6, 1993, p. 1.
26. Benson, comments, April 12, 1992.
27. Imse, "American Know-how," p. 31.
28. Ibid., p. 30; comments at seminar, Russian Research Center, Harvard University Oct. 25, 1993.
29. *Pravda*, Feb. 12, 1992, p. 2.

Bibliography

Alexeev, Michael, Clifford Gaddy, and Jim Leitzel. "Economics in the Former Soviet Union." *Journal of Economic Perspectives* 6, no. 2 (Spring 1992): 137–48.

Allison, Graham, and Robert Blackwill. "America's Stake in the Soviet Future." *Foreign Affairs* 70, no. 3 (Summer 1991): 77–97.

Åslund, Anders. *Gorbachev's Struggle for Economic Reform: The Soviet Reform Process, 1985–88*. Ithaca: Cornell University Press, 1989.

———. "Gorbachev, *Perestroyka*, and Economic Crisis." *Problems of Communism*, Jan.–April, 1991, pp. 18–41.

Berend, Ivan T. *Hungarian Economic Reforms, 1953–1988*. New York: Cambridge University Press, 1990.

Blanchard, Olivier, et al. *Reform in Eastern Europe*. Cambridge: MIT Press, 1991.

Borovoi, Konstantin. *People, Events and Feelings: The Price of Freedom*. Moscow: Novesti, 1993.

Diamond, Douglas. "Soviet Agricultural Plans for 1981–85." In *Russia at the Crossroads: The 26th Congress of the CPSU*, ed. Seweryn Bialer and Thane Gustafson. London: Allen and Unwin, 1982.

Dornbusch, Rudiger, and Holger Wolf, "Monetary Overhang and Reform in the 1940s." Cambridge: MIT 1990. Photocopy.

Estrin, Saul, Paul Hare, and Marta Surányi. "Banking in Transition: Development and Current Problems in Hungary." *Soviet Studies* 44 (1992): 785–808.

Fischer, Stanley, "Stabilization and Economic Reform in Russia." *Brookings Papers on Economic Activity*, 1992, no. 1.

Fischer, Stanley, and Jacob Frenkel. "Macroeconomic Issues of Soviet Reform." *American Economic Review—Papers and Proceedings* 82 (1992): 37–42.

Gerschenkron, Alexander. *Economic Backwardness in Historical Perspective.* Cambridge: Harvard University Press, 1962.

Gluck, George. "Privatisation: The Hungarian Example." *International Company and Commercial Law Review,* Aug. 1993.

Goldman, Marshall I. *Gorbachev's Challenge: Reform in the Age of High Technology.* New York: W. W. Norton, 1987.

———. *The USSR in Crisis: The Failure of an Economic System.* New York: W. W. Norton, 1982.

Goldsmith, Raymond W. *The Financial Development of Japan, 1968–1977.* New Haven: Yale University Press, 1983.

Gurley, John G. "Excess Liquidity and European Monetary Reforms, 1944–1952." *American Economic Review* 43 (1953): 76–100.

Hardach, Karl. *The Political Economy of Germany in the Twentieth Century.* Berkeley: University of California Press, 1980.

Hewett, Ed A. *Reforming the Soviet Economy: Equality versus Efficiency.* Washington, D.C.: Brookings Institution, 1988.

Institute of Politics Proceedings, 1990–91, 1991–92. Cambridge: John F. Kennedy School of Government, Harvard University, 1992.

Ito, Takatoshi. *The Japanese Economy.* Cambridge: MIT Press, 1992.

Jasiewica, Krzysztof. "Polish Elections of 1990: Beyond the 'Pospolite Ruszenie.' " In *Polish Road from Socialism: The Economics, Sociology, and Politics of Transition.* ed. Walter D. Connor and Piotr Ploszajski. Armonk, N.Y.: M. E. Sharpe, 1992.

Joravsky, David. *The Lysenko Affair.* Cambridge: Harvard University Press, 1970.

Keren, Michael, and Gur Ofer. *Trials of Transition: Economic Reform in the Former Communist Bloc.* Denver: Westview Press, 1993.

Klopstock, Fred H. "Monetary Reform in Western Germany." *Journal of Political Economy* 57 (1949): 277–92.

Kornai, János. *Contradictions and Dilemmas.* Cambridge: MIT Press, 1986.

———. "The Hungarian Reform Process: Visions, Hopes, and Reality." *Journal of Economic Literature* 24 (1986): 1687–737.

———. "The Postsocialist Transition and the State: Reflections in the Light of Hungarian Fiscal Problems." *American Economic Review—Papers and Proceedings* 82 (1992): 1–21.

———. *The Road to a Free Economy: Shifting from a Socialist System: The Example of Hungary.* New York: W. W. Norton, 1990.

Kornai, János, Merton J. Peck, and Thomas J. Richardson, eds. *What Is to Be Done?* New Haven: Yale University Press, 1991.

Kuttner, Robert. "The Dustbin of Economics." *New Republic,* Feb. 25, 1991.

Layard, Richard. "Russia in Transition." *LSE Magazine,* Spring 1993.

Lutz, F. A. "The German Currency Reform and the Revival of the German Economy." *Economica,* n.s., 16 (May 1949): 122–42.

Makarevich, Lev. "Commodities Are the Key." *Business in the USSR,* July–Aug. 1991.

Mann, Jim. *Beijing Jeep: The Short Unhappy Romance of American Business in China.* New York: Simon and Schuster, 1989.

Marer, Paul. "Economic Reform in Hungary: From Central Planning to Regulated Market." In Joint Economic Committee, *East European Economies.* Washington, D.C.: Government Printing Office, 1986.

McKinnon, Ronald I. *The Order of Economic Liberalization: Financial Control in the Transition to a Market Economy.* Baltimore: Johns Hopkins University Press, 1991.

Medvedev, Zhores, *Soviet Agriculture.* New York: W. W. Norton, 1987.

Mendershausen, Horst. "Prices, Money and the Distribution of Goods in Postwar Germany." *American Economic Review* 39 (1949): 646–72.

Milanovic, Branko. "Poland's Quest for Economic Stabilisation, 1988–1991: Interaction of Political Economy and Economics." *Soviet Studies* 44 (1992): 511–32.

Morrison, John. *Boris Yeltsin: From Bolshevik to Democrat.* New York: Dutton Books, 1991.

Murrell, Peter. *The Nature of Socialist Economies: Lessons from Eastern European Foreign Trade.* Princeton: Princeton University Press, 1990.

Nurske, Ragnar. *Problems of Capital Formation in Underdeveloped Countries.* New York: Oxford University Press, 1961.

Poznanski, Kazimierz Z. "Privatisation of the Polish Economy: Problems of Transition." *Soviet Studies* 44 (1992): 641–64.

Pringle, Peter. "Gaidar and Company." *Moscow Magazine*, June–July 1992.

Rosenbluth, Frances McCall. *Financial Politics in Contemporary Japan*. Ithaca: Cornell University Press, 1989.

Rostow, W. W. *The Stages of Economic Growth*. Cambridge: MIT Press, 1960.

Roxburgh, Angus. *The Second Russian Revolution: The Struggle for Power in the Kremlin*. London: BBC Books, 1991.

Shiller, Robert J., Maxim Boycko, and Vladimir Korobov. "Popular Attitudes toward Free Markets: The Soviet Union and the United States Compared." *American Economic Review* 81 (1991): 385–400.

Shmelev, Nikolai, "Avansy idolgi." *Novy mir*, June 1987.

Solovyov, Vladimir, and Elena Klepikova. *Boris Yeltsin: A Political Biography*. New York: G. P. Putnam's Sons, 1992.

Sterling, Claire. *Thieves' World*. New York: Simon and Schuster, 1994.

Stolper, Gustav, Karl Häuser, and Knut Borchardt. *The German Economy, 1870 to the Present*. New York: Harcourt, Brace and World, 1967.

Tsuru, Shigeto. Japanese Capitalism: Creative Defeat and Beyond. Cambridge: Cambridge University Press, 1993.

Wegren, Stephen K. "Private Farming and Agrarian Reform in Russia." *Problems of Communism*, May–June 1992, pp. 107–21.

Wellisz, Stanislaw, "Poland under 'Solidarity' Rule." *Journal of Economic Perspectives* 5, no. 4 (Fall 1991): 211–17.

White, Stephen. *Gorbachev and After*. Cambridge: Cambridge University Press, 1992.

Winiecki, Jan. "The Polish Transition Programme: Underpinnings, Results, Interpretations." *Soviet Studies* 44 (1992): 809–35.

Yeltsin, Boris. *Against the Grain: An Autobiography*. New York: Summit Books, 1990.

———. *The Struggle for Russia*. New York: Random House, 1994.

Zaslavskaia, Tatiana. "The Novosibirsk Report." *Survey* 28, no. 1 (Spring 1984): 88–108.

Index

Abalkin, Leonid, 68–71, 73, 74, 75
Academy of Sciences, 64, 65, 66, 87
  Institute of Economics, 68
Adenauer, Konrad, 148
Aganbegyan, Abel, 67, 76–77
Agency for International Development (AID), 219–20
agriculture:
  in China, 192, 198–200, 202
  in Hungary, 162
  Japanese land reform, 151–52
  in Ukraine, 128
agriculture in Russia:
  brigade contract system, 66
  communal history, 123
  garden plots, 124, 128
  perestroika and, 123–25, 126, 194–95, 200–201
  planned command economy and, 15–16
  privatization in, 118, 123–28, 199, 200, 210–11
  Yeltsin's missed opportunity for reform, 201
Allison, Graham, 80, 81, 82–83
Alphagraphics company, 224–25
Andropov, Yuri, 31, 65–66
Andrus, Gordon, 247
Anglo-Suisse company, 247
Armenia, 22, 53, 58, 247
Åslund, Anders, 191
Atwood, J. Brian, 220
Aven, Peter, 106
Azerbaijan, 22, 54, 58, 120–21, 247
Baker, James, 6–7
Balcerowicz, Leszek, 82, 88, 180, 181, 186
Balcerowicz Plan, *see* Poland's economic restructuring
Baltic states, 25, 53, 56
  see also Estonia; Lithuania
banking industry:
  in Hungary, 168
  in Russia, 208, 243
Batterymarch Financial Management, 218
Belarus, 55, 56
  shock therapy in Russia and, 118
  see also Commonwealth of Independent States
Beltway bandits, 220
Bessmertnykh, Aleksandr, 7
Bielecki, Jan, 184, 186
Blackwill, Robert, 80, 81
Bogomolov, Oleg, 71, 73, 102
Borovoi, Konstantin, 140–41
Boycko, Maxim, 18*n*
Brandt, Willy, 1
bread subsidies, 98–99
breakup of Soviet Union, vii, 2–3, 96–97
  Commonwealth of Independent States and, 55–57
  coup attempt of 1991 and, 27–28, 55
  decentralization of authority and, 52–55
  economic consequences, 60–61

breakup of Soviet Union (*continued*)
economic factors, 7–8, 23–24
Gorbachev's efforts to avoid, 24–25, 53
nationalism and, 58
referendum on, 53
Russian support for, 24
violent episodes, 54–55
Yeltsin's anticipation of, 44–45
Yeltsin's efforts toward, 52, 54, 55, 61
Bretton Woods Conference, 155
Brezhnev, Leonid, 65, 66, 178
brigade contract system, 66
Bunich, Pavel, 73
Burbulis, Gennady, 89
bureaucracies, 165
Bush, George, 5, 6, 7, 57, 217

capital flight, 112–13, 115
censorship of newspapers, 4–5, 50
Center for Research into Economic Transformation, 87
Central Economic and Mathematical Institute (TsEMI), 72, 86
centrally planned systems, *see* planned command economy
Chechens, 61, 62, 97
Chernenko, Konstantin, 32, 67
Chernomyrdin, Viktor, 92–93, 130–31, 138, 211
Chiang Kai-shek, 192
China:
Cultural Revolution, 193, 194
demographics of, 191
ethnic makeup, 192, 193
Great Leap Forward, 193, 196
Tiananmen Square demonstration, 27
China's economic reforms, 8, 130, 131, 190
agricultural reforms, 192, 198–200, 202
bureaucratic obstructionism, decline of, 211–12
as capitalism with Chinese characteristics, 191
credit creation by enterprises, 111*n*
economic growth and, 203–5
exports and, 207
facilitating factors, 192–94
foreign investment, 206–9, 215–16
goal of, 203
industry's role in economy and, 196–97
mafia-like operations, avoidance of, 204
odds against successful reform, 191–92
political reforms and, 212
Russia, lessons for, 210–12
small-business formation, 202–3, 205
state enterprises, transformation of, 197–98
work culture and, 195–96
Chornovil, Vyacheslav, 56
Chubais, Anatoly, 87, 88, 89
privatization and, 132, 133, 134, 138
Clay, Gen. Lucius, 148, 159
Clinton, Bill, 3, 217
Clinton, Hillary, 20
Coca-Cola company, 227
Combustion Engineering, 225
commercial codes, 243
Committee on National Salvation, 59
Commonwealth of Independent States (CIS), viii
breakup of Soviet Union and, 55–57
Central Asians and, 58
ineffectiveness of, 57–58
Communist Party (Soviet Union), 26, 55
Nineteenth Party Conference (1988), 41–42
conditionality, 156, 157
Conoco company, 218
Corrigan, Gerald, 217
Council of Mutual Economic Assistance (CMEA), 168, 169, 172, 181
coup attempt of 1991, 4, 6–7, 25–28, 46, 49, 55, 84
credit creation by enterprises, 110–11
crime problem, 4
see also mafia
currency reform, 116–17, 139, 236, 240–43

Deng Furong, 197, 207–8
Deng Xiaoping, 130, 131, 192, 193, 194, 203, 204, 206, 207
depressions, economic, 21–23
Doder, Dusko, 66
Dodge, Joseph, 148, 153–54
Du Pont company, 218

East Germany, 177, 179, 214, 215
economic assistance for Russia, 213
  aid requirements, 213–14
  donor countries, consequences for, 221
  IMF and, 155–56, 222–23
  for infrastructure, 219
  misuse of funds, 219–20
  priorities for, 227–28
  privatization, assistance for, 218–19
  ruble stabilization fund, 220–21
  see also foreign investment in Russia
economic assistance for Soviet Union, proposed, 78–84
Economic Commission for Europe, 114
Economic News Agency, 141
economic reform:
  political reform and, 29–30
  prerequisites for, 29
  see also specific reforms
energy crisis of 1970s, 166–67
Enterprise Funds, 217
environmental problems, 220
Erhard, Ludwig, 148, 159
Estonia, 61
  see also Baltic states
ethnic tensions, 192–93
excess-wage tax, 242–43
exchange rates, 231
exploitation tax, 242
export taxes, 113–14

Fathers and Sons (Turgenev), 236
Fedorov, Boris, 74, 138
Fedorov, Valentine, 252–53
Fischer, Stanley, 13, 82
500-day plan, 74–77, 95
foreign investment, 214
  in China, 206–9, 215–16
  in Hungary, 171–72
  investment decisions, factors influencing, 215
  in Japan, 211
  labor costs and, 215–16
  market access and, 216
  in Ukraine, 218
foreign investment in Russia, 172, 211
  investment climate, 114, 208–9
  mafia and, 226–27, 251
  nationalist opposition, 114–15
  in oil industry, 209–10, 218, 227, 246–50
  priorities for, 227–28
  public-private programs, 217–18
  risks of, 223–27, 246–50
  short-term investment, 225
  successful ventures, 251
Friedman, Milton, 79

Gaidar, Yegor, viii, 29, 95, 96, 138, 208, 248
  on China's economic reforms, 190
  dismissal from office, 92, 93
  economic beliefs, 86
  economic reform program, *see* shock therapy in Russia
  editorial work, 89
  finance minister, appointment as, 90–91
  political activism, 93
  privatization policy, 129, 132
  promotions for, 91
  on Russia's lack of economic growth, 204
  writings of, 85–86
  Yeltsin and, 89–90, 91
garden plots, 124, 128
Gdansk shipyard, 183
General Electric, 171
General Motors, 172, 215
Georgia, 53, 54, 56, 58
Gerashchenko, Viktor, 107, 112, 113, 139, 143, 236, 240
Germany, *see* East Germany; West Germany *headings*
Gierek, Edward, 177
gigantomania, 13
Glaziev, Sergei, 88
Glazkov, Gregor, 87, 88
Goldman, Marshall I., 79–80, 87, 113, 118–19, 122, 128, 194, 202, 203
Gorbachev, Mikhail, 1, 56, 94–95, 193–94
  Abalkin and, 68, 69
  agricultural policy, 66, 123–25, 126, 194–95, 200–201
  breakup of Soviet Union and, 24–25, 53, 54
  Commonwealth of Independent States and, 57
  coup attempt of 1991, 6, 25–26
  early years, 39–40
  economic advice, solicitation of, 64–65, 66–68

Gorbachev, Mikhail (*continued*)
  economic reform program, *see* perestroika
  elections, avoidance of, 47–48
  final weeks as president, 84–85
  Hungary's economic restructuring and, 169–70
  imperial lifestyle, 48
  local party involvement, 40
  missed opportunity for economic reform, 238–39
  ouster from power, 1, 5–7, 28
  Poland's economic restructuring and, 178–79
  political reforms, 194–95
  popular attitude toward, 1–2, 4, 5–6
  rise to power, 31
  see also Gorbachev-Yeltsin relationship
Gorbachev, Raisa, 7, 48, 67–68
Gorbachev Foundation, 1
Gorbachev's Challenge (Goldman), 128
Gorbachev-Yeltsin relationship, 44, 52
  common characteristics, 39–40
  falling out, 36–37, 38, 41
  political partnership, 32–33
  Yeltsin's campaign for Russian presidency and, 45–47
  Yeltsin's humiliation of Gorbachev, 50
  Yeltsin's political comeback and, 41, 42, 43
Gore, Al, 228
Gosplan, 22, 103
Gossnab, 13, 103
gradualist approach to economic reform, 230–32
  see also Hungary's economic restructuring
Grand Bargain, 78–79, 80–84
Great Britain, 217
green-fieldization, *see* small-business formation
Grishin, Viktor, 32–33
Group of Seven (G-7):
  economic assistance for Russia, 219
  perestroika and, 78, 83
  Poland's economic restructuring and, 180
Gvishiani, Gherman, 88

Hartman, Arthur, 80
Hewett, Ed, 72, 204–5
Hungary:
  industrial monopolies, 163
  uprising of 1956, 161
Hungary's economic restructuring, 160–61, 190, 217
  achievements of, 173
  agricultural reforms, 162
  banking reform, 168
  bureaucracy and, 165–66, 167
  energy crisis of 1970s and, 166–67
  foreign investment, 171–72
  Gorbachev's reforms in Soviet Union and, 169–70
  industrial reforms, 162–65, 173
  Kádár's role, 161
  moderation of planning system, 161
  New Economic Mechanism (NEM), 163–65
  political reforms and, 169–70
  price liberalization, 172
  privatization, 170–71
  "reform of reforms," 167–69
  Russia, lessons for, 174–75
  trade initiatives, 168–69, 172–73
  unemployment and, 173

industry in planned economy, 12–14, 15, 161
inflation:
  Japan's economic recovery and, 152–54
  shock therapy in Russia and, 96, 97–99, 105, 106–7, 108, 110, 111, 120, 256
  in Ukraine, 108
Institute for Economic Policy, 89
Institute of National Economic Forecasting and Scientific-Technical Progress, 74, 86
International Institute for Applied Systems Analysis (IIASA), 88
International Monetary Fund (IMF), 80–81, 82, 228, 248
  approach to economic reform, 100, 156–57
  economic assistance for Russia, 155–56, 222–23
  origins of, 155
  results of reform efforts, 157–58
investment vouchers, 134–35
Iran, 237
Ishibashi, Tanzan, 153

Japan, 219
  foreign investment in, 211
  foreign investment by, 215–16
Japan's economic recovery, 145, 150–51, 190
  imposition of reform by outside force, 154–55, 158
  inflation problem, 152–54
  institutional framework, 155
  labor laws, 152
  land reform, 151–52
  pre-World War II conditions, 151
Jaruzelski, Gen. Wojciech, 175, 177, 178, 179, 180
Jeep-American Motors joint venture, 207, 209
Johnson, Lyndon, 51

Kádár, János, 161, 162, 164, 170
Kagalovsky, Konstantin, 87–88
Kazakhstan, 58, 210, 226
Khasbulatov, Ruslan, 28, 55, 62, 201
Khizha, Georgi, 92, 138
Khlystun, Viktor N., 124
Khrushchev, Nikita, 6, 34, 38, 39, 65, 178
Klaus, Václav, 88
Kommunist, 89
Korean War, 154
Kornai, János, 157, 165, 166, 167, 230, 231–32
Korobov, Vladimir, 18*n*
Koshkin, V., 85
Kosygin, Aleksei, 65, 88
Kovalev, F., 85
Kravchuk, Leonid, 55, 56, 57, 96
Kryuchkov, Vladimir, 25

Labbe, Giles, 247
labor costs, 215–16
Latsis, Otto, 89
LeBaron, Dean, 218
Leningrad economists, 86–88
Leontief, Wassily, 79
Liberal Democratic party, 114
Liberman, Evsei, 13–14, 65, 164
Ligachev, Yegor, 8*n*, 126
  Yeltsin and, 35–36
Lithuania, 27, 54, 59
  see also Baltic states
Lobov, Oleg, 90, 138, 236
Luzhkov, Yuri, 131
Lysenko, Trofim, 65

MacArthur, Gen. Douglas, 151–52
McKinnon, Ronald, 230–31
mafia, 119–20, 141, 204
  currency reform and, 116
  foreign investment and, 226–27, 251
  perestroika and, 11, 22, 23
  privatization and, 102, 129, 131, 135
  Yeltsin, threats against, 34
Malenkov, Georgi, 6, 38
Maley, Mikhail, 90
Mao Zedong, 192, 193, 196, 206
Marrese, Michael, 167
Marshall Plan, 146, 149, 214
Marx, Karl, 17
Maslyukov, Yuri, 75
Matlock, Jack, 6
Matyukhin, Georgi, 222
Mazowiecki, Tadeusz, 179, 184, 186, 187
Mikhaylov, Aleksei, 73, 74
military expenditures, 99
Ministry of Medium Machine Building, 61
Moldava, 53, 58
Molotov, Vyacheslav, 38
money supply, shock therapy and, 107–10, 111, 120
monopolies, 12–13
Moscow, Yeltsin's administration of, 32–36
Moscow Convention of Entrepreneurs, 141
Murrell, Peter, 230
mutual investment funds, 135–36

National Bank of Hungary, 168
nationalism, 58–59, 114–15
NATO, 187, 188
Nechayev, Andrei, 91, 220
Nemtsov, Boris, 140
New Economic Mechanism (NEM), 163–65
New Economic Policy (NEP), 9, 17
New York Times, 196, 203
Nixon, Richard, viii, 256
Nizhni Novgorod, 140
Number One Beijing Textile and Dyeing Plant, 197

Ofer, Gur, 105
oil and gas industry:
  currency reform and, 241
  equipment shortage, 120–21

oil and gas industry (*continued*)
  foreign investment in, 209–10, 218, 227, 247–50
  planned economy and, 13, 18–20
  shock therapy and, 117
  smuggling oil out of Russia, 117
oil shock of 1973, 166
Overseas Private Investment Corporation (OPIC), 218

Paine Webber Incorporated, 218
parliamentary revolt of 1993, 4–5, 55, 62
Party of Economic Freedom for Business, 141
Pavlov, Valentin, 75, 77, 84, 240
perestroika (Gorbachev's economic reforms):
  Abalkin's reform proposal, 70–71
  agricultural policy, 123–25, 126, 194–95, 200–201
  breakup of Soviet Union and, 7–8, 23–24
  central planning, maintenance of, 69–70, 72
  cooperative and private enterprises, 9–11, 128–29
  criticisms of, 71–72
  economic decline under, 20–23
  experts' advice, Gorbachev's reliance on, 67–69, 72
  500-day plan, 74–77, 95
  implementation failures, 9–10
  joint Soviet-Western reform effort (Grand Bargain), 78–79, 80–84
  machinery production, focus on, 8, 67
  mafia and, 11, 22, 23
  missed opportunity for economic reform, 238–39
  Petrakov's reform proposal, 72
  price liberalization and, 70, 72–73
  psychological obstacles, 16–18
  structural obstacles, 12–16
  summary of economic plans, 76
  Western assistance and, 78–84
  Yavlinsky's reform proposal, 73–74
Petrakov, Nikolai, 72, 74, 86
Petro-Canada, 225
Petrov, Ivan, 141–42
Phibro Energy Products, 247
Philip Morris company, 224
planned command economy:
  psychological impact, 16–18
  raw materials exports, reliance on, 13, 18–20
  structural impact, 12–16
Poland's economic restructuring (Balcerowitz Plan), 30, 82, 160, 190
  achievements of, 175–76
  communist government, ouster of, 179
  conditions preceding reform, 176–78
  Enterprise Fund for, 217
  excess-wage tax, 242–43
  facilitating factors, 188–89
  foreign debt and, 177
  Gorbachev's policy on, 178–79
  initiation of, 180, 181–83
  institutional framework, 105–6
  Jaruzelski's reform efforts, 178
  opposition to shock therapy, 186
  popular mandate for, 179-80, 186
  price liberalization, 73, 180–81
  privatization, 184–85
  production increases, 185
  Russia, lessons for, 186–88
  small-business formation, 184
  trade situation, 183
  unemployment and, 185–86
  Western orientation of Poland and, 187–88
  y stabilization fund, 220–21
Polaroid company, 251
Polozkov, Ivan, 48
Potemkin, Count, 20*n*
Prague Spring, 164
Pravda, 89
price liberalization, 3
  in Hungary, 172
  perestroika and, 70, 72–73
  in Poland, 73, 180–81
  shock therapy in Russia and, 99, 100, 118–19
privatization:
  in Hungary, 170–71
  in Poland, 184–85
privatization in Russia:
  achievements of, 139–42
  in agriculture, 118, 123–28, 199, 200, 210–11
  alternative routes to enterprise privatization, 136–37
  currency reform and, 139

foreign assistance for, 218–19
initiation of, 122
investment vouchers, 134–35
mafia and, 102, 129, 131, 135
managers' control through ("grabitization"), 137–38
mass participation in market, 129–30
mutual investment funds, 135–36
opposition to, 130–31, 138–39, 143
perestroika and, 9–11, 128–29
political motivation, 133–34
political party for, 141
regulation of, 137
small-business formation, 128–31, 140–42, 211
Sakhalin reform effort, 252–54
of state enterprises, 132–38
structural obstacles, 101
Yeltsin's decree on, 118
Promyslov, Vladimir, 33

Reagan, Ronald, 95, 217
Reconversion Finance Bank, 153–54
Romanov, Grigori, 31, 87
ruble's collapse, 115
ruble stabilization fund, 220–21
Rumania, 111*n*
Russia:
autonomy demands of republics, 61–63, 97, 233
banking industry, 208, 243
censorship of newspapers, 4–5, 50
change, receptivity to, 237
China's economic reforms, lessons of, 210–12
commercial codes, 243
crime problem, 4
see also mafia
environmental problems, 220
ethnic tensions, 192–93
exchange rates, 231
factories problem, 149–50
foreign debt, 115–16
foreigners blamed for economic problems, 254
future of reform, 256–57
GNP collapse, 96
Hungary's economic restructuring, lessons of, 174–75
manufacturing enterprises, 253
military expenditures, 99
nationalism and, 58–59, 114–15
parliamentary revolt of 1993, 4–5, 55, 62
phone system, 18*n*
Poland's economic restructuring, lessons of, 186–88
political anarchy, 103–4
presidential election of 1991, 47–48
successful economic ventures, 251–54
summit meetings, 3
tax policy, proposals for, 242–43
trade barriers against, 221
trade barriers by, 222
transfer of money between banks, 243
Westerners and Slavophiles, struggle between, 236–37
work culture, 196
see also agriculture in Russia; Commonwealth of Independent States; economic assistance for Russia; foreign investment in Russia; oil and gas industry; privatization in Russia; shock therapy in Russia
Russian Central Bank, 107–9, 111, 112, 113, 115
Russian Commodity and Raw Material Exchange, 140–41
Russian Congress of People's Deputies, 44, 91, 92, 125, 130
Russian National Commercial Bank, 141
Russian Supreme Soviet, 44, 45–47
Russia's Choice party, 93
Rutskoi, Aleksandr, 52, 55, 62, 93, 113, 138
agricultural reform and, 125–26
Ryzhkov, Nikolai, 68, 70, 74, 75, 77

Sachs, Jeffrey, 82, 83, 105, 106, 184
Saikin, Valery, 33
Sakhalin reform effort, 252–54
Sakharov, Andrei, 236
Schwalberg, Barney, 135
Shatalin, Stanislav, 74, 77, 86, 95
Shevardnadze, Eduard, 6, 85
Shiller, Robert J., 18*n*
Shleifer, Andrei, 132
Shmelev, Nikolai, 71
shock therapy:
in Poland, *see* Poland's economic restructuring

shock therapy (*continued*)
theories of, 232
in West Germany, 148–49
shock therapy in Russia, viii, 29
abandonment of, 91–93
capital flight and, 112–13, 115
credit creation by enterprises, 110–11
currency reform, 116–17, 139, 236, 240–43
foreign debt and, 115–16
goal of, 100
inflation and, 96, 97–99, 105, 106–7, 108, 110, 111, 120, 256
initiation of, 99–100
institutional framework, 101–4
missed opportunities for reform, 239–46
money supply and, 107–10, 111, 120
nationalist opposition, 114–15
oil industry and, 117
political conditions and, 103–4
pre-breakup reform efforts, 85, 88–90
price liberalization and, 99, 100, 118–19
public's displeasure with, 105
ruble's collapse, 115
simultaneous implementation of various reforms, 97–98
supply-side failure, 104, 119–20, 204–5, 255–56
tax policy and, 113–14
theories and methods, development of, 85–89
as top-down program, 100–101
unemployment and, 110
uniqueness of Russia's problems and, 106, 111
wholesaling infrastructure, 103
Yeltsin's announcement of, 96
Yeltsin's political concessions and, 111–12
see also foreign investment in Russia; privatization in Russia
Shultz, George, 82
Shumeiko, Viktor, 138
Shumeiko, Vladimir, 92
Shushkevich, Stanislav, 57
Silayev, Ivan, 85
Sivac, Anatoly, 247
Skokov, Yuri, 85, 90
small-business formation:
in China, 202–3, 205
as initial step in reform programs, 230
in Poland, 184
in Russia, 128–31, 140–42, 211
Sakhalin reform effort, 252–54
Sobchak, Anatoly, 88
Solidarity movement, 176, 177, 178, 179
Solzhenitsyn, Aleksandr, 58, 236
Soskovets, Oleg, 236
Soviet Congress of People's Deputies, 42–43, 55
Soviet Union:
coup attempt of 1991, 4, 6–7, 25–28, 46, 49, 55, 84
economic policy process, 64–67
Gorbachev's ouster from power, 1, 5–7, 28
highway system, 198
Hungary's economic restructuring and, 169–70
oil and gas industry, 13, 18–20
political reforms, 194–95
private enterprise, public's attitude toward, 16–18
reactionary culture, 2
see also breakup of Soviet Union; perestroika; planned command economy
Stalin, Joseph, 12, 65, 101, 146, 211, 240
State Committee for State Property (GKI), 137
Stockdale, William, 91
Stolypin reforms, 123, 134
Strauss, Robert S., 93
Suchocka, Hanna, 187
summit meetings, 3
supply-side failures:
of perestroika, 21–23
of shock therapy in Russia, 104, 119–20, 204–5, 255–56
Supreme Soviet of the Soviet Union, 43
Suslov, Mikhail, 31
Sverdlovsk (Ekaterinburg), 31–32, 33, 35, 40

Tajikistan, 58
tax policy:
proposals for, 242–43

shock therapy and, 114
Texaco, 218
"traffic problem" story, 10
Truman, Harry, 153
Tungsram electric bulb factory, 171
Turgenev, Ivan, 236
Turkmenistan, 58

Ukraine, 23
agricultural privatization, 128
breakup of Soviet Union, 53–54, 55–56
foreign investment in, 218
inflation problem, 108
presidential election of 1991, 56
shock therapy in Russia and, 108, 118
see also Commonwealth of Independent States
Ukraine Fund, 218
unemployment:
in Hungary, 173
in Poland, 185–86
in Russia, 110
United States, 188
agricultural credits for Russia, 115–16
China, trade with, 207
economic assistance for Russia and Eastern Europe, 217–20, 221
Enterprise Funds, 217
Japan's economic recovery and, 151–55, 158
large-scale enterprises, 13
Marshall Plan, 146, 149, 214
summit meetings, 3
West Germany's economic recovery and, 146, 148, 149, 154–55, 158
U.S.S.R. in Crisis, The (Goldman), 80
Uzbekistan, 58, 61

Varyegan Oil and Gas Production Association (VNG), 247, 248, 249
Vasilyev, Sergei, 87, 88
Vladimir tractor factory, 22
Vlasov, Aleksandr, 45, 46–47
Vneshekonombank, 112
vodka controversy, 8, 36, 71

Walesa, Lech, 176, 177
Wall Street Journal, 226
Washington Post, 66
Western assistance, *see* economic assistance *headings*
West Germany, economic aid to East Germany, 214
West Germany's economic recovery, 145, 190
economic assistance and, 149
economic reforms, 147
imposition of reform by outside force, 154–55, 158
institutional framework, 155
investment priorities, 149
post-World War II conditions, 146–47
production increases, 147, 150
shock therapy approach, 148–49
World War I experience and, 146
White Nights joint venture, 246–50
Window of Opportunity, *see* Grand Bargain
work culture, 195–96
World Bank, 80–81, 82, 140, 156
wrapping paper, Russian, 214

Yakovlev, Aleksandr, 6
Yarmogaev, Yuri V., 87
Yavlinsky, Gregory, 73–74, 81, 82, 83, 84, 85, 89, 95
Yeltsin, Boris, viii, 1, 2, 3, 4
as activist reformer, 33–34, 35–36
agricultural reforms, failure to implement, 201
autonomy demands of republics, 62–63
breakup of Soviet Union:
anticipation of, 44–45
efforts toward, 52, 54, 55, 61
censorship of newspapers, 4–5, 50
communist ideology, abandonment of, 43–44
condemnation of (Nov., 1987), 37–38
coup attempt of 1991, 26, 27, 49
decree, governance by, 60, 118
democracy, commitment to, 59–60
disappearance in fall of 1991, 51–52
early years, 39, 40
economic advice, solicitation of, 64–65, 74
economic assistance for Russia and, 222
exile from public life, 38–39
Gaidar and, 89–90, 91

Yeltsin, Boris (*continued*)
Gorbachev's ouster from power, 28
health problems, 37–38
impetuousness of, 50–52
Ligachev and, 35–36
market reforms, support for, 94–95
media exposure, 42
Moscow party positions, 32–36
nationalism and, 58–59
parliamentary revolt of 1993, 4–5, 62
perestroika and, 74, 77
Poland's Western orientation and, 188
political comeback, 41–43
political skills, 94
popular mandate, 47–49
privatization policy, 118, 125–27, 129, 130, 132
public image, 33–34, 41, 48
resignation from Politburo, 36–37
in Russian Congress of People's Deputies, 44
Russian presidency, 45–49
in Soviet Congress of People's Deputies, 42–43
Sverdlovsk years, 31–32, 33, 35, 40
see also Gorbachev-Yeltsin relationship
Yeltsin-Gaidar reforms, *see* shock therapy in Russia
Yurchyshyn, George, 218

Zadornov, Mikhail, 73, 74
Zaslavskaia, Tatiana, 14, 66–67
Zhirinovsky, Vladimir, vii, 30, 114, 143, 216, 222, 257
zloty stabilization fund, 220–21